Chicks in
TANK TOPS

BAEN BOOKS
edited by
JASON CORDOVA

Chicks in Tank Tops

Chicks in
TANK TOPS

Edited by
JASON CORDOVA

A Baen Books Original

Baen Publishing Enterprises
P.O. Box 1403
Riverdale, NY 10471
www.baen.com

ISBN: 978-1-9821-9235-8

Cover art by Dave Seeley

First printing, January 2023

Distributed by Simon & Schuster
1230 Avenue of the Americas
New York, NY 10020

Library of Congress Control Number: 2022948062

Printed in the United States of America

10 9 8 7 6 5 4 3 2 1

For my sisters
Jessica, Jenny, Kristin, Nikki, and Courtney

Contents

Chicks in
TANK TOPS

A Modest Foreword
(or, Mistakes Were Made)

⊕

Esther Friesner

Gentle Reader, it behooves me to wonder, because it beats doing actual work, whether you picked up this slim, sensibly sized volume because you have some familiarity with that gem of Western Literature, the effervescent and delectable Chicks in Chainmail series, another fine Baen Books production.

What in the name of Hades' hand sanitizer do you mean, "Uh, never heard of it"? Wretched child, you shame your cats! (Not your ancestors. Your ancestors don't really care about stuff like this. Sad but true.)

(PS: If you don't have cats, forget I said anything and pick your own whatever for you to shame. Go on. I'll wait.)

(Okay, who suggested "You shame your breakfast"? *sigh* Well, if that's the best you can do, fine, I'll work with it because I don't have all day. We proceed...)

The germ of the first Chicks in Chainmail book made itself manifest unto me at a science fiction convention. I was at the art show and for no logical reason thought of those old, exploitative movies about women in prison. Hey, *Orange Is the New Black* actually has cinematic *ancestors*. (Which it does not shame.) My mind not only wanders, it hires a tour bus and tootles all over the landscape, in this case turning to thoughts of potential anthology themes. In this case, the possible title "Babes Behind Bars" presented itself. I gnawed this over, trying to come up with a way to adapt the title to the world of science fiction and/or fantasy.

Fantasy! By the great horn spoon, *fantasy*, of course! But no longer *Babes Behind Bars*, nay, for had I not just meandered away from a gaggle of my friends busily criticizing artwork that insists on garbing perfectly innocent bloodthirsty women warriors in itsy-bitsy, teeny-weeny bits of a chainmail bikini? At this point, the aforementioned mental tour bus jumped the guardrail, plunged into the Ravine of Creativity, and I ran back to my friends exclaiming, "Chicks in chainmail! Chicks in chainmail! *In hoc signo*— Oh, wait, not that, but do I ever have an idea for an anthology about women! In armor! And funny! Gotta be funny! Wheeeee!"

Eureka, kiddies. *Eu*-freakin'-*reka*.

From this point on, the publishing history of the first Chicks in Chainmail anthology becomes a looooong visit with Our Friend, Plausible Deniability.

First, albeit Baen Books embraced the concept of the anthology, when it came to the *title* . . . Well, there was some *hesitancy* on the part of the publisher himself regarding it. He was at length persuaded to let it stand, Because Reasons, but he insisted he be given an Out, also Because Reasons. So the first book appeared with a Disclaimer on the back, absolving him of all responsibility for that title.

By the time the third book in the series stood in need of a title, he was the person who provided, of his own will and skill, *Chicks and Chained Males*. So I'd say he got over his qualms, wouldn't you?

This time *I* wanted (and got!) the Disclaimer.

Ever since then, your Humble Correspondent has found herself repeatedly insisting that various things connected with the Chicks in Chainmail series were Not My Fault. For one thing, none of the titles in the Chicks in Chainmail series after *número uno* was my doing, and considering some of those titles—!

Now we come to *this* book. For once it looks like I will not have to fear encountering any *connoisseur* of fine literature who might encounter me at a convention and say, "What a wonderful book! So many brilliant stories, each of them a treat. But honestly, Esther, that *title*?" (Cue more-in-pity-than-in-anger sigh and expressive rolling of the eyes.)

I am to be spared this, because this time there is so much proof beyond my mere claim to innocence that I find myself gleefully distanced from responsibility for this book, title and all! It ain't me, babe. It's that guy, over there (and with his name on the cover). Jason Cordova, *j'accuse*!

How was I to know that the already cited germ of inspiration (which blossomed into a glorious sneeze of five—count 'em, five—anthologies) was contagious? Our Noble Editor has not stopped at mere body armor as a theme, oh mercy cupcakes, no. He has boldly upped the ante, giving the ladies far more than a jingly g-string to shield them as they charge into battle.

I do find it cool that my Chicks were the—I dunno, Muses?—for his, but he can tell you all about that himself. I am responsible for one of the stories, but that (and this foreword) are as far as I'll go to admitting complicity. For one thing, when I was asked to come frolic in Mr. Cordova's literary backyard, I wanted to play but realized that I knew nigh nothing about tanks and the women who drive them.

So I did some research. I *had* heard of *Tank Girl*, but I knew nothing about it, so I looked it up and—

Oh dear.

Ohhhhhh *dear*.

On a less traumatic front, I found out that real-world women and tanks have an interesting and inspiring history.

In the USSR, Mariya Oktyabrskaya's husband was killed in combat during World War II. She vowed revenge against the Nazis, and she didn't stop at words alone. She sold all of her possessions and used the money to have a tank built. Then she demanded to be allowed to ride that tank into battle, which she darn well did. She took a big toll on her enemies before her own death. She was posthumously honored as a Hero of the Soviet Union.

Oh, and she named her tank "Fighting Girlfriend." Hey, her money, her tank, her rules.

The World War II USSR also knew the heroic service of other women and their tanks. There was Yekaterina Petlyuk whose tank, "Little One," was paid for by contributions from schoolchildren. There was Alexandra Samusenko. There were many more.

Are you noticing a little tongue-in-cheek trend in tank naming? Then you're going to love what Captain Jillian Collins of our own nation named *her* tank:

"Barbie's Dreamhouse."

Stop looking at me that way; *I* didn't do it!

Speaking once more of the viper-infested rabbit hole that is internet research, not only did I pick up TMI about *Tank Girl*, I also learned that there is a perfectly sensible, practical, reasonable underlying principle that goes into the naming of tanks, at least US Armed Forces tanks. No, I don't have a website URL to offer, because you will never thrive if you get everything spoon-fed to you (and also because I am too darn lazy to go back and fetch it), but if you search for articles about the sorta-kinda hooraw that sprang up online over one crew naming their tank after Dwayne "the Rock" Johnson, you well may find it.

And here's one more Aha! moment I enjoyed while educating myself preparatory to writing my story and this foreword: since I wanted to find out about women-and-tanks, those were the words I plunked into my Search program.

Result: A stampede of sites offering to sell me *women's tank tops*.

I thought that if I changed my search terms to women-*fighters*-tanks that would clear things up nicely.

Result: A fresh plethora of sites selling women's tank tops *emblazoned with the logo for the Foo Fighters*. (Come on, don't be snarky; even I know who they are!)

And so I close my remarks secure in the knowledge that our esteemed Editor is not fully to blame for the title of this book. *Chicks in Tank Tops* was inevitable, foreordained, the internet would have it so, Manifest Destiny at its finest! He couldn't help himself, poor lad.

Or maybe he could, and he chose this title on purpose, perchance with a wicked laugh upon his lips. I could not say and really, it's not important in the grand scheme of things.

What IS important is for all of you to know beyond all doubt that despite *Chicks in Chainmail* to the contrary, *Chicks in Tank Tops* is . . .

Not

MY

Fault!

And I'm back to the whole Plausible Deniability thing again, amn't I? Such is my fate.

But *your* fate is to read this book and enjoy the bejabbers out of it. You will. That's an order! And a very easy one to follow, once you figure out where you left your bejabbers.

Fighting Writer, over and out.

PS: When I was asked to write this foreword, I in turn asked Mr. Cordova if he wanted to set any . . . boundaries. His response was:

I'm not going to say "write whatever strikes your fancy" because, as an author myself, those are the second-most dangerous words, following "Hold my beer. I've got an idea . . ."

I forgot about that until the moment I finished writing this piece. Oops. Sorry.

My fault.

Editor's Note

Jason Cordova

Esther is correct. You can't blame this project solely on either of us. It was inevitable. After careful deliberation, a thorough investigation, and multiple castings of the bones, it was determined that this anthology is all Toni Weisskopf's fault.

(Note: what follows is a highly dramatized version of events which may or may not have actually occurred.)

I was being snarky one December evening on social media after rereading *Fangs for the Mammaries*. I casually mentioned Baen Books had missed out on a golden opportunity to add to the series. I mean really, who doesn't like the sound of "Tanks for the Mammaries"? It was gold! Gold, I tell ya! The title sold itself! Money, hand over fist! The cover would shock and awe the world! Multiple people added to the discussion, which quickly barreled downhill into regions best left unsaid, and then Toni made the mistake of commenting on the (at this point) long thread.

Let me tell you—there's nothing like hearing "Pitch this to me" to really get your heart racing and cause a minor freak-out.

After some discussion with Toni, the project was green-lit. However, I already knew the anthology wouldn't feel right unless I had the person who inspired this mad creative endeavor aboard in the first place. So with the help of a mutual friend, I was introduced to Esther Friesner. Who, after five minutes of conversation, not only agreed to participate with an introduction, but also asked if she could submit a short story since she already had the title in her head.

I think that was the quickest "yes!" I've said in my life, ever.

I don't think she knew what she was getting into at the time. Poor dear.

With Esther on board, picking up the rest of the authors was a straightforward process. I really only had one requirement: instead of the historical trope of a boy and his dog, I wanted a girl and her tank. I didn't care if it was science fiction, fantasy, or whatever in between. Give me a brave, strong girl and her tank. That was my one and only request from everyone invited to participate.

Luminaries such as Sharon Lee and Steve Miller joined David Drake and Esther, while I went to people I knew personally and asked them if they wanted to be part of my insanity. Robert E. Hampson, Marisa Wolf, Philip Wohlrab, and Kevin Ikenberry all brought their unique styles and voices to the project, all wondering if I'd lost my mind. Jody Lynn Nye has the distinction of being in all five of the "Chicks" books with Esther and there was no way I was going to tell her "no." Joelle Presby offered up a story which felt similar to my own experiences in the Navy. (Side note—no, we did not sail directly into a tropical depression on purpose so we wouldn't have to scrub the upper decks, sir. Honest. Simple navigation error.) A.C. Haskins used his real-world experience as a tank commander to draw upon for his short story. Lydia Sherrer sent in an amazing story of daring rescue coauthored with her husband, David Sherrer, and who doesn't love a good G. Scott Huggins story involving Leonardo da Vinci, Machiavelli, and a villainous Borgia?

They say editing an anthology is like herding cats. If that's the case, then these were the best-behaved cats in the history of the world. It was both a pleasure and an honor to work with each and every one of these authors throughout the process. I would gladly do it again.

Thank you, dear reader, for picking up this anthology. We hope you enjoy it as much as we did creating it. Because really, who doesn't like the idea of *Chicks in Tank Tops*?

Gadreel's Folly
A Liaden Universe® Story

⊕

Sharon Lee & Steve Miller

ANGEL

Somewhere out in the sweet bye 'n' bye, there's a place made all of bright crystal, folding back on itself 'til it's pleated like a fan, over, under, and around, containing the universe and everything in it.

I see it in dreams, though I think it's real—or was. A perfect place, cold, unchanging, breathlessly clear, with nothing warm to taint its perfection.

I'm imperfect; all us vessels of blood and electrons are. We fought *against* crystal perfection; committed the sin of Change. Took flight in our tattered armada of lifeboats, mining rigs, holiday ships, and surplus troop transports, going from crystal *there* to dusty *here*.

We *wanted* imperfection, and we pushed through the transition: heretics, sure, but alive.

The Liadens call the transition the Great Migration. Terrans are closer to the truth—they call it the Great Escape. To the Churchly— that's me—it's The Choice.

I'm no novice; I've had my training, and swore my final vows. I'd done well in combat training, strategy, tactics, but my Calling wasn't the ministry of the High Command. I was Called to repair armor, and the wearers of armor, everything from the brave clanks on the front line, to the soldier fitted out as a turret-gunner. I was attached to field battalions as Sister Mechanic, or, as the soldiers called me— the Repair Angel.

⊕ ⊕ ⊕

I was attached to the forward base at Scythe Seven, a small worldlet around a tiny red star. For the last dozen Standards, I'd been working out of Garages and Mobile Units, but there was a full Cathedral on Scythe Seven, funded, so the Sexton told me, by a pious believer named Kobara Zeldin.

I went into the chancel to pray. The Cathedral reviewed my vows, my record, and my Calling, and opened to me.

I rose, bowed to the altar, and left to bring in my supplies and the Big Rig.

The last action had been bad, though it would've been worse if it hadn't been for the soldier right now in my care, his carapace shredded like tinsel, and most of the rest of him, too. I'd had to do repairs, by which I mean *repairs*. I had a feeling he wasn't going to like some of the choices made on his behalf, but, then, I couldn't exactly ask his preferences.

He'd joined up. I was on contract. I had a little wiggle room, and I *could've* let him go with a prayer, if he'd taken even the smallest knock to his head. His bad luck that he'd been wearing a premium helmet— not standard issue, so *some*body loved him, and I sent a blessing to them out on the prayer wind, put on my gloves, and got to work.

The hero wasn't the only casualty of that particular action, though he was the most complicated. Part of that was the extent of the work to be done, and because I had to machine the pickier parts. I *could've* gone with what I had in inventory, and the contract would've preferred it, but there was just that little bit of wiggle room. I did pray on it, which the contract stipulated was my duty in cases where I stood at Cusp. Prayer wasn't as informative as I might've liked, but I logged it, and kept on fabricating the fine parts, around the repair of the others—the *relatively few* others—who'd been wounded in this latest of too many battles.

I prayed over three and released them, set their helmets and what was left of their armor aside for when I had leisure to clean and mine them for working components. Eight more had needed repair, though nothing as extensive as the hero, and I got them up and out just in time for Troop Rotation, even if they rotated out and no one else rotated in.

The rotation wasn't an event this time, no marching of forces, circling the Cathedral where it sat commanding a view of the plains and the distant ring of hills. In this season, the rivers—one wide and shallow, the other deep and furrowed—were dry at the confluence and the trees droopy. The troops marched straight out to the transport without so much as a drumroll in farewell.

The Sexton had come out onto the parapet with me to overlook the departure.

"They won't be back," he said, barely nodding in my direction. "I'll watch the doors, Sister. You keep the souls."

The hero was in Purgatory, on standby while the ceramics set.

I was in the north transept, tinkering with the Big Rig. The Rig was set to accept me as motivator. I had all the circuitry and modules to accept a full merge, though I'd only done that once since training. Still, the contract stipulated that the Big Rig and its operator be prepared, so prepared we both were.

"Sister Mechanic?"

She spoke quiet, out of respect for the place. She shouldn't have had to speak at all, but I'd been concentrating on the Big Rig, and hadn't heard the Sanctus bell.

"Sister Mechanic?"

The sound was hollow and empty like the building.

"Right there, Commander," I called, climbing out, sealing the access and checking the tie-downs. The local star was small and the Jump points only a few hours away, so the commander tended to be elsewhere and then drop in, expecting me, armor-mending specialist that I was, to be beck-and-called whenever.

I took off my gloves, and headed for the nave, only to catch sight of her in Purgatory, where the hero rested.

"Ma'am?" I said, stepping around the aide to her side.

She continued to study the readouts above the hero's drawer. I folded my hands and waited.

The silence stretched. Maybe she prayed. I didn't—just waited—and finally she turned to look at me.

"A lengthy repair, Sister Mechanic."

Commander Alifont always gives me the full formal. She treats me like we're equals, which I used to think was a fine, heady fiction.

Lately, I've come to realize she's right. My actions are constrained by the terms of the contract. Hers are constrained by the orders of the High Command. Both of us would do things different, left to our own hearts and heads.

"A lengthy and difficult repair," I said.

"How long until it is complete?"

"Assuming we don't attract anyone's attention, I'll finish the build tomorrow, then put it through the trials. If everything's good, I'll attach, calibrate, and resuscitate. That's seventy-two hours, best case."

"Best case," she murmured, looking again at the readouts. "I wonder, Sister Mechanic, why you chose this therapy?"

She knew the terms of the contract as well as I did, which meant she was asking something else. Often, I can figure what it is, but this time, I didn't see it.

I turned my hands palm up.

"Soul and mind were intact," I said piously.

"Soul and mind *alone* were intact," she said, a gentle correction, but I thought I saw what she was getting at now.

"He's a hero, Commander. If he hadn't grabbed a ride on that Grinder and hit the most vulnerable spot, the base wouldn't be here, now, nor any living thing."

I paused, decided against adding anything more, and refolded my hands.

Commander Alifont sighed.

"That is very true, though it could be argued just as neatly that he disobeyed orders and deprived the High Command of a valuable piece of enemy tech."

I blinked.

"We were ordered to *capture* a Grinder?"

She met my eyes.

"Why, yes, that was the mission."

Capture a Grinder? I thought about that; recalling the battle as first I heard it over the scanner in the nave, and as I reviewed it, later, when the Observer's cache had been dumped and distributed. I saw in my mind's eye the lines dropping—not back from its invasion, but *away*. Obvious *now* that they had meant to enclose the Grinder, but how they had ever meant to capture it defied my understanding, despite my training. I *hadn't* been a full turret commander in a real war, and so in no position to dispute the High Command's orders. Not in so many words.

Anywise, it had been that falling away that had given the hero-soldier his opportunity, which—not knowing the High Command's true intent, and their willingness to see him vaporized, if necessary—he'd seized.

Putting himself between his comrades and annihilation, he had destroyed the Grinder, preserving his battlemates and the base, not *quite* at the cost of his own life. Which was a blade with two edges, as Sister Fariette used to say.

If I were to own the truth, it was the *how* of that destruction that puzzled me. Grinders are well-named, and while we haven't captured one, we have captured lesser engines. I'd worked on a few, and can attest that, of all the wrongs the enemy embraces, sloppy engineering isn't one of them. So, I was looking forward to learning the *how* of that particular heroism.

I considered the readouts above the drawer where the hero, what was left of him, awaited resurrection, and I examined my actions and my conscience.

I had, I decided, made the correct choice, not for my curiosity, but for the unit and the souls of the soldiers in my care, because—

I thought about the spine I'd grafted into the titanium gridwork, hoping I hadn't gone too far, wasting resources on someone they'd turn off before putting back in the field again.

"Did he disobey orders?"

Commander Alifont shook her head.

"He didn't get a full briefing. The line soldiers were told to do the best they could."

I nodded, relieved.

"So, the best he could was take a Grinder out to full destruct sequence."

"Yes, that seems to be the case, doesn't it?"

I nodded, struck by a thought that I might have to pray over, or worry about, or both.

"The enemy's going to pay special attention to us, now," I said, hearing Truth in my voice. I nodded at the drawer. "We're going to need him."

Commander Alifont sighed.

"I believe you are correct, Sister Mechanic," she said softly. "Well done."

KAS

"You sent for me, Grandmother?"

Kas hesitated on the threshold of the workshop, reluctant to go in, knowing she was angry, knowing he deserved it; not wanting anger to be his last memory of her.

"Yes, young Kasagaria, I did. Come in and close the door."

That . . . was remarkably mild, despite the use of his full name. Kas stepped up to the counter, the door banging shut behind him. She was at the workbench, her back to him, facing the forge. He waited for whatever came next.

"So, you're for a soldier, is that what I'm hearing?"

He should have told her himself; he had *meant* to tell her himself, but the transfer had hit the account before he'd even gotten on the train, and everybody knew what he'd done by the time he got home.

"Yes, ma'am," he said carefully. "It's soldier for me."

"Not the trade I would have chosen for you. I had librarian in my mind."

So had he. He'd trained for librarian all his life. Which is how he'd come to know that Saijmur Village needed money to pay the generation tax, and what was the penalty for nonpayment. He loved his grandmother; he loved his village; and it was, after all, a librarian's duty to shield the ignorant from harm.

It hadn't been so large a sum, saving that Saijmur Village didn't have it. The signing bonus for a soldier willing to go to the front had been just as meager. Almost *exactly* as meager, the debt balancing the tax balance so perfectly that they might have been made for each other.

Which he did not doubt they had been. Librarians were suspicious creatures, after all.

"Well," said his grandmother, turning around at last to face him. Backlit by the forge, he thought she was holding a head cradled in her arms until she leaned over and put it on the counter between them.

"Made that helmet for your grandfather, when *he* went off for soldier."

Kas stared. His grandfather had been a librarian. Saijmur folk didn't hire out as soldiers. They were artificers, with a side in information.

"I . . . didn't know that," he said.

His grandmother nodded.

"Felt the responsibility to buy us out of a previous trouble." His grandmother sighed. "We either birth stupid librarians or brave ones." She extended a hand and patted the helmet. "This is what got him home, or so he told me. Saved his head, though not his leg, and they shipped him home. I'm backing it to do the same for you."

Kas woke, kept his eyes closed and took stock. That was an old lesson, born of Saijmur's past, when raids had been common.

He didn't hurt. He'd *expected* to hurt, and hurt bad. He'd remember why in another minute or two. What he did feel was . . . heavy, which suggested that he might be drugged into a pain-free state. That in turn suggested that he was in Purgatory, which was . . . hopeful.

One of the first things he'd learned on coming to the front line was that soldiers were expendable, nothing more so. The carapace, and the equipment—*those* was expensive, and cared for appropriately.

If he was in Purgatory, his wounds must be relatively trivial. That was unexpected. He'd had a moment there, right before the Grinder staggered under him, when he'd thought it was too much, too dangerous, that *he could die here*—but he'd been committed by then—overcommitted, if he was telling the truth—and there wasn't anywhere to go but onward.

If he was in the hospital, then . . . he'd *succeeded*, the Grinder hadn't destroyed the base. That was a relief, though—truth again— he hadn't done it for the base or his comrades.

He'd done it for himself, out of raw anger that the enemy sent such things against living people, against defenseless planets, and villages like the one he'd grown up in.

He heard something just then—a rustle, or a soft burst of static. Reasonable, if he was under medical repair. He should really establish that.

Kas opened his eyes.

ANGEL

The build had tested well—better than well, which is what you get when you take the time to machine the parts, and don't depend on items from inventory that'll do well enough. And, most times, they *do* well enough, because most repairs aren't extensive, and most soldiers won't be depending on them for long, one way or another.

This soldier was going to be depending on the repairs I'd done for the rest of his life, which, given Gadreel's blessing, would far outdistance three score and ten. I was careful, like Sister Fariette had taught me. I prayed, and ran three complete test suites, though the contract barely called for one.

The numbers were good, the seals, hydraulics, and onboard spin-systems better than good.

I made the attachments, and initiated wake-up.

Done right, wake-up is a slow process, and there wasn't any reason to do it wrong.

I had a notion about the Big Rig that I wanted to test, given the likelihood we were due for a lot of close attention from the enemy, but I didn't want the hero to wake alone. Eventually, he'd *need* to be in there as turreteer, but building that connection would take info from Training Wheels sessions. So, once everything was sealed and settled, I walked him over to the north transept, which was easier than trying to shift the Rig.

The scanner wasn't getting anything but the occasional burst of static, which could either be good news or bad. The noise helped keep me grounded in the present. It was easy to get involved in the Big Rig and forget there was anything else.

The scanner fizzed and popped. Somebody nearby said, "Hello? Medic?"

The hairs rose right up on my arms, hearing that clear, commanding voice. The voice of a god, though according to the contract, that would be blasphemy.

I turned on the ladder, and saw him for the first time, by which I mean, I saw *him*. I'd seen his face often enough he seemed familiar, but seeing *him*, the beautiful soul looking out through those deep, dark eyes, was enough to make me doubt prayer.

"Hello?" he said again, and I heard the beginnings of panic in his voice. He'd noticed that he couldn't move, and that would be frightening. Admittedly, not as frightening as the reality, but that was exactly why I hadn't wanted him to wake alone.

"I'm here," I said, and his eyes moved, tracking the sound of my voice, and widened when he saw me.

"I can't move," he said.

"That's temporary," I assured him. "I didn't want you hurting yourself."

Some of the panic eased out of his face. "I'm restrained."

"That's right," I told him, which wasn't a lie. "What's your name, child?"

"Kas," he said, then his mouth quirked, and he expanded it. "Kasagaria Mikelsyn, Unit Soldier, OHV440-43-14-33-60N."

I grinned at him.

"I like Kas better. You mind if I use it, or is it only for friends?"

"Friends, family," he said, warily.

I nodded. "Friends and family call me Angel," I told him. "You, too. You're in for repairs. Last bit of action left you pretty torn up. You remember anything about that?"

He frowned, then blinked.

"It *worked*?" he asked, looking only slightly up at me.

"Didn't you expect it to?"

"More . . . *hoped*," he said slowly. "I had a bad few seconds right before the engage, when I thought maybe I'd been a damn fool."

"Your actions saved the unit from annihilation," I told him, putting conviction and pride into my voice. "You're a hero, Kasagaria Mikelsyn."

There's a lot of ways to answer something like that. Kas Mikelsyn laughed. I liked him for that.

KAS

A hero, was it? Kas laughed. He had to. Saijmur folk weren't heroes, not by any measure. Saijmur folk were sneak-abouts and secret-finders. Which was how he'd known where the kill-switch for the Grinder was.

Somebody'd found or stolen a manual, sometime years ago, and brought it home to Saijmur. The librarian at the time—maybe his grandfather, maybe another generation back—had accessioned it, and Kas had processed it as part of his training. The Saijmur bred for librarians; bred for an eidetic memory and the ability to machine-learn.

But there was the Nurse Mechanic still standing there on her ladder next to the big mech, watching patiently, like she expected something more than a laugh.

"Just trying to save my own life, if it comes to that," he said.

"Right. You did a good job there, Kas. Where'd you get that helmet, if it can be told?"

"Told easy," he said. "My grandmother's a smith. When my grandfather went for soldier, she made the helmet, hoping it would keep him safe—which it did. He lost a leg, but didn't even get a headache."

"Glory to your grandmother. She does good work." She tipped her head. "Lost a leg," she murmured. "Had a rebuild?"

"That's right," Kas said, wondering why she cared—but, there, maybe it was a test, to see how well the helmet *had* protected him. He was tempted to run a test himself, but an inventory of the library inside his head would have to wait until he'd been released back to his own quarters.

"If your grandfather had his leg rebuilt," the Nurse Mechanic said, "you're familiar with the concept. That'll help us move along."

That caught his attention. Had *he* lost a leg? Two legs? An arm?

Kas took a deep breath to quell the rising panic.

Say instead—he *tried* to take a breath.

Which was when he realized he wasn't breathing.

"Kasagaria Mikelsyn, don't you flatline on me, all the work I put into patching you back together!" Her voice reminded him of his grandmother when she was about to lean into a scold.

"I'm not breathing!"

"Sure you are," she said brutally matter-of-fact. "Gotta breathe to talk."

Well, that was true, but—

"I'm not breathing in-between talking."

"Now, that's so, and I'll explain why not, but you have to let me tell it."

It was the willing offer of information that calmed him. There was something here to learn, and information was a currency he understood.

"Tell it," he said.

She nodded and eased down onto the rung of her ladder. It struck

Kas then that they were eye to eye, with her halfway up, and the big unit looming behind.

"Quick tell, Kas. You saved the base from annihilation. That's *true*. You're a hero. *That's* true. You thought you'd been a damn fool—and that's true, too. Your helmet served you just like it did your grandfather. The rest of you . . . well. Grinders are called Grinders for a reason."

Kas thought.

"So I had a rebuild?"

"You did. More extensive than your grandfather's leg. You're *mostly* rebuild, is what I want you to appreciate, Kas."

"My head," he said, because what was in his head made him who he was more than anything else.

"Your head's in good shape," she said, and gave him a sidewise grin. "I should say, as good as it ever was, given it told you to take out a Grinder on your own, in standard armor."

"And I did," Kas said, stung.

Her grin got wider.

"And you did," she agreed. "That's why I patched you up good and tight."

He considered her. "I'm not following."

She pointed her work gauntlets at him.

"I want to see what you can do now you've got the means to carry through."

Kas stared at her, brain working, and looked up at the monster unit rising behind her, like an honor guard.

"I want to see," he said. "I want to see what you did to me."

"Fair."

She pulled a stick out of an overall pocket and tapped it.

A screen slid down from the ceiling. Kas looked up and met his own eyes.

Dark Saijmur eyes set deep in a craggy, beetle-browed face. His nose was broad, cheekbones sharp, chin square and determined. His mouth was narrow, lips tight. Rusty red hair clustered tight against his head in tight, springy ringlets.

He saw tears rise in his eyes—relief, it might've been to see everything so normal.

Then, he looked further.

Face, ears, chin, neck, shoulders, chest . . .

No, *not* his chest, but . . . armor, sort of.

He closed his eyes and concentrated.

He decided that yes, he could *feel* his shoulders and he could feel motion at the extension of the arms that ought to be depending from those shoulders. He felt and heard vibration when he flexed his fingers. He *felt* the fingers but not the scars and fingernails that belonged there, not the itches . . .

He didn't hear his heartbeat, but something like the whir of a pump working.

Ceramics and isolloy. He knew the theories, at least. He took a breath he didn't need and then one he did. Opened his eyes and looked at—Angel.

"How long does something like this last?"

"Organics are the weak points," Angel said, like she was giving a lecture. "But, given reasonable upkeep, repairs or replacements as needed, I'd say the whole unit's good for a hundred-fifty, two hundred Standards, easy. Could be more."

"Brains are organic."

She grinned like he'd given her a present.

"So they are, and that'd be a worry for you if I'd forgotten to do the circulatory hookups. We're using the same cerebrospinal fluid you grew up with, along with a couple additives that work better and last longer. Your brain tissues'll stay supple and in good working order for at least as long as the chassis, and you'll be processing faster, too." She paused. "Unless you take a high-voltage hit, naturally; anything that dries out the organics is going to be problematical. So, be careful, Kas."

He snorted.

"Not exactly my strong point."

"You'll have time to learn," Angel said comfortably. "Other questions?"

"What if I go unstable? The . . . chassis looks like it could do some serious damage."

"There's protocols in place to take care of that kind of thing," she said, and gave him an earnest look. "You wouldn't want to be destroying a station full of innocent people or anything like that, would you, Kas?"

"No," he said truthfully, "I wouldn't. Thank you for thinking of that."

"No problem at all," she said. "Other questions?"

"When will I be able to move?"

"Couple minutes, if you think you're ready. I'll warn you there's work ahead. That brain of yours has to learn how to manipulate the new interfaces. Ought to have you walking by suppertime. What'll take longest'll be fine motor control."

She squinted thoughtfully. "You knit?"

He considered her: a lanky woman in overalls, shaved head covered in tattoos; her sleeves were rolled, revealing more tattoos, down her arms, over her wrists and fingers. Her blue eyes were round in a round pale face, lips full, chin soft. More tattoos ran down her throat, vanishing beneath the overalls.

"Knit?" he repeated.

"Or embroider? Make models? Something that requires precision finger-work, is what I'm looking for."

"I play the *rastfeener*."

She blinked.

"And that would be, exactly?"

He tried to raise his hands, to show her the shape against the air. An alarm shouted, high and unnerving. Angel tapped the stick and it stopped.

"Alarm can't tell the difference between a man who talks with his hands and one who's trying his strength," she said apologetically. "So . . . *rastfeener*?"

"Musical instrument," he said, suddenly missing his, back home in his room. "Five strings, strum or pluck."

"You any good?"

He grinned.

"The best."

She grinned back, and stood up on the ladder.

"All right, Kas, here's what we're going to do. The contracts—mine and yours—prefer you to go back to barracks. I'd rather not see my work go to waste, but—you being the work—you get to choose.

"What's your preference: back to the barracks and learn as you go, or stay here for physical therapy and learning how to take care of yourself?"

"Physical therapy." Kas didn't even have to think.

"That's it, then."

She raised the stick, inputting commands with a rapid patter of fingertips against ceramic, slipped it away into a leg pocket, and slid down the ladder.

"Let's get you walking."

ANGEL

There hadn't been any action to speak of, though we did get one ambulance come in with casualties from a skirmish. Kas assisted. His fingering still needed work, but there was plenty of gross work, and research, for him.

I'd given him full permissions for the library, and there wasn't anything I could've done to make him happier, except hand over the *rastfeener* I'd signed out of the Cathedral's stasis storage room.

"Gift of the Grancino Family, it said on the record," I told him while he turned the instrument over in his hands like it was his own child.

He looked up. "The Grancinos were master luthiers, back a hundred, hundred-fifty Standards."

"Then it's a good instrument?"

He grinned. "Oh, *yes*. Thank you, Angel."

We ran sims, and when he had the protocols clear, I introduced him to the equipment.

"This here's your Fariette-Kelsin Tactical Acquisition Heavy Operations armor. Which I find a mouthful, so from me, it's the Big Rig. There's three ways in—for most, the standard inputs. For you, the spine interface. For me, these—"

I held out my arms, showing him the tattoos.

"Before I found my Calling, the Order had me trained as a turreteer. I was good enough, technically, and got the whole set of implants."

"Good enough—technically," Kas said, that quick mind of his at work. "What happened?"

"Live targets happened. I'm better at healing than I am at killing."

He nodded, and I turned away.

"Training Wheels," I said, putting my hand on the chassis. "This is where you'll learn about the spine interface, and the systems. Once you're easy, we transfer you to the Big Rig."

I grinned up at him, and patted the Training Wheels one more time.

"Mount up, soldier. Let's see what you can do."

Pride's a sin, but it's no more than factual to say that Kas was good. The rebuild was my finest work to date—another fact—but what brought it to excellence was Kasagaria Mikelsyn—his brain, his heart. His soul.

Where we'd run sims, now we ran in truth: races down the wide empty halls below the Cathedral, him in the Training Wheels, learning to control the spinal interface, me running the Big Rig on manual. In another hundred hours, Kas would be as good you could get, and ready for full turreteer.

Except for that one ambulance, there was only us, and we might've indulged ourselves: racing, sparring, listening to Kas make music, his fingering ever finer.

There were some things to worry about. Troops were rotating out, but none were rotating in. There was a skeleton crew at the barracks, and the Cathedral guards had been relocated, leaving me, the Sexton, and Kas to guard her.

"We're gonna be pulled," I said to Kas, and realized how much I'd come to love the Cathedral, and how much it would hurt to leave.

Right in the present, though, I was as happy as I'd ever been.

We were sitting in the choir, for the acoustics, the pair of us singing a song I'd just been taught, while Kas played his *rastfeener*.

So, we were singing, and Kas was playing, me sitting on the steps, and him standing by the rail.

That was where Commander Alifont found us.

She stopped, her aide at her side, and a laden-down carrier 'bot behind them both.

She looked at me, and at Kas, immersed, the strings holding his concentration.

"Therapy?" Her voice held doubt.

"Coordination of assisted vocal apparatus, communications protocol test and certifications, finger and hand dexterity testing, testing of the bio resource management interface, and utilization of new sensors testing and confirmations."

Her lips quirked as Kas let his playing fade away with the last line of the song, his voice strong and true.

"Your glory shall be ever ours."

The commander's face was stern again. She tipped her head, and the mech aide moved one step forward.

"Attention!"

I stood. Kas straightened, the *rastfeener* held down at his side, eyes forward.

"Sister Mechanic, to your office with me, please. Unit Soldier Mikelsyn! You will map the Cathedral defenses, and send it to me before I leave."

Kas saluted. "Commander." He strode off, taking the *rastfeener* with him.

I came down the steps to accompany the commander to my office.

I pulled up Kas's records for her, and stood aside, hands folded, while she reviewed.

"Has he done any live fire in this configuration? I don't see a check-off."

The Big Rig's main weapons, that would be.

"He's been with the Training Wheels, and worked with the basic launchers. We were slow getting coordinated—my fault. Turns out that helmet of his is more than I knew. It can interface directly with the weapons systems, which gives him an edge, even over the spinal interface."

"The sim scores are adequate," she said, which was a lie. The sim scores were superlative.

I didn't correct her.

"We've been out on the surface a few times when the defense lights have shown green, but that hasn't happened much lately, given staffing. He's a hundred hours from taking on the full load, I'd say, maybe just almost a hundred."

The commander turned away from the screen.

"He needs live fire experience with the Borefours before he faces combat."

"I need permissions," I reminded, "before I can have the auto base-crew load those."

She looked at me oddly, like I'd made a joke.

"Area commander's got to approve the Big Rig going fully live. It's still in my fix-it file, and still set up for me. All the test rigs are mine, so I can figure out what's still to be fixed. On top of that there are fresh neural attachments and the like that need to be inserted before he can sit in there, and they have to be right and tested fully so he don't blow his brains out. It falls to me, and I got to have those permissions."

Her face went odd again and she gently shook her head, letting out a breath.

"Very well, Sister Mechanic. There will not be a problem about your permissions."

She motioned to the carrier 'bot, which unloaded itself on the worktable. It opened the first box, and I felt a sudden chill. Ceramics and crystal, the shape just slightly *wrong*. The Order had some devices that were . . . similar in construction, though not, I thought, this particular device.

"I have brought with me a mark of the High Command's recognition of your work and your prowess, Sister Mechanic."

KAS

He'd not understood that the Cathedral was a museum as much as a military base until the *rastfeener* came to his hands. Angel had taken him to the warehouse when he asked, showing him not only rare musical instruments but other things looking like furniture and weapons in their see-through sealed wraps on shelves and pallets and piles. He hadn't known that a stasis box the size of a warehouse was even possible, but yes, such things *were* possible if the Cathedral it was housed with sat upon a bed of timonium able to power it for centuries.

And it came to him that the Cathedral was the reason Scythe Seven had military importance. Too far from convenient travel lanes to be a proper guardian fort, too strong to be overwhelmed with easy weapons, not strategic enough to turn the course of a war, but of too much use to just abandon whole. It was old, and had survived several wars, so it had value, maybe, as a fallback point.

The new . . . *configuration* required minimal downtime. His organic brain needed sleep, but much less than the previous . . . *configuration* had.

He'd put that extra time to use. Angel had given him full access to a vast, varied, and ancient library.

"You're trained in information—that seems to be what's got you this far. You've got lots of duplicate storage onboard, and backup processors. Feel free to access what's here, copy what you need—but you can't share what's classified with someone besides me."

He was a librarian. Of course, he needed it *all*.

"You're on all my comm channels right now. I expect that when the next flight of casualties comes in you'll be right there with me— you can do fine work with those hands! Meanwhile, about the history files . . . so much of it will never be touched again, you know? Take it or leave it, as you will. Someone ought to get use of it."

It warmed him that she thought he'd get use of it. He'd tried to imagine the Saijmur library holding the Cathedral's info, and saw ruin and raiders. He tried to imagine himself in the Saijmur library, and heard his mother weeping and his grandmother cursing.

He'd tried to think of going someplace else, then put it aside. First, he had to survive to the end of his contract.

And right now, he had orders to fill.

He'd left the *rastfeener* in his quarters, and proceeded to the defense area.

"I have brought with me a mark of the High Command's recognition of your work and your prowess, Sister Mechanic." Commander Alifont's voice.

Kas checked his systems, found Angel's comm green. He was on all her comm channels, hadn't she told him that?

Maybe he should've shut it down, except—

"The High Command wishes to duplicate this fortress."

Kas frowned. They couldn't duplicate the fortress, not unless they duplicated Scythe Seven. How did they not know that?

"Sister Mechanic, we are withdrawing the bulk of forces from Scythe Seven to concentrate on an incursion elsewhere. The High Command feels it is best for us to maintain a visible presence here. We see in your records that you have experience in Proto-armor Command. You and your office will provide the visible presence we need. We seek a pretense of normality, assuming a certain amount of monitoring of this location is ongoing."

"I'm a nurse, Commander. I fix the injured—"

"And you protect those under your care. You have a patient, you have a mandate. And you have your orders."

A pause that went long, before the commander spoke again.

"An unmanned fleet ambulance will arrive soon, from the Residal battle area. It is empty."

Kas frowned. Angel had been expecting incoming wounded, and had taken time from the rigs to train him in repair. But—an *empty* ambulance?

"Understand, Sister Mechanic, that the preprogramming extends to leaving the system. That ambulance is intended to be *your* exit if the enemy broaches the Cathedral's defenses."

Angel was thinking, he could tell by the way she didn't say anything. The commander continued.

"This is not the whole of the situation. Now, this device was recently acquired from an enemy cache of Old Tech. It has been studied, and its functions are well understood. You will find the information on your mission key."

Kas looked at his wrist screen. The object looked vaguely like a helmet, inset with . . . jewels?

"You'll wear this while we test. We want to know why you're such a good body mechanic, Sister, and this—it records what's happening in your head, why you make certain choices, where your points of decision are located, and so on. This record can be downloaded and studied. The device also creates a profile, which can be directly shared with another mechanic. We are making recordings of the most successful across a variety of fields.

"I do not wish to lose your expertise, Sister Mechanic. You will, therefore, be made directly available to my home staff at High Command. The war has come to a difficult turn. Command will be augmenting so that we may interface directly with captured enemy equipment. This will improve our position, and keep the High Command safe."

Kas stopped moving. Relying on organic memory rather than going for a playback—he still wasn't used to all the things he could do with those buttons, controls, and screens built into the new arms—

Yes, he had just heard Commander Alifont explain that the High Command was to be adopting more of the enemy's techniques and equipment . . . in order to stay abreast of the enemy. They'd *become* the enemy in order to fight it.

It was about then that Kas gave up and pressed the privacy switch. The information Angel was getting was being stored, if he needed it, but for now, he would study what there was of the landscape.

He had his orders, after all.

ANGEL

The ambulance came in and docked, just like normal. There was nothing there for me this time: just empty beds and an operating emergency set up—could have been the one that brought me Kas, because he'd been that close to the beyond when he got to me.

Commander Alifont was gone, on her way to Jump almost a dozen hours out, but Cathedral systems thought Commander was still here. Live. I'd never wanted command, but it hung on my vest in three new keys, each one far too much power for a failed turreteer who'd rather fix than break.

I had a headache. Had it since the ceramic headset had come off, and Commander Alifont packed it away with her own hand. Neither one of us believed it was just a calibration; I'd spent a half dozen and more hours having my brain invaded, memories checked, thoughts explored and somehow sucked elsewhere. It'd been painful, then, not much less, now.

Before she'd left, Commander Alifont handed me a fourth key.

"Your copy, Sister Mechanic. In case of need."

She handed me a fifth key.

"As you have invested so many resources in his therapy, you will now install this device in the larger mount that you are prepping; it will do the same for that driver."

She watched me install the recording device in tandem with the regular driving helmet even though I pointed out that it was currently my seat and not his.

"I'm still tracking a problem spot on this thing. Could take me hours more."

"Then concentrate there, Sister Mechanic. Your skill is known throughout the quadrant and you have only your patient and this device to care for. Any insights we gather can only further our cause."

⊕ ⊕ ⊕

"The place runs itself, mostly," I told Kas when he'd found me in my office, looking at his records, and the records of dozens of others. Commander Alifont had taken copies of all my files, as well as copies from the Sexton's office and even Kas's own notes, where he'd been thinking he might eventually be able to send something to family to let them know.

"But she removed the rest of the garrison, Angel. What's going to happen?"

"We're supposed to make the place look lived in, so that's what we'll do. You and me'll get some practice out on the dunes by the outer walls; we'll let you work up to the Big Rig like you're supposed to. I told her one hundred hours, but you know, all things considered, if we just work like there's nothing else to do, I'd say in forty hours, maybe twenty-five, since you're so canny. I'll certify you for the Big Rig—I ought to have your tie-ins done by then. You'll be able to run patrols to make up for who's not here."

"You know," he said, admitting what I knew already, "our comms were all live. It sounds like the High Command *wants* Scythe Seven to be attacked—like they're going to let me go down fighting, like they're offering you the *appearance* of an out, once they have your brain copied, but the assumption is that they will own your skills, regardless."

I gave him a salute, right then.

"We're bait, right enough. But we're not *stupid* bait, Kas. And we're not easy, either."

I patted the Big Rig.

"Once you're properly mounted, we'll both be more than we were. We'll do the best that we can, and maybe there's a future in it. You and the Sexton are my troops, I'm not going nowhere without you.

"Now, let's get busy. It might be we have enough time to get it right."

KAS

There wasn't enough time. The commander had known what was coming in before she'd left the Cathedral.

The commander was two days gone when the Sexton called the first alarm: the Cathedral's sensors saw the ships incoming.

"I have the doors, Sister. And the Cathedral fights for itself. We'll hold, like we've always held before."

Kas had studied the Cathedral's history; knew the Sexton was right. The *Cathedral* had held, but soldiers had died.

It sat on a plain where in three seasons of five two sluggish rivers met after they'd wandered down the world's only big mountain and a line of foothills. An easy target at first glance, but down in the vaults there were some powerful shields that would take major busting to get through.

The superstructure, though, and anything above the stasis warehouse level, and the heaviest shields, was vulnerable. And that meant the ambulance sitting attached to the Purgatory Unit was at risk, even hidden under the portico.

"There's no dreadnought incoming," Angel said, studying the data field. "This could go on a long time. Not even really a heavy bombardment. But they have the high ground, and I got nothing but you and me. I think they must have come in to scout, probing to see where they went wrong last time, maybe looking for the Grinder-killer. Meanwhile, Commander Alifont took everything but the building so the target's something they got to be careful of. Things that are holy might be held by fanatics!"

Kas snorted a laugh.

"Angel, right now I'm for saving you, me, the *rastfeener*, and the Sexton, if he'll come. I'll be fanatic about that. You're not going to order we charge them, are you?"

He knew that in the long run, maybe she'd need to. For the moment, as the dim afternoon sky gave way to dusk, the automatics were shielding and tossing back what the incoming ships threw at them.

Waiting, waiting, waiting... Kas read and reread what he knew of the projectile weapons, practiced with the strongest waldo, making it throw punches against the air.

Finally several of their ships peeled off, one laid down fire across a blameless plain of mostly dust and scrub vegetation while the other took out the core of the landing field big ships used—or had used—in the days before Scythe Seven was a forward base. That ship pulled away while the first seemed bent on setting down, perhaps unleashing soldiers on their own. The automatics were pickier now, so it might have been a matter of them waiting it out...

Came an alert across the speakers and sensors, too close to what followed to have been an aid to any but a fully armor-installed soldier.

The nearest foothills lit up like new stars, the tallest mountain went blue. Noise roared around even deep within Purgatory where they stood armed, armored, and stunned.

"Gadreel speaks!"

The Sexton's voice rose like a prayer across the ether.

"Sister Mechanic," he said, across the comm, "it is my belief that there may be one more such outburst available. I have faith that the enemy has encroached too far and too long for the Cathedral to feel itself secure without strong measures . . . but it can clear the skies only so often, and the enemy has landed! I to my post!"

The view screens showed vid from atop the tower: the enemy *was* landing, the ship that had strafed the land finally settling down.

Kas still reeled from the power, the Training Wheels vibrating as the ancient shields strained—and held.

Down on the plain, the enemy ship disgorged a ragged line of five units quite similar to their own rigs—high-speed tractor bases with an armored cabin nestled deep between. Where the Big Rig had four projectile tubes arrayed in a tight diamond shape on a turret above the cabin, and Training Wheels a double, two of those oncoming units had triple large tubes turreted, and the other three a dozen or more smaller side-mounted tubes stacked one above the other, with no turret at all. They seemed clear what the target was: the portico beneath which the ambulance ship, clearly marked as such, lay parked.

Angel said, "Move out," and they took the camouflaged relief door opposite the narthex while the Sexton moved to the narthex itself, his rudimentary armor little more than ceremonial, like his rifle.

ANGEL

I hear there are things you're not supposed to forget how to do: making love, fixing breakfast, breathing . . . but I hadn't expected I'd feel that way about taking the Big Rig's turret live, with live ammo, with a mission, and full permissions. I'd dreamed about being back in command, distant and indistinct dreams where, sim-wise, the ride was the thing and there was no game plan except to keep moving while the enemy got melted around me.

Now, I could feel my heart beating faster, the breath coming harder, feel some sweat. But I was calmer than I expected—this time I knew exactly where my help was, and the Cathedral's tactics module was showing to be closer to AI than I expected.

So, the Cathedral protected itself and, as an afterthought, shielded us. My local reference sensors showed no ships in the sky anywhere near us, an amazing help and unexpected, but we had no idea of what they might have that could stand off and fire. I could feel the Big Rig's shield vibrating, heard my heart, wondered, not for the first time, what combat was like for the rebuilds I'd done, people with no human heart and just enough fringe of adrenal analogs to be physically thrilled as they faced a battle.

I guessed we needed to do the test, with Kas, and neither of us experts, both leaning on the Cathedral's comm links.

"You got the basics there, Kas, you know the theory. I've got heavier shielding here, and more zap when I fire; I want you to watch the tactical screens and make sure where the smaller rigs are headed, if you can. Don't want them ganging up on either of us . . ."

It was probably truer than he knew when I told Kas he had the basics; my links not only had the plains but also gave me some minor theater views. The enemy been brought down hard with whatever the Cathedral had done and aside a couple of smaller orbiting objects that might be anything from planet-busting bombs to simple comm relays, there wasn't anything aloft that drew attention. If Kas could keep up—

"I've got matches from the records," I heard him over secure comm. "The smaller units are basically crackers. They can fight but they're mostly after opening things up—they carry actual rams besides the firepower. The others are hunters."

"Heard that," I offered. "Your unit's really fast and you've got good reactions. We'll see if we can't isolate one of those crackers—watch your screens, arm everything that arms, and remember, you owe me a song."

With that Kas began circling the trainer toward the plains, where the enemy moved toward us. Then weapons locks showed on the screens, and plans became chaos.

KAS

Kas's unit was moving faster than the Big Rig when they came out from the radar shadow of the Cathedral; perhaps it was the speed that drew first attention because almost immediately his tactical screen showed radar lock-ons for his unit. The larger hunter fired a projectile weapon in his direction and then the second, but both shots blew up in mid-flight as some shield within the gray pile of stone came to the fore.

Kas saw the hunters turn together then against the Big Rig, and it was clear they saw that unit as the danger: they fired again, this time an energy weapon in the mix, shields sparking and coruscating in defense. The three crackers, though, were trying to sneak behind the action and Kas wheeled, locking on the trailing one and firing a solid shell that exploded just short, and another, which nearly struck. Shield or luck he didn't know but in the midst the middle of the crackers halted and twisted, perhaps target seeking, the narthex in sight.

The Sexton!

He stood in his light armor in the opened narthex, pointing at the cracker Kas had aimed at . . .

It was in fact a point, for where he lit the side of the still vehicle with his rifle's weak beam there followed a lightning strike of stunning power from the tower top, and additional lightnings nearly too bright for Kas, even through the filtered vids.

In the aftermath that vehicle was obliterated, a wide shallow crater all that remained.

Kas fired on the next cracker, this one furiously turning away . . . again, his efforts were deflected but the Sexton's quick point brought another flash and rumble of energies. This was not as potent, perhaps, for the turning continued and it looked like several survivors exited before the thing stalled where it was. The third cracker, spinning, rushed away, apparently seeking refuge around the building's corner.

Kas turned the trainer to follow, heard whines of power through the trainer's sensors, thought he heard a gasp on the comm . . .

The tactical map showed the heavy hunters bearing rapidly down on the Big Rig where it was backed into a natural defile formed by the deepest dry watercourse. Not a long-term solution, Kas thought, but no side-fire against her position now.

"Took a hit, turret's sluggish. Watch the narthex, Kas, they're staying away from me. The Sexton's in danger!"

Kas fired after the third cracker, but left the aftermath of those shots to the winds of the dark as he altered the trainer's course toward Angel's side of the war.

ANGEL

I'd thought the Cathedral had defenses, but so far it had outdone itself. The Sexton, in his way as holy as me, hadn't let on that his keys were quite so potent.

Being holy wasn't going to be enough, I was afraid, and I *was* afraid, sweat running down my back and under the helmet, my hands trying to run with the need for accuracy as well as speed.

My messages to assorted gods and assorted bases were long gone and I prayed now to luck and more luck. I'd sent Kas to watch for the Sexton, but here we were barely started and truth told I was wishing for repair rigs and two battleships to back me up.

I hit the switch then for my backup plan. It'd hardwire me to the unit until I could pull out, but it gave us all better chances.

The hard thing was being down where I was, depending on video from the tower. The enemy had begun lobbing random test fire at the walls from somewhere beyond my sightings; it wasn't like they needed to range things so much as to judge reactions. I realized soon enough that more than armor deployed from that landed ship: there were smaller vehicles racing toward the walls now, darkness only a modest cover, but it wasn't like we'd been left with infantry of our own . . .

"Presence, Kas," I said. "There's groundlings out here, moving your way. Also—"

That's when they came at us, the hunters having located the Big Rig and a swarm of smaller vehicles rushing the building itself, the sensors showing energy weapons and projectile fire. I saw from the tower's vantage three small ATVs run into the Sexton's light and dissolve in fire, but there was return fire, the narthex glowing . . .

The Big Rig's sensors began lighting up—small-arms fire was banging off my shell while a sapper made a run with a hand-mine and my fire took him down. I needed time to—

"Angel!"

They'd charged then, the assembled ground forces heading for the narthex, Kas running intercept there while the pair of hunters came

at me one from the back and one obliquely from the front, firing
rapidly, having discovered my slot.

"He's down," Kas said, and I knew he meant the Sexton, and by
then it appeared all his weapons were on auto, but my spot was even
more precarious now that I was fully located.

I fired straight on against the heavy shielding of the oblique
enemy, felt the fabric of the Big Rig shudder as it absorbed an energy
weapon's blasts.

The rig behind me was closing rapidly—while my best shields
were there and in direct front the turret wouldn't answer at all now
to turn. Sound and vibration were relentless; I could smell
overheated components, I could hear things breaking as the enemy
from behind rammed the Big Rig and moved to do it again—

My headache was back.

"Angel?" I knew the voice.

"Keep it dark, the head hurts so bad. Is it a head wound?"

Then the headache was gone and the dark remained for awhile.
I've been sedated and it was like that, but more. Not even the
phantom of a headache, not the phantom of a dry throat's itch.

"Angel? We won. They're gone. All gone. So's the Sexton and the
Cathedral."

I knew the voice. I should be sad about the Cathedral and the
Sexton, but I was drained, too drained for multi-thought threads.

"Where?"

"Ambulance, Angel. I got us to the ambulance. We're in Jump."

"You've got me restrained?"

He laughed, sort of, then he was quiet and I heard equipment
noises, sounds I knew. There was that undertick I knew, too.

"I'm on life support? How?"

He laughed sort of, again.

"I'm a librarian and didn't have much else to do. I got you to the
ambulance but it took...awhile...to dig it out. Put you on the
automatics here."

"What's happening?"

"Listen. Here's that song."

And it was a song of home, comfort, love even. Joy even. He had the
rastfeener, was strumming it with his own fingers, singing along quietly.

The song echoes around me sometimes now when I wake up.

"What's happening, Kas?"

"I'm going to have to let you sleep for awhile, Angel. We're going to have to work around to a rebuild, when I can get all the parts together. We're going to be awhile on this, since I've got to rebuild the rig."

I thought about it, and knew that took a long time. The ticking kept me company, while I worked it out.

"I don't need a rig, Kas. You can—"

"Angel. When you hardwired yourself to the rig, that was smart. Kept you going, kept you alive. But the recorders—we're depending on them, Angel, to get you back, and what they know, what they recorded, is you in the rig. I'm going to do a rebuild from scratch, backward. We gotta start with a rig."

And I'm awake now, which means there's been another find, maybe a working turret this time. Kas is a hardworking man, and I'll be back to myself.

Hold the Line

Kevin Ikenberry

"L'audace, l'audace, toujours l'audace!"
(Audacity, audacity, always audacity!)
—attributed to General Napoleon Bonaparte

Middleton
2154

The Buzzers charged with their armor in front and ten million infantry behind them. Captain Vanessa Ransom, commander of Alpha Troop, Regimental Cavalry Squadron for the Fighting 79th Tank Regiment, climbed up through the commander's cupola of her MR-110 magtank, gently patting its armor as she did. Never superstitious, she'd always felt it necessary to appreciate her mount. In ancient times, a cavalry soldier was nothing without their horse. Ransom held the belief close to her heart more from necessity than nostalgia. A non-mission-capable vehicle meant a lack of combat resources. Since they'd named the beast *Reprisal*, stenciling the letters along the length of both gun tubes, she'd kept up the ritual. Aside from routine preventative maintenance, an appreciative tap was the least she could give her tank on a daily basis. Her life, and that of her crew, depended on it.

With practiced ease, she locked the hatch open with one hand as she detached her communications and oxygen lifelines. She hauled herself up to the angular turret deck and stood. She wanted a look at the situation herself, not trusting anything other than her good human eyes. The young combat veteran couldn't help but think the whole damned lot of aliens were charging straight at the Earth Maneuver Forces lines. Again. Yet, something about the sight of the massed attack unsettled her.

The insectoid enemy hadn't stooped to the level of using chemical or biological weapons, but she wouldn't put it past them. For the last ten years, Earth had been at war and the Buzzers—what humans called the insectoid, wasplike aliens—hadn't stopped coming. After suffering stunning defeats on Honalee and Spira-Two, there was speculation the Buzzers would withdraw and regroup. Instead, they attacked, advancing toward the galactic core with a hundred divisions of infantry and armor. Middleton was their first objective.

The rumble of artillery fire from the division's artillery battalion caught her attention. The volume of indirect fire along the front was louder and more insistent than it had been the previous three days. Buzzer positions at the forward edge of their advance seemed to writhe like a living carpet of beings on the valley floor below. They were indeed massing to attack. Ransom studied them for a moment and then turned her attention to the friendly units she could see, which weren't many. There was time for a more detailed look. She pulled her knife from her lower-right-leg sheath and rapped its handle twice on the auxiliary hatch. It swung open a moment later and her communications specialist, Sergeant Vines, stared up at her.

"I'm going up on the hill again. Make sure nobody tries to kill me," Ransom said as she sheathed her knife and checked her pistol in its shoulder holster.

"Yes, ma'am," Vines said. The young woman was already on the radio with the adjacent unit on the far side of the hill. Ransom stood and moved swiftly down the turret to the lower hull. At the front of the vehicle, she jumped down from the left front skirt and made her way up the rocky incline immediately west of her cavalry troop's position. She'd placed her vehicle there to be able to use the terrain to her advantage. If the uneasy sensation in her stomach was any indication, she'd need every possible advantage soon.

From the top of the craggy knoll, she studied the Earth Maneuver Forces lines. Condensation from her breath fogged the inner faceplate. She moved behind an outcropping of rocks and removed her helmet. Without the constant, albeit unnecessary, flow of cool oxygen, the faceplates notoriously clouded. She activated the external faceplate control and swung it open before pulling the helmet again over her close-cropped black hair. Some females wore their hair longer, but she used the clippers like the men in her unit. Easier to handle. No muss. And, most importantly, it enabled her combat vehicle crewman helmet to fit snugly. She stopped and adjusted the helmet, leaving the sliding faceplate open to catch what breeze there was on Middleton. Having a breathable atmosphere was a blessing in more ways than one. While the oxygen-laden Middleton air also allowed fires to burn, it enabled a modicum of freedom she could not overlook.

Tanks of the 2nd Brigade of the 1087th Armor Division filled the position adjacent to her unit's to the west. Beyond them, she found the EMF line intermixed with the alien forest as far as she could see. Her squadron commander, Lieutenant Colonel Peffers, said the visual had to rival the Maginot Line. She'd managed not to laugh. Things hadn't gone too well in France in 1944 against the Blitzkrieg. Two hundred and ten years later on a different planet and facing a numerically superior enemy was not the time to bring up failed attempts at human engineering and strategic blunders. There was a war to win.

Rounds from the division artillery battalion ripped overhead as they streaked north into the Buzzer formations. The rules of engagement authorized the use of harassing artillery fire while the Buzzers moved significant portions of their units into attack positions. Action was coming, and while the division's plan to receive and repel the Buzzer attack sounded solid, there were far too many unknowns. Given her troop's position overlooking the nearby narrow draw, away from what was supposed to be the main effort, she should have been elated. Whether it was the division commander's dislike for her methods or simply the staff failing, once again, to understand the use and application of cavalry forces, her unit's position was a terrain feature away from the center of the line.

Out of sight and out of mind.

Unless they feint.

Ransom snorted. *Of course they're gonna feint. It's exactly what I'd do.*

Behind her and past the rock formation, overlooking the draw all she saw of her camouflaged vehicles were their yellow guidons. She'd ordered the small flags and had them flown from the main communications antenna on the rear deck of each magtank. The flags were against every regulation in the book, and every time they ordered her to remove them, she gave the order to her crews. The guidons bearing two Celtic lions would disappear for a day or two and then magically return. Peffers had wisely given up asking for their removal. She'd heard, secondhand of course, that he actually approved of them for their visual references on the battlefield. He always knew where his lead cavalry troop fought.

Ain't that hard to find us. We're always in the middle of the shit.

"Ma'am!" First Sergeant Juan Lopez called from down the hill. She turned and saw him scrambling toward her. "What's wrong?"

Lopez was smaller than her, but all muscle. His face scarred from a bomb blast on another shithole of a Buzzer planet, his dark eyes glinted like chips of obsidian. He closed the distance between them quickly and brushed his dusty hands on his coveralls.

"Change in orders?"

"No, Top. No change." Ransom stopped and took a deep breath.

As the troop's first sergeant, Lopez was her partner in running the troop. The leadership manuals all said the relationship between a commander and their senior enlisted leader was professional and solely focused on the troop. When leaders actually assumed a role of leadership at that level, they learned differently. Lopez was her friend and confidant as much as he was her partner in leadership. He felt the same way about her, and the impact on both of their leadership styles and outcomes had been palpable. The troop loved and respected them, just as they loved and respected each other. Together, the troop was better than the sum of its individuals, which was all she could have asked for.

She met his eyes. "I don't think our position is dumb luck anymore. I think they put us out here on purpose. To keep us from mucking up the general's plans."

Lopez snorted and then grinned. "I mean, it's not like any of their plans have survived contact recently. And how do they call winning the battle mucking up anything?"

Crump! Crump!

Several explosions came from the western side of the rock formation they occupied. Ransom looked past Lopez and tried to see the impacts. Buzzer artillery rounds found their range on the far edge of the 1087th's position.

"Guess we're going to find out soon enough."

Lopez didn't reply. They stood there for a moment taking in the sight of the battlefield below them without saying anything. Nothing Ransom saw gave her hope for the outcome of the battle. The Buzzers would keeping charging until they broke the EMF line.

And we fall back. Again.

"Ma'am?" Sergeant Vines called through a direct laser connection to her helmet's receiver. "Division is preparing to engage forces. They want all commanders on the line."

She frowned and turned to Lopez. "Here we go again."

"You got that right."

Together, they made their way down the hill. The sound of an approaching tank from the right caught their attention. Ransom turned to glance over her right shoulder at the tank commander and frowned inside her helmet. Their eyes met and her gut twisted on itself. Not only was Peffers visibly upset, it was clear his anger was directed at her.

What did I do this time?

Peffers hadn't wanted her to attend the most recent briefing, and with good reason. The previous operations order briefing had ended badly. Seeing the staff in their clean coveralls receiving their third hot meal of the day, when her troops had eaten cold rations only for the last seven, set off her simmering anger and ended her attendance at future briefings. No one in the staff wanted to hear what life was like on the front line. For them, it was a video game. Detached. Impersonal. They knew nothing of warfare or had forgotten what they'd learned as a result of their relative comforts. Their attitudes infuriated her and their deference to command pushed her over the edge.

Peffers dismounted his tank and climbed off the front skirt. Ransom, with Lopez at her side, met him.

"Sir? What can I do for you?"

Peffers opened his faceplate to stare at her and then at Lopez. His mouth worked silently. Lips pressed into a thin white line, he took a sharp breath. "The division commander has ordered you to hold this position. You are to hold the line and not—I repeat, not—pursue the initiative unless specifically ordered."

The frown on Peffers's brilliant red face said it all. General Higashiyama's scorn wasn't something easily shed. While she'd toed the line of insubordination on numerous occasions, she'd never crossed it—in garrison. In combat, the situation dictated everything, including when to deviate from plans and orders.

Plans never survive contact with enemy forces.

"Vanessa?" His deep voice was low and firm. "You heard what I said?"

"I did." She suppressed the attitude and her exasperation threatened to erupt. "Sir, I've never taken a chance that didn't—"

"You've been lucky." Peffers's eyes bored a hole through her. "Yes, you've been successful to this point, but luck doesn't always work on the battlefield. It's bound to run out. The next time you think you see something and you act, it's going to bite you in the ass."

Ransom swallowed. Peffers stared at her, and it was clear he expected some type of response. She sucked in a breath. "It might, sir. But this army can't move without a general's approval, and they're so out of touch with what happens on the line that people die while they fuck around."

"They're not fucking around."

"Oh, please, sir, you can't expect me to think they actually give a fuck about anything other than their next star. Really? They don't want to look bad. That's why he said that."

Chickenshit motherfuckers, generals. All of 'em.

"Just—" Peffers stopped. The cords in his neck tightened and then released. His eyes flashed to Lopez at her side and then returned to her. The coloring in his face eased, slightly. "Hold the goddamned line, Ransom. You better hope you're right. The next time you *gain the initiative*, the general's going to court-martial your ass. You can't keep hoping he won't."

"If it makes the difference and gives hope for my troopers, sir, I'll take that proposition." Ransom smirked. "I know full well that hope isn't a method. That doesn't mean there ain't a place in the universe for it, even on a hellhole like this."

A deafening fusillade of artillery from the line behind them covered everything with a blanket of sound. All of them turned to it. The battle had been joined.

"Hold the line. Good luck, Vanessa," Peffers said and turned back to his tank.

"You, too, sir."

She turned to Lopez. She watched him try not to grin. "Orders, ma'am?"

"Stay with the combat trains. Move headquarters back to them and stay there. When the shit hits the fan, you'll need to be ready to receive us and pass the division reserve through."

"If they make it on time, I will." Lopez stuck out a gloved hand. "Be safe, Vanessa."

"Conquer or die, Top." She shook his hand and slapped his shoulder. Their unit motto never failed to make her smile.

"Give 'em, hell, ma'am."

Without looking back, Ransom boarded her magtank and settled into the commander's station. In front of her was the Commander's Information Display System. The display enabled her to not only see and track the status of all the vehicles in her command, it gave her the opportunity to communicate directly with them on a variety of frequencies. Each tank had a crew of three: driver, gunner, tank commander. However, both her tank and the one commanded by Lopez were command variants and carried a crew of four. The additional crew member served as communications specialist in charge of maintaining the network between the troop's vehicles and higher headquarters. With a series of taps, she called up a topographic map of the area showing their current position and the information about the enemy's location, which came directly from division headquarters intelligence.

That's almost an oxymoron.

Ransom studied the enemy's displacement and immediately theorized a couple of courses of action. The first was the most likely, and that meant the enemy was going to charge headlong into the center of friendly lines. They'd seen this type of attack repeatedly. It was as if the Buzzers wanted to fight a war of attrition. They had the replication rates to do just that and given the biological makeup of their armored vehicle's systems, what humans would have thought insanity seemed to be the Buzzer method of warfare.

The second course of action was the least likely. Given their experience, it was unlikely the enemy was just going to harass friendly positions. Between every major engagement there'd been some type of harassing fire from the Buzzers. Whether it was artillery barrages or strikes that looked like an attack but were just designed to harass friendly intelligence, they never failed to lob mostly harmless rounds at the Earth Corps. She didn't think that was going to happen today. Given the concentration of forces and the preparatory artillery fires falling on the main line now, they were gearing up for something larger.

The most dangerous course of action was that the Buzzers were setting up for an attack but would employ a very different tactic than a straightforward penetration attempt. Given what she could see of the terrain occupied by the friendly line, there were two options. If she were the enemy commander, she'd look at probing the line to the far west or to the far east of the center of the human defense. The far western edge introduced much more significant terrain restricting their movements. The Buzzers' vehicles, unlike her own magtanks, actually touched the ground. Given that, the restrictive terrain to the far west didn't seem a likely course for an attack. The valley facing her, though, looked like a reasonable avenue of approach. While she wasn't holding the flank, her position slightly forward of the friendly line could present an opportunity to a determined enemy.

"All Typhoon elements, this is Typhoon Six." General Higashiyama's voice was soft but firm. "Prepare for attack. Do not fire until fired upon. When that happens, give them hell."

Ransom heard several other commanders, including Lieutenant Colonel Peffers, chime in with exuberance on the division's main frequency. She verified she received but kept her mouth shut. The business of war was not about cheerleading and grandstanding. She wasn't excited to put her troopers at risk. She would never be excited about the potential for anyone to die.

Ransom resumed tapping the screen and prepared a hasty plan based on the most dangerous course of action. When it was complete, she tapped the transmit button to send the graphic to all her vehicles. Verification came that everyone had received the message. She touched her communications button and activated the local laser communications network.

"Guidons, this is Black Six. You've got new graphics. Red One and Blue One, I want you to move forward down the slope to provide a screen. Push out as far as you can to maximize your cover and concealment. I think the enemy might send an attack in this direction. I want them to see we are not fully displaced along the line like Division wants us to be, give them a little depth to worry about. White One and Green One, orient your tubes in the kill box. Hold your fire until Red One and Blue One withdraw by fire. If we do this right, any enemy that comes this way, we can suck them in. That might be the break we need. Acknowledge, over."

Lieutenant Winters, leading the first scout platoon, replied, "Red One, over."

The next call came from Lieutenant Hinata, second tank platoon, who replied, "White One, over."

Lieutenant Nguyen, the third scout platoon leader, replied, "Blue One, over."

And, finally, Lieutenant Savon from the fourth tank platoon replied, "Green One, over."

As she hoped, Lopez chimed in at the last. "Black Six, this is Black Seven. Copy all. Good hunting. Steel on target."

As she watched her two scout platoons push forward, Ransom turned her attention to her own vehicle. "Crew report?"

"Driver, ready," Zeno called from the hull.

"Comms, ready." Vines didn't bother looking at her. There was a ton of information coming in and it was partially her job to get it sorted for Ransom to decipher.

"Gunner, ready," Fellrath whooped on the frequency.

<<Interface, ready.>>

Technically, the Interface wasn't crew, but the automated command-and-control system made it much easier for her to monitor the tank's internal vehicle and communication systems, as well as maintain situational awareness from its onboard sensors. In a pinch, the Interface could take over for the gunner or the communications specialist. Redundancy was a good thing.

Her headset chimed and Ransom turned to the communications display to her right. First Sergeant Lopez was calling on a private frequency.

"Go, Top."

"You think they're coming this way?"

"You know I do. When have they ever disappointed us before?"

Lopez chuckled. "Division intelligence seems to believe they'll try to spearhead through the center of the line again."

Ransom frowned. "You know they said that of the last three attacks, right?"

"I know," Lopez replied. In all three attacks, they'd eventually probed for weaknesses along the line, either with air support or with swift movements of tactical forces. "I think you're right."

I hope I'm not.

Over the whine of the magtank's systems, Ransom heard, and felt the tremors of, an increase in the volume of fire from the adjacent units. Contact reports came in over Division's operations network in rapid succession.

She relayed the information to her units. "Guidons, Black Six. Contact to our west. Keep your eyes open. Red One, deploy an Oscar Papa atop the hill at your seven o'clock. Over."

"Black Six, this is Red One. Copy and acknowledged," Winters replied instantly. There wasn't a question or a need for clarification.

Her intent in pushing an observation post team to the top of the hill was simple: she needed eyes on the full measure of the enemy formation. Where she was, she couldn't see all of their activity. While the sensor feeds and the intelligence network provided excellent information, it was not a total picture. An observation post would provide her live video of what the enemy attack looked like. It would also give her the opportunity, through other sets of well-trained eyes, to detect any change in the enemy's movement or disposition. It took a couple minutes longer than she expected because of the terrain, but the reconnaissance post team set up their sensors and engaged direct laser communication to her.

"Black Six, OP One. The feed is live and the sensor is yours."

"OP One, Black Six. Visually scan anything I'm not looking at. I want to know the whole situation as you see it. Anything goes. Be ready to un-ass your position."

Click-click.

The clicking of the microphone, something they'd learned from the aviators and their exocraft, transmitted both an affirmative and an acknowledgment without saying anything.

The first thing she did was study the enemy formation. The Buzzers tended to put their armor up front in a stacked column formation with at least two regiments of the heaviest armored vehicles forward. Their purpose was to break the line behind their strongest and most resilient armor. In typical Buzzer fashion, their armored vehicles resembled those of twentieth-century Earth. Ransom had to admire their intent to deceive humans by using the iconic forms of wars past. The sleek, angular shape of the Abrams or the Leopard were readily identifiable, as were the T-80 and Challenger analogs. While they were nowhere near as capable as those vehicles had been, they caused confusion far too often because of how close they were in appearance to the modern magtank. They'd placed the Abrams-like vehicles in the front of their attack formation on more than one occasion.

From what she saw of this attack, they'd done the same thing. She studied the units immediately behind the lead regiments and something didn't look right. Typically, Buzzers deployed their heaviest units forward and used their infantry and lighter vehicles toward the middle and rear of the formation. This time, there appeared to be millions of infantry immediately behind the tanks. The presence of the infantry wasn't necessarily unexpected, but the sheer number of them took her breath away. Over what looked like eight or ten square kilometers, the ground was completely invisible underneath a blanket of moving Buzzers. There were far more infantry than she'd ever seen in one single operation.

Our frontline units are having kittens about now.

The camera swung violently back to the right as she heard the young soldier at OP One call, "Ma'am, I've got movement to the north."

Ransom steered the camera and found what the soldier was looking at. Another regiment of Buzzers, with their heavy armor up front, had peeled off from the main effort and appeared to be on a parallel course.

Second wave. They must be facing more resistance than they expected. We're holding up well for a change. Maybe that bullshit rock drill was really worth it.

Another regiment pulled away from the main effort and took up a parallel course on the eastern side of the first regiment. Not only were the Buzzers building a second wave, they were throwing a lot of combat power toward the Earth Maneuver Forces line. Ransom steered the camera back to the south for the main attack and saw that another group, mostly lighter reconnaissance vehicles, had broken away from the enemy formation and appeared to be oriented on her position.

Not unexpected. They're probably looking for ways around. Now is where we give them hell.

A plan formed quickly. She depressed her radio transmit button and said, "Guidons, this is Black Six. Prepare to execute staggered withdrawal. Red One, I want you to move forward—I say again, move forward—roughly four hundred meters. That should keep you masked terrain-wise from friendly fire. Break."

She released the transmit switch for a few seconds and then depressed it again. "Blue One, I want you to move forward two hundred meters. Prepare to engage the enemy and then withdraw. Conduct hasty passage of lines through White and Green elements. We want to pull them in. Acknowledge?"

Her platoon leaders checked in in rapid succession. Her intention was to make the Buzzers think they'd found a weak point in the line. They'd pursue her withdrawing forces, and then she'd hit them with her tanks and give them no quarter.

<<Orbital gunfire warning. Thirty seconds.>>

"OP One, Black Six. Leave your post and take cover," Ransom called over the laser connection.

Twenty-six seconds later, the Interface chimed, <<OP One has been recovered.>>

The valley in front of them erupted in a cloud of dirt, smoke, and Buzzers. Each impact of the tiny tungsten slugs dropped from the Earth Maneuver Forces destroyers in orbit tore through the Buzzers like canister rounds from the nineteenth century.

"Targets obscured," Fellrath reported.

"Interface?" Ransom asked.

<<The Buzzers are preparing to move.>>

The enemy movement took only a few minutes. As their combat reconnaissance patrol turned the corner of the exposed rock formation, first scout platoon engaged. The firefight lasted only a few seconds, and then Lieutenant Winters pulled their troops back toward the center of the tank platoon to their rear. Emboldened, the

Buzzers sped up their pursuit. Within another minute, her third scout platoon was engaged. The firefight lasted two seconds longer than the first, but the effect on the Buzzers was noticeable. Ransom watched as two Buzzer tank regiments paralleling the main attack turned her direction.

"Wabash Six, this is Wabash One." Ransom used the squadron's standard radio coding instead of her troop's color-coded scheme. "Large contingent of enemy forces moving in my position. Over."

"Wabash One, Six. Understood. Wait one." In her helmet, Ransom heard Lieutenant Colonel Peffers take the information to the regimental network. From there the regiment passed it to the division along with a direct video feed from her observation post. In the time it took for those messages to traffic, the two enemy regiments were now facing her cavalry troop at a distance of six thousand meters and were closing.

Ransom heard the commander-in-chief himself, General Higashiyama, reply, "Wabash Six, this is Typhoon Six. That's a feint. I'm directing close air support to the area. We'll pull them back in line."

A private laser connection dinged. "Ransom? Did you hear that?" Peffers asked.

"I did, sir. I disagree."

"Noted. Hunker down to prepare for close air support."

Like I can do anything else.

Twenty seconds later, another orbital strike rained down on the valley. Choking clouds of dirt, smoke, and fire rose and obscured everything she could see. Even though the observation post camera was still on, the sensors could not see anything. All they could do was wait.

Ransom stared into a billowing cloud of dirt and debris from the orbital strike looking for any sign of movement. Something moved in the dust, but she couldn't be sure. The dark shape moved again.

"Contact front! Contact front!"

Ransom glanced at her display and saw the square icons for first platoon flashing. In rapid succession, each of the four icons turned from green, meaning systems were nominal, to red, showing damage.

Ransom punched the transmit button. "Open fire. Open fire. Weapons free. Support first platoon."

It was too late. First one, then a second, and then a third first platoon vehicle icon turned black, indicating the vehicle was dead. Only Red Three was still operational. A heartbeat later, that icon also turned black.

Ransom fought the bile rising in her throat. "Blue One, Black Six. Do you have eyes on first platoon?"

What's left of them, that is.

"Negative, we can't see a thing. All targets are obscured."

"Understood, orient your tubes toward Red platoon and open fire. Turn your fratricide limiters off and open fire. That's a direct order."

Let the legal assholes chew on that if I make it through this mess.

"Roger, Black Six. Understood."

Her remaining scout platoon opened fire and Ransom worked to direct her two tank platoons forward. If she was going to save her scouts, they'd have to directly engage. She was crossing the forward line of troops again and if she survived the next ten minutes, a court-martial was almost certain.

None of that mattered. The twenty-two troopers in her third scout platoon mattered, as did their loved ones on Earth.

"White One and Green One, move forward. Maintain line abreast and hold that line. We can't support Blue One by fire from where we are. Turn on your thermal viewers and engage anything in front of you."

She didn't wait for an acknowledgment. Instead, she changed frequencies to the squadron's frequency. "Wabash Six, this is Wabash One. Contact my position. Taking heavy fire and moving to engage."

There was a hiss of static across the frequency and the transmission died in a burst of harsh noise. She attempted a direct laser connection, but there was too much debris in the air attenuating the signal.

"Vines?"

"Ma'am, we're being jammed on all frequencies. Laser is relay only—I have our troop including Black Seven locked but that's it. Otherwise, all I've got is super-low-frequency resonators to nearby vehicles."

With a maximum range of about fifty meters. Shit.

As the two platoons moved forward, Ransom directed her crew in a similar fashion.

"Driver, move out. Hold position between second and fourth platoons. Gunner, index heat fire and adjust. You are weapons free on everything in front of you. Comms and Interface, monitor the field and find a connection to higher or else this is going to be a quick DIP."

Her attempt at humor failed. No soldier, regardless of their branch of service or occupational specialty, ever wanted to *die in place.*

Ransom engaged a private laser communications channel. "Top, can you hear me?"

"I've got you. Move out. I'll hang back and tell Division what's going on."

<<White and Green elements are reporting contact. Both platoons are taking heavy fire,>> the Interface reported.

Suddenly, Ransom felt the magtank rock from an impact somewhere on the left front of the vehicle.

<<Impact front. All systems nominal.>>

"You okay down there, Zeno?" she called over her one-on-one connection to the hull.

"Roger, ma'am. Still can't see anything. I'm on thermals and my ears are ringing."

"Understood, just keep us out of any ditches."

"No guarantees, ma'am." The young driver laughed.

Fellrath called, "Going to high rate. Multiple targets. There's at least a battalion of heavy tanks in front of us. Can't see past them yet."

Ransom frowned. Lopez and his tank were more than fifty meters away now. There was no way to relay the information division. Their enemy feint was anything but—it was an attack.

"Guns hot," she reported over the crew intercom. "Fire and adjust, Fellrath. You're on your own."

"Yes, ma'am." Fellrath called. A half second later, the magtank's railgun released another hypersonic round in the enemy's direction with a *thump.* "Scouts are falling back. I can see third platoon."

She leaned forward and looked through her extension of the gunner's primary sight so she could see what Fellrath was looking at. He was right. The remaining Rippers from Third Platoon had turned and were accelerating toward friendly lines. Behind them, at least twenty enemy tanks were following in a simple line-abreast formation. While the Buzzers typically were no match for the human magtanks, they relied on suppressive fire to allow their infantry to close with the enemy. Buzzer infantry armed with antitank weapons did far more damage to human forces than their somewhat capable tanks could do. Yet behind the line of tanks it didn't appear there was any infantry.

And then she saw them. But instead of a couple of regiments' worth there seemed to only be a few hundred of the aliens.

A hole in the Buzzer line materialized and she hesitated for a heartbeat. And then another.

Hold the line, Ransom.

To hell with that.

"Gunner, get ready to cut me a wide path through that line. Comms, prepare to get up on your guns. We're going through and hitting their infantry at close range. If you can get us CAS, get it. I don't give a damn about danger close. You hear me?"

Fellrath didn't reply. Her communications specialist looked at her incredulously.

"Yes, Vines. I want you to unbutton and get up on your machine guns. I'll be up there, too. We'll need every barrel we have once we cut through the armor."

"Yes, ma'am."

"Driver, move out in Gear Five. Stand on that pedal. Don't stop until we're in the middle of their infantry."

The tank lurched forward on its repulsors. Gliding a meter off the ground, they rocketed toward the line at over thirty kilometers per hour. The magtank had a top speed of almost one hundred and ten, but she didn't think they'd need that much.

"White and Green elements, follow me," Ransom said into the radio.

<<Low frequency resonators successful. All vehicles auto-linking by SOP.>>

Even in the jamming field, everyone in the attack heard the orders. As they closed the distance to the line, Fellrath blasted two tanks to their immediate left and swung the gun tube violently to the right to dispatch a third.

They were through the line.

Simultaneous impacts on either side of the magtank rocked

Ransom and the others hard enough that she saw stars after hitting her head on the gunner's sight extension.

Motherf—

<<Multiple impacts. Both sides. Battery compartment alpha, minor penetration. All systems nominal.>>

"Fellrath, give me all your coax. Save the tube for any vehicles you see. Up on your guns, Vines."

Ransom activated and swung the commander's hatch upward. She stood in the seat and brought the dual barrels of the .50 caliber machine gun to bear on the first of the infantry she could see amid the dust and haze. Fellrath opened up with both coaxially mounted cannons alongside the main gun. The rate of fire impressed her.

"Wish we had a beehive round, ma'am." Fellrath said. The Armored Corps brass requested the round, most reminiscent of ancient canister rounds, several months earlier. EMF Intelligence said the effect on the enemy would prove negligible even though the armored commanders knew otherwise. It didn't matter. They had other firepower to exert.

"Let's go, Vines. Up on your gun." The opposite hatch opened. Her comms specialist came up, grabbed the smaller machine gun controls and opened fire.

Small-arms rounds impacted the tank and rocked it as she fired on the prancing Buzzer infantry. Tanks to her left and right opened fire, but they took a heavy volume of it in return; several were destroyed. Ransom didn't listen to the radio. Every single ounce of her focus was on training the machine guns and dispatching Buzzer infantry to save herself and her soldiers.

A series of chimes sounded in her headphones.

"We've got comms!" Vines yelped and dropped into the turret.

"Get your ass back up here!" Ransom roared. Vines popped up and looked at her, wide-eyed. "Get on your goddamned guns, Vines. They're all around us!"

At that moment, a Buzzer rocketeer leapt to the front slope of the tank. Ransom swung her barrels toward it and cut it in half with a salvo of rounds. A volley of rounds from her left confirmed Vines had manned her weapon. Together, they worked to cut down the infantry.

"Black Six, Black Seven. On my way to your position. Open a hole. I've got reinforcements."

Ransom looked to her left and right. Amongst the smoking, damaged vehicles of her tank platoons, she saw all of them were still functioning in one way or another.

"Guidons, spread the formation. I'll go with White. Leave a hole in the middle," Ransom called. The Buzzer infantry hesitated and fell back. She recognized their movement and its likely result.

"Vines. Get down there and get close air support on the infantry. They're going to push more of it our way and try to get us to fall back. We will not let them. Danger close is authorized. We're gonna hold the line and—"

A flash from her right side and—

WHAMM!

WHAAMM!

WHAAM! WHAAM!!

Ransom crumpled into the turret as she was trained to do. Her ass bounced off the seat and as she fell forward across Fellrath's back, she snatched at handholds and caught herself. Vines did the same. There was a sensation of wet and cold on her face. Her helmet's faceplate was shattered and most of the lower left half of the protective shell was gone. She touched her skin below the helmet edge and saw her fingertips stained with blood. Beyond them, the tank's caution and warning system flashed yellow and red system icons.

Come on, baby. Hold together.

<<Multiple impacts. Forward repulsors damaged. Communication antennas have been severed. Vehicle is seventy percent combat effective.>>

You hold together, baby. Just a few more minutes.

Tugging off her helmet, Ransom scrambled into her seat and reached for the display. There was so much blood.

"You're hit, ma'am!" Vines said. "Holy shit!"

The communications specialist scrambled over the autoloading mechanism of the main gun with a combat field dressing in her hands. Vines pressed the dressing to the side of Ransom's face and neck and held it there.

"It's pretty nasty, ma'am. Hold still."

Ransom shook her head and pushed Vines away. "Get up on your guns! Come on!"

With one hand on her bandage as it worked to seal her wound, Ransom stood in the commander's cupola and charged her weapons. The Buzzer infantry were fewer and she saw, and heard, the Fleet close air support dropping antipersonnel munitions on the Buzzers.

Vines tugged on her coveralls and handed Ransom a spare communications headset. She worked it over her head. Her face and neck hurt. Every movement was agony, but she depressed the transmit switch. "Guidons, Black Seven is on the way with reinforcements. Prepare to cease fire when friendlies are present. Acknowledge."

Her remaining platoon leaders checked in, but she wasn't really listening. She raked the Buzzer infantry with machine gun fire, her sole objective to put them all down.

Once and for all.

The enemy's rate of fire increased. Ransom felt her tank shudder from multiple impacts. The Interface tried to keep up with damage reports, but it was no use. One particular jolt was hard enough it slammed her forward, toward the machine guns.

<<Hull penetration, forward quarter.>>

Ransom called, "Driver, report."

<<Sergeant Zeno's vital signs are negligible. He appears to be dead.>>

Goddamnit.

WHAMM!

<<Hull penetration, right side.>>

"Motherfucker! I'm hit! I'm hit!" Fellrath screamed.

Ransom couldn't see him, nor could she stop firing to help him. Doing so would mean death and her options were limited. "Vines, see what you can do. I'll stay up."

"Yes, ma'am."

The main gun and its coax cannons fell silent. The adjacent machine gun on the auxiliary hatch was quiet. The Buzzers sensed the weak spot in her line and descended on her tank.

"Wabash One, this is Wabash Six. Standby for close air support. Danger close. Button up."

Ransom refused. If she dropped into the turret now, the Buzzers would get past her and gain an advantage. Once behind her they could do serious damage.

"Interface? Status of adjacent platoons?"

<<Second platoon is thirty-six percent combat effective. Fourth platoon is thirty-four percent combat effective. Elements of third platoon are eleven percent combat effective and remain in the fight.>>

"I told them to withdraw." She ran out of ammunition on one of the dual machine guns.

You know they're not going anywhere. Just like you wouldn't.

A blur of motion caught her eye. She recognized in a microsecond the promised close air support had arrived. Reflexively, she dropped into the turret, snatched the handle for the hatch, and slammed it closed over her. Nearby explosions rocked the tank violently from side to side. She heard a shower of debris and shrapnel raining against the outside surface of the armor. It sounded as if the bombs were falling in the seat next to her. Dozens more warning lights appeared on the tank's system board.

Come on. Hold together for me, baby. One more time.

Thirty seconds later, the bombardment stopped. Ransom opened the hatch and rose to her machine guns as before, the entire valley obscured by dust and smoke. She looked at her ammunition stores, but there was nothing to load into the empty weapon. With one barrel and a few hundred rounds of ammunition remaining, she realized any subsequent attack would be her last.

"Fellrath? I need you back on the gun."

There was no response. "Vines?"

"I'm trying, ma'am," Vines replied. "He's unconscious. Lost a lot of blood."

"Release the guntube to the Interface. Master switch is above Fellrath's primary sight. See it?"

Vines didn't respond. <<I have control of the main gun. Do I have permission to fire?>>

"Interface, you have permission to fire and adjust. Vines? Get Fellrath stabilized. Give him a combat coma shot and get up to your guns."

"Doing it now."

Trying to find an identifiable target was impossible as she swept the guns over her field of fire without squeezing the trigger. She risked a look to her left and right. Many of the adjacent tanks were badly damaged; several appeared dead. Through the earphones tied to the outside microphones of the tank, Ransom heard the screaming buzz that gave the aliens their name. They were massing for an attack. She heard them so clearly that she knew they were close and there was a shit ton of them.

Not this time, motherfuckers.

Ransom squeezed the trigger and the now single-barreled machine gun roared to life. Taking her as an example, the adjacent tanks—at least those that could—did the same. With methodical precision, she walked the rounds through the smoke, hoping to take a few more of the Buzzers out before they swarmed. The main gun fired automatically at a target she couldn't see. It didn't matter now.

"Wabash One, Wabash Six. Cease fire. Cease fire."

Ransom continued to fire.

On the private channel, First Sergeant Lopez chimed, "Six?"

"Not now, Top."

"We're coming! We're right behind you, Vanessa. Cease fire and let us through."

I hope there's a hell of a lot of you.

Vanessa stopped firing but kept her eyes on the smoke-filled valley below. The frightened side of her expected the Buzzers to swarm up the terrain in a cloud and demolish everything around her. She did not safe her machine gun, nor did she clear it. Her thumbs rested on the trigger, waiting to open fire again. One heartbeat became two, and then three, and then a vehicle shot past her position, its guns blazing. She recognized the magtanks that belonged to the 53rd Armored Brigade. They were Division's reserve element. As she watched, the brigade roared past, took up wedge-shaped assault positions, and plowed into the Buzzers.

More tanks came. Scout vehicles came. She was aware there were at least two ambulances and four maintenance vehicles gathering at her position. Soldiers were out of vehicles and crawling over her unit's tanks. They pulled Zeno out of the hull alive. He was moving, but obviously in tremendous pain.

Thank God.

Vanessa turned her eyes skyward and saw a flurry of close air support aircraft approaching to attack the Buzzers. They were giving the aliens hell, and it made her smile. Vines appeared in the other hatch and handed her another set of bandages, which she pressed to her bloody face with shaking hands.

Vines glanced over Ransom's shoulder and her eyes went wide. A lone tank approached her side and decelerated. Vanessa turned, expecting to see Lieutenant Colonel Peffers frowning at her.

Instead, the magtank's antennas flew red flags bearing the four white stars of the Earth Maneuver Forces commander-in-chief. General Higashiyama stood in the commander's cupola and stared at her.

This is where he ends my career for doing exactly what I should've done.

After a long moment, the general nodded. There was a hint of a smile on his grim face as he raised his right hand and saluted.

Maybe not.

Her left hand pressed against the bandages on her face, Ransom returned the salute.

"Well done!" he shouted over the din as his tank roared down the valley and into the fray.

Ransom closed her eyes and leaned against the machine gun mount. She patted the tank's armor with her free hand and took a deep breath, and then another. Middleton's star shone through a break in the battlefield smoke and warmed her skin.

For a moment, the pain subsided and the war drifted away. They'd held. Maybe it would be enough. When the medics came, they mistook her smile for the onset of shock. Vanessa Ransom simply knew better. This war had only just begun.

A Girl and Her K't'ank

⊕

Jody Lynn Nye

Someone must have known they were coming, because Detective Sergeant Dena Malone saw absolutely no one amid the towering stacks of containers on the Tri-City dock. The waterfront normally bustled with thousands of workers. No one steered copters or flying loaders overhead in the wide blue sky. Not even a drone hummed overhead to spot the small brown-haired woman riding in a very fancy, bronze-hued floatchair or the tall man walking alongside her. A single pigeon's coo echoed for blocks in the concrete-and-steel landscape.

"There aren't even any AIs moving cargo," said her partner, Detective Sergeant Ramos, a good-looking man with tawny skin and thick black hair. His voice was muffled in the depths of the clear helmet he wore over a white hazmat suit so bright they probably could have seen it from Moonbase. The police transport van had been left behind at the edge of the docks.

"They're all union, too," Dena said. Her white protective suit crackled whenever she moved. She sat back in the lush padding of her chair, a perquisite of being a host for an intelligent alien species known as Salosians. Dr. K't'ank occupied her peritoneum, which approximated the salinity and temperature of the seas on his homeworld. It was designed to protect her—or rather K't'ank—anytime they went out in public. It was like a light all-terrain vehicle with antigravs. Its comforts came in handy considering that she was

61

also several months pregnant. Hosting a Salosian came with a number of benefits as well as responsibilities, including an allowance that supplemented her never-generous city salary and ongoing maintenance of the floatchair. The complex update that it had undergone that morning had taken a couple of hours, under the supervision of Alien Relations' Deputy Ambassador Sardwell Marin himself, to assist on the callout she and Ramos had been assigned.

Despite Marin's fussy briefing about the new features, her throne-like conveyance seemed pretty much unchanged. The ambassador had showed her a bunch of new controls on her skinnypad and assured her it would be "adequate for the parameters of the mission," whatever that meant. She didn't trust the bureaucrat as far as she could throw him, and he knew it, so she had laserproof, slugproof armor on underneath her hazmat suit to protect her and her two occupants.

"If the humans get called off, so do they. The Equal Employment Act of 2085, you know."

"Forgot that," Ramos said, snapping his fingers. With the glove on, the movement sounded like two balloons rubbing.

The skinnypad on Dena's lap buzzed. She glanced down at the screen. Their two red dots on the electronic map were within two rows of the purple star—purple for chemical or biological hazard that Patrol had reported. She couldn't get any readings inside the building itself, meaning it was heavily shielded against scans.

Around her, she spotted the dozen or so dots representing the other officers on the operation looking distressingly far away. Hundreds of tiny black spots indicated other life-forms nearby, almost certainly rats or roaches that had no interest in the comings and goings of humans. She and Ramos were on their own.

"We're coming to the location," she said. "Better circle around." She steered the chair to the left, cutting between two towers of shining containers that looked newer than the others.

"You getting this, Control?" Ramos asked his audio pickup.

"Captain Potopos here," the voice crackled over it. "The other units are covering you. Be careful. Those smugglers are ruthless. Those two bodies Patrol picked up this morning are deteriorating already. The medical examiner thinks they swelled up like that while they were still alive. And those purple blisters! They had to hurt like hell until it killed them. Make sure you don't come in contact with any of that stuff, all right?"

"Duh," Ramos said. "I mean, 10-4, Captain. Sheesh, you'd think this was our first rookie assignment."

I should not be here, Dena thought, for the millionth time since they left the station house. *Ningustan toxin exposure could kill me or the baby. I'm just a few weeks from maternity leave. I could have refused . . .*

Then, a kick against her ribs from the inside broke her concentration.

"Are we there yet?" Dr. K't'ank's voice came from the heavy platinum bangle on her wrist.

"Stop asking that!" Dena exclaimed.

Ramos laughed hollowly inside his hood. "You're gonna hear that sentence a lot more in the future, Mama."

"The increase of excitement is becoming overwhelming! I must know. If you issued more frequent updates, I would not have to ask."

"Here." Dena tapped on her skinnypad. "I'm giving you access to the map. Besides, you can see out of my eyes. You already know where we are."

The fact that he asked added to Dena's nervousness. As if having an alien Salosian occupying her peritoneum with his eye-filaments drilled into her spinal column so he could tap directly into her optic nerves wasn't enough, he was the one who was the most in danger from the toxin. Ningustan was a native parasite on the ocean world of Salos. Customs had received information that a quantity—no one knew how much—had been brought to Earth. Infiltrating and capturing the people involved ought to have been their job, not that of a couple of cops from the Tri-City area. They'd managed to convince Alien Relations that Dena, as a Salosian host, should be involved in taking down the operation. As big a pain in the butt as K't'ank could be, she could handle his endless observations on human nature—and on hers, in particular. The part she hated was being the poster child for Earth-Salos interaction. It wasn't the first time she'd been trotted out to represent the program, but it was by far the most dangerous. Purple blisters!

"So many windowless buildings," K't'ank said, as Dena scanned the landscape for his benefit. "Does no one live here?"

"These are all cargo containers. There's stuff inside them waiting for ground transport across the continent. But people sometimes live here, just off the grid. Maybe not even with electricity or running water."

"That is inconvenient," K't'ank said. "I prefer the comforts that are afforded in your domicile."

"Me, too," Dena said. "Anyhow, shut up. They'll already be able to detect our footsteps. I don't want them hearing your voice."

"But...!"

"No more buts! I'll drop the bangle here and go on without it if I have to."

"Don't make me turn this chair around!" Ramos added, in a mocking tone. Dena glared at him. "I told you, Mama. It's good training."

"Stop calling me Mama. I'm getting so sick of it, I'm going to teach the baby to call me Detective." Dena drew her sidearm, a slugthrower with eleven explosive rounds in the magazine. She knew the floatchair had other protective gear hidden in its framework if she—or rather K't'ank—needed it. Guns and a mesh shield had popped out of the pillars when the chair detected danger in other cases. In a pinch, she could pull Ramos into her lap and book the hell out of there if it got too bad. He'd tease her until the end of time about it, but that was better than attending his funeral.

"I will comply," K't'ank said, with what passed for contrition for him. He fell silent, leaving Dena to worry if he was sulking or going into observation mode. She was pretty sure he had written several articles about life inside her that she doubted she would find complimentary.

"Moving in," the audio pickup crackled. On the scope, the other dots approached the purple star.

"We don't have enough information," Ramos said in a low voice. "How many people are in there? What kind of hardware are they packing?"

Dena shook her head. She glided closer and closer to the corner. She sent a hand-sized drone out and watched through her skinnypad as it surveyed the container stack in question. She sent the video to Ramos. No guards. The criminals must be relying on their shielding and probably some lethal tricks when they tried to break in.

Fortunately, Ramos had a laser drill that could also be operated remotely and silently, apart from the obvious red line that would appear on the other side as the door was being cut away.

Closer and closer they crept, hearing the chatter from the remote teams. Dena was nervous enough to chew nails. Ramos's usually ebullient personality had retreated, leaving him all instinct and watchful dark eyes. He held his laser rifle upright but ready in both hands. Closer. Closer. Twenty meters. Ten. Five . . .

"Aaaaaand we're here live from the top secret sting operation currently under way on the Tri-City dock front!" a cheerful female voice burst out. Suddenly, a slim figure in a bright red skirt suit dropped down right in front of them, landing on a pair of sky-high patent-leather heels. Lauren Sigdaller, the bubbly bright blond reporter for *What's-Up Evening News*, shrugged expertly out of her harness and her drone chopper flew away. Four hovering cameras positioned themselves in the air, one pointing at her. The others moved in on the police officers. Dena swatted at the one practically in her face. "Detective Sergeant Dena Malone, you're about to move in on the hideout occupied by the alleged ningustan smugglers. Please give the What's-Up viewers your feelings about penetrating into a den possibly reeking of fatal fumes?" She smiled brightly into her eyeline camera, and stuck an oversized microphone toward Dena.

"Wha . . . ? What are you doing here? How did you know where we were?" Dena demanded, gathering her scattered wits with both hands.

"A trusted informant," Lauren said, with that smooth, confident smile that millions of viewers had come to know and, in the police's opinion, loathe. "Just like our brave people in the police force use. The public has a right to know, Detective Malone! Dr. K't'ank, how are you coping with this situation? This is a threat that issues from your own star system! Do you feel any sense of responsibility for putting human beings in danger from the arrival of ningustan toxin?"

"What responsibility could I have for criminals?" K't'ank asked, outraged.

Ramos reached into one of the pouches on his ops belt and took out a palm-sized device. He aimed it at one camera after another.

The little drones dropped to the ground, trilling and moaning like wounded birds.

"Get out of here!" he growled at the reporter. "You've alerted them to our presence. Our mission is totally blown!"

"Oh, they knew you were coming already," Lauren said, brightly. "How do you think I knew where to be when?"

"They have a mole in the station?" Dena asked, aghast.

"Nobody has to be in any physical location anymore," Lauren said, with a pitying look. "We get information from all kinds of places. Hints 'R' Us, Amazeballs.com, the Old Busybodies Network, you name it!"

"Who told you about this mission?" Dena asked, trying to keep her voice down.

Lauren tossed her long blond locks smugly. "That's confidential. So, when are we going in?"

"One," Ramos said, with superb self-control, "you are not going in. Two, you're not dressed for it anyway. Three, we're not insured if something happens to you."

"I am absolutely going with you," Lauren said. "Two, I am *always* dressed for every occasion." She pulled a tab concealed in the collar of her pristine jacket. From every seam, bright red fabric billowed, until she was covered in a hazmat suit that matched her attire. "Three, I have no intention of dying. And one, they promised me safe conduct! I'll bring *you* in with *me*. That way, I get an exclusive." She glanced at the chronometer on the wrist of her puffy suit. "We've got about six minutes before Bob Colchik from Satellite News Network gets here. I have the solo scoop if I beat him inside. Can we get going, please?" Plunking a clear helmet over her head, she spun on her heels and marched toward the entrance to the container. Her drones rose humming from the ground and followed.

"Why do I think we're in the wrong business?" Ramos asked. He scrambled to catch up with the reporter.

"Her profession is information, not enforcement," K't'ank replied. "Malone, you did not answer, so I did."

Dena shook her head. She punched the forward control on the floatchair.

Lauren stood on the threshold of the target container, microphone at the ready. The two officers stayed three meters back.

"Password 84-36-22-1796-Cronkite!" she chirped. The door retracted downward. The reporter shot Dena a triumphant look, and stepped inside. "Come on!"

Surrounded by floating drones, Dena urged her throne inside. As soon as Ramos entered, the door swooped up and clanged into place, leaving them in utter darkness.

The floatchair's systems reacted faster than Dena could. Six floodlights erupted on the pillars like brightly glowing pimples, two facing forward, two to the side, one upward and one to the rear. The top light's beam seemed to disappear into the gloom. Dena caught glimpses of pierced metalwork and incised art in the walls around her.

"Holy Butlerian Jihad!" Ramos exclaimed. "This place is gigantic!"

"How did they build something like this in the middle of a working dock?" Dena asked.

"Oh, there's dozens of places like this here," Lauren said, with a dismissive wave. "Some of these containers have been here centuries, and none of the freight companies notice they never get moved, so they hollow them out and furnish them. The dockworkers know all of them. One is their clubhouse. Very fancy inside. You'd never get an invitation, but I've been there. You'd be welcome, Dr. K't'ank," Lauren added, winking flirtatiously at Dena's bracelet. "They've got some of your treatises in the data library. Is anybody out there?" she called.

A sliver of yellow light in the distance appeared and widened into a rectangle. Lauren immediately minced toward it. The two detectives trailed her.

"My sensors are not getting any traces of ningustan here," Dena whispered, showing Ramos her skinnypad. "I also lost the traces of the units outside. The shielding here is too thick to penetrate. No wonder we couldn't sense anyone in here."

Her partner grunted. "I don't like it. This is getting fishier by the moment."

"There are no fish, but there is sea life," K't'ank said. "I am picking up communication box signals used by my kind. There are Salosians here!"

"Can you talk to them?" Dena asked. She kept her eyes on the open door ahead, but couldn't see anything inside.

"I am getting nothing but HOLD music and out-of-office replies,"

K't'ank said. "I am concerned for their well-being. None of my people can resist contact with our own kind. It has been days since I communicated with Ambassador Haihatsu's occupant."

"Do you think they're free to move around?" asked Ramos. "I mean, inside people."

"That is all the information I can glean. I will try to cross-reference the communication codes to discover their names."

"Oh!" Lauren exclaimed as she reached the doorway. "Well, I never expected to see *you* here!"

"Who?" Dena asked. Her sight was blocked by the mass of the reporter's puffy red suit. "Who's here?"

Lauren turned to answer, but mechanical arms swooped out of the opening and scooped her up like a doll. She kicked and shrieked with fury, trying to wriggle out of their grasp.

"Help me!" she cried, and disappeared.

Dena and Ramos plunged forward, but the door slammed in their faces. Dena pounded on it with the butt of her service weapon. Like the surrounding walls, it was solid metal. No amount of pounding or rattling the door handle made it move even a millimeter.

Dena backed up a couple of meters, unlimbered her laser cutter, and set it to work on the door frame.

"Can we trace her?" she asked. "Do we have a comm code for her?"

Ramos worked furiously on his skinnypad. "Got one, but I can't raise her. All I've got is her moving away from us really fast. This place is huge! It must take up hundreds of shipping containers laid out for blocks."

"Customs ought to know about these," Dena said. Her temper rose with every minute that it was taking her to cut her way inside. She wasn't that fond of the reporter, who tended to harp on even innocent mistakes made by officers in the field. Still, she had the motto of the police force engraved on her heart, "To serve and protect, and not make bad headlines for the department." "When we get out, I'm going to send a full report to Potopos. He needs to inform the commissioner that these things should be dismantled! How's it going to look that we've got a neighborhood of archvillain lairs right on the waterfront?"

"Is it not convenient to where goods arrive in the city?" K't'ank asked. "For such entrepreneurs to prosper, they require direct access to free-market trade."

"That's not the point!" Dena exclaimed. "They're taking over private property for illicit purposes."

"But no one else is making use of them. Is there not a commercial property shortage in this city?"

"I think it's kind of cool," Ramos said, his fingers flying. "What it's costing me for my apartment, when I could link a dozen or twenty of these together for the cost of welding? Admit it, you and Neal could use a bigger place pretty soon."

"Yeah, we could," Dena said, a dreamy vision of extra rooms coming into her mind unbidden. Her husband's home office took up half of their living room with his computers and monitors. The second bedroom had already been transformed into a nursery, and with the robot valet that she had acquired by accident, the place was a tight fit.

"Never mind! Come on, we have to save Lauren and find the cache of ningustan."

As soon as she said it, the laser cutter switched off and flew back to her lap. Ramos walked up to the wall with a red glow still outlining it, and pushed with one finger. The door fell backward with a deafening clang.

Ramos brought his rifle around and undid the safety.

"Let's go."

The light that had drawn them forward was gone, but the spotlights on Dena's floatchair provided plenty of illumination. She guessed by the style of the complex reliefs on the wall that this particular habitation had been in use for centuries. The ningustan smugglers were only the latest tenants. The smooth floor was deep with dust that showed trails of footprints as well as machine tracks like that of an earthmover.

"Can I use the laser cutter?" Ramos asked. "I want to carve some graffiti on one of these walls."

"I don't have time to arrest you for vandalism," Dena said. "Maybe later."

Her lights hit a wall that stretched for dozens of meters in both directions. Five doors were cut into it at regular intervals.

"Pick your labyrinth," Ramos said. "I bet there's a warren of rooms behind every one."

"I detect heat emanating from the fourth door," said K't'ank. "And I have just received a different message from one of the Salosians!"

"Saying what?"

"It translates as 'please stop calling,'" K't'ank said.

"Maybe the recorder ran out of room," Ramos suggested.

"Salosian message systems never run out of room." K't'ank sounded offended. "We have much to say that is of value. Our systems record every phrase."

Dena frowned. "I bet it's trying to tell you that it heard your messages but it's afraid to respond. I think we're dealing with prisoners."

"Let's hit doorway number four," Ramos said. "You want to cut through it?"

"Try the handle," Dena said, nodding toward the metal tongue. "I think these mysterious smugglers want us to come to them."

Warily, the tall detective pulled up on the latch. Just as she suspected, it wasn't locked. It creaked like a lost soul, but the big door swung inward. Like the other chambers, it was black inside. Dena started to glide toward it.

"Wait a minute," Ramos said, stepping between her and the looming portal. "You're acting like it's safe to go in."

"If they wanted to kill us, they would have tried before," Dena said. "I've been thinking about it since we got here. This is all too easy. They want something, but they're not asking directly. So, my guess is it has to do with K't'ank. And Sardwell Marin would never have sent me in here if he thought there was any chance it would hurt K't'ank."

"That man really hates you," Ramos reminded her.

"The feeling is mutual. But he'll ensure I'm protected as long as it keeps K't'ank safe." She took a deep breath. The knot in her stomach tightened. "I just hope I'm right."

Setting the spotlights on a wide sweep, she pushed ahead. No sense in delaying the inevitable. Who knew what was happening to Lauren? If she could set the reporter free before the evening broadcast, it would look good for the department.

"Swishing noises are ahead," K't'ank said, sounding happy. "They are reminiscent of the seas of my youth. Such pleasant memories, squirming intertwined with hundreds of my friends."

"Eyagh," Ramos said. "Sounds like an orgy I was at in college."

"That's where they're holding the prisoners," Dena said. "Look at that door. It ought to have 'Big Boss Battle Ahead' printed on it in neon letters."

"I didn't get to level sixty of *Interstellar Bug Conquest* for nothing," Ramos said. "Cover me."

He flung open the portal and sprang through it to the left. Dena followed, angling to the right. No one fired at them. Nothing jumped out and attacked them.

The chamber beyond was so brightly lit it hurt Dena's eyes for a moment. The main feature was a huge glass tank that occupied more than half of the room. A dozen or so skinny pink Salosians swam to the glass and stared at her with their big black eyes. They reminded her of K't'ank's desperation when he had been pulled from the corpse of his previous host.

They weren't alone in the water. Two smaller glass chambers nestled side by side behind them. In one, a cloud of bright blue glittering particles circulated. In the other, Lauren Sigdaller hammered on the glass with both fists. A big, very good-looking man with a sweep of chestnut brown hair going elegantly white at the temples sat on the bottom with his chin on his fist, looking dejected. They both recognized him at once.

"Bob Colchik," Ramos said. "He must have gotten here first."

"Get us out of here!" Lauren yelled, her voice muffled.

"Okay!" Dena moved to the center of the room and shouted to the Art Deco ceiling. "We're here to talk to the Arch-Supervillain! Come on out! What do you want?"

A resonant female voice that seemed to come from everywhere at once emitted a throaty laugh.

"You're everything that I thought you were," she said. "You are brave and intelligent. You'll suit my purposes exactly."

"Do you always talk like a twenty-first-century movie villain?"

"What does she mean?" the voice asked.

"She's comparing you to a trope from early Earth entertainment," a very deep male voice said. "It's a derisive term."

"Am I talking to a Salosian?" Dena asked.

"It would seem so," K't'ank said, alarmed. "She is not one of these in the tank. Only two of them have communication implants. The others must have been captured on my home planet. They are hostages, like the two entertainers."

"We made a mistake in coming here," Ramos said. "It's not K't'ank they're after. It's *you*."

With growing horror, Dena realized he was right. She spun the floatchair around on its axis and headed toward the door. It emitted a loud clanking before she laid a hand on it.

"Locked," Ramos said.

"Your partner is correct," the female voice said. "I am not letting you leave. I have been observing other Salosian hosts that are in the Alien Relations files, but they rely entirely on their technology to preserve their symbiote's life. You are resourceful and clever. I have business to do with many humans, and you will assist me in that enterprise. My physician will remove Dr. K't'ank and replace him with me. He will remain here to ensure your cooperation."

"No way!" Dena said, both arms across her belly. "I'm tired of you people treating me like I'm a taxi! I've had enough to put up with carting K't'ank around! Besides, there are dozens of law enforcement officers outside about to break in. They'll take you and your host into custody."

"If they do, I'll shatter the tank containing the ningustan parasites," the female said, sounding bored. "Your humans and the other Salosians will die horribly. There will also be residual toxin in the air. It will likely kill you, too. That is a shame."

"I've *seen* this movie," Ramos said, his mouth in a wry twist. "It sucked. It was only interesting when the hero ends up tied to an operating table . . ."

"Not you, too!" Dena said. She turned back to the door and turned on the laser cutter. "Well, it's been fun, but we're leaving." The floating device began to draw its red line around the heavy portal.

"Wait, what about us?" Lauren shrieked. "You can't leave us here!"

Dena glanced back. Both the reporters were on their feet, their eyes desperate.

"Sure I can," she said, sounding as nonchalant as her pounding heart would let her. "You came in here of your own free will. You interfered with a police investigation. You are concealing a leak in the department that could cost lives one day. But I bet you're smart enough to get yourself out of this. Maybe they could use *you* as a host."

"I'll give you names! I'll cooperate!"

"Sorry," Dena said. "My responsibility is to Dr. K't'ank. I have to get him out of here. Alien Relations will do a number on me if I let him get into danger."

"I'll get you!" Lauren said. "I'll haunt you until the end of your days!"

"Too unstable," the female voice said. "Guards, stop Detective Malone! Take her to the operating room!"

"Told you so," Ramos said.

A slug pinged off the door. The floatchair backed away from the point of impact, an egg-sized crater. A heavy, fine-mesh metal curtain lowered into place around Dena, and she heard the cocking of weapons from the pillars. The floatchair was going into action, spinning in the direction the bullet had come from. Just in time, too, as eight burly men in green hazard gear rushed into the room. One of them rode a cargo lifter with waving octopus-like arms. That had to have been what snagged Lauren. It was coming straight toward Dena.

"Finally," Ramos said, bracing his rifle. "I was getting bored. I assume you have a play."

"I think I do," Dena said, uneasily. "Whatever you do, don't take off your helmet."

"Got it. Hey, you guys! Surrender now, and nothing bad will happen to you!" Ramos called.

The whole gang turned to shoot at him. Ramos was already running. He made a dive behind the corner of the huge glass tank. A cluster of bullets ricocheted off the surface and went off in all directions. The Salosians inside fled to the far end of the tank. Some of the slugs hit Dena's protective shield. They bounced off, but left dents in the mesh. All solid projectiles, she noted. No lasers meant that the tank's glass could be melted. She filed that fact for her Master Plan.

Her skinnypad's screen changed to the floatchair's weapons control panel. The intense training in its use that Alien Relations had put her through kicked in immediately. With a swipe, Dena turned automatic tracking on the slugthrowers. They started spitting out bullets, making the thugs on foot duck out of her way. If they had to dodge her guns, they wouldn't be concentrating on Ramos or the cutter.

The one she had to worry about was the cargo lifter. If it got its claws on her, it could disable or crush the floatchair. She made the chair dodge from side to side, keeping her gaze fixed on the operator's eyes. It would take about eight minutes before the cutter had finished removing the door. She needed to keep him distracted for that amount of time. How long before he got so impatient that he made a stupid mistake?

"The Salosian wishes to steal you?" K't'ank asked, worried. "But I am used to you!"

"Not now, K't'ank! I want to get us all out alive."

Dena feinted to the left, then slid right so that her back was against the tank. The cargo lifter operator must have been ordered not to break the glass. He trundled toward her, jointed arms reaching for the frame of her chair. She dodged from side to side, then scooted out from her position. Her trajectory knocked two of the green-suited thugs away from Ramos. He managed to get to his feet, but two more were heading for him.

"Behind you!" he shouted.

Dena turned the chair, just as the first pair leaped onto the chassis. They started tearing at the mesh over her head. They'd never get through it, but it hampered her vision. She activated the switch that sent electrical current charging through the mesh. It ought to have fried their hands, but the green gloves must be insulated. Dena shook the chair from side to side, hoping to dislodge them. Three more of the thugs grabbed at the floatchair frame. She found herself bouncing against one after another, until she was trapped in place. Ramos went down, using the butt of his rifle to defend himself. The cargo operator, with a look of glee, homed in on her. One claw froze onto the pillar of the chair. The other started to tear at the mesh, dislodging the other ruffians. The floatchair let out a moan as it was slammed from one side to the other.

"We shall be torn apart!" K't'ank wailed.

"No. They want me," Dena said. She held onto the skinnypad, reaching for the laser controls. As long as she aimed away from the tank, she could use them.

"Surrender!" the Salosian archvillainess, as Dena thought of her, demanded. "Your partner is now in my grasp. I will have my humans throw him into the ningustan tank if you do not stop resisting right now!"

"He knew the job was dangerous when he took it!" Dena said. "So did I!" She flicked the controls. The slugthrower barrels withdrew, replaced by shorter and narrower tubes.

The Salosian's minions knew what those meant. They scrambled off the body of the chair. Hot red light streaked after them, leaving charred black lines across the backs of their suits.

But the cargo loader didn't retreat. He continued to shake her back and forth. Dena was afraid that K't'ank was right. The floatchair might come to pieces. Her only hope of saving all of them would be lost.

She had no choice.

Mentally crossing her fingers, she activated the new screen that had been installed on it only that morning. Really, she hadn't been paying close attention to what the annoying bureaucrat had been blathering at her. She had heard "protective shell," "heavy-duty motivators," and "superior weather resistance," but that was about it. Since Alien Relations always did things with triple and sextuple redundancy, she had to believe that what she was going to do would work.

All right, Deputy Ambassador Marin, I'm trusting you!

"Hang on, K't'ank," she said, flicking controls as fast as she could. "It's going to be rough."

"What do you mean by rough? Why are you heading for that glass wall? It must not be breached! The lives of my fellow Salosians are at stake!"

His tail pounded her insides as Dena took aim at the direct center of the tank. She hoped her suit contained enough air to last the next few minutes.

She pressed the control that activated the new motivators. The floatchair settled to the ground and rumbled forward. Without her having to take any action, clear panels flipped up from underneath the seat itself and surrounded her. The loader lost its grip as the smooth sheets of maxiplex plastic knocked the claws away. It battered at her in vain. Dena ignored its pounding. Now for phase two.

No control existed for the "weather resistance," so either that was automatic, or she was going to be treading water pretty quickly.

"Hang on," she said, and aimed all the lasers at the glass. The pane began to glow. All the Salosians retreated to the sides away from the hot beams.

"Don't! Don't ruin my tank! You will kill my subjects!"

The bubble of glass started to quiver. Dena stuffed the skinnypad down beside her where it couldn't get washed away, and held tight to her armrests. She wished, too late, that she had a safety harness. The glass shimmied, then opened up like a bursting balloon.

Water washed over her in a wave that would make any surfer crow with glee. The green-suited minions went tumbling away like seaweed. Dena braced herself, worried the floatchair would go tumbling, but the new treads seemed to hold the ground as if they were cemented there. She lowered the protective shell to her waist. Water flooded in and with it came one of the Salosians. She grabbed it and shoved it into the well around her feet. She urged the vehicle forward, searching for all of the pink-skinned aliens.

"There!" K't'ank said, as her eyes swept to the left. "Underneath the filter housing!"

Three of the aliens had knotted themselves together, trying to resist the outgoing tide. Dena swooped down on them and gathered them up in both gloved hands. They struggled, fearing the air, but she plunked them down into the pool. The others already there gathered them into a protective mass.

"Is that all of them?" Dena asked, scanning the ruins of the tank.

"It seems so," K't'ank said.

"You will die for this!" the archvillainess screamed. "I will break open the ningustan tank!"

"Oh, don't bother," Dena said, with a grin. "Let me do that for you."

She turned her makeshift war machine toward the smaller tank, closing the protective shield over herself and her passengers as she rolled. The human minions saw what she was doing and fled. The cargo operator practically ran them over trying to get away.

"No! No! Humans, return to the tank room! Stop her!"

"I don't think they want to be here when I do this," Dena said. She turned her lasers on the square enclosure. She held her breath, just in case some of the ningustan escaped. It wouldn't help, but it made her feel better.

"Stop, stop!" the Salosian pleaded over the speaker. "Everyone is leaving!"

"No! You're going to kill us!" Lauren bellowed, pounding on the tank.

"Wait, look!" For the first time, Bob Colchik stood up. He aimed his personal skinnypad at Dena and the ningustan enclosure. Under fire from the lasers, the tank began to glow, but from the inside. By the time the beam breached the wall of the container, all of the blue particles had turned black and floated up to the surface of the water. It gushed out harmlessly onto the big tank's floor. "That was awesome! I've got the best exclusive for this evening's broadcast!"

"Bob, you have to share with me," Lauren pleaded, reaching for the skinnypad.

"Are you kidding?" he asked, raising a perfect eyebrow at her. He held the device up to avoid her grabs. "You tried to get my informant to delay me so you would get in here first! Suck on it."

Dena wished she had been able to record their argument. It would be great trade goods to prevent either newscaster from giving them bad publicity, at least for a while.

"Stay there until the emergency crews arrive," she told them. "We have to make sure the air is clear before we let you out."

"We owe you our lives, Sergeant," Bob said, still stiff-arming his fellow broadcaster. "I'll make sure that gets into my report."

"*Our* report!" Lauren insisted.

Chuckling, Dena turned her back on them, and went to look for Ramos.

She found him head down against the wall in the corner near the minions' escape route. She breathed a sigh of relief to see that his helmet was intact, with no trace of water inside.

"Are you okay?" she asked, as he pulled himself to his feet.

"What is all that?" He stared at the new configuration, and let out a whistle. "Did Marin do all that?"

"I guess so," she said. "It worked. My chair now really is a tank. Can you get up? If I open this bubble, I'll expose all these Salosians to what's left of the ningustan."

Ramos looked around. "Don't we have to get after the guys in green? And the man with the Salosian symbiote?"

Dena grinned. "I will bet you next month's pay that Potopos

already has them in custody. If you knew the air was about to be full of fatal toxins, you'd get out of there as fast as you could."

"Next month's pay?" K't'ank piped up. "Next month you will be on leave. It will be a reduced sum."

"She ought to get hazard pay," Ramos said, smacking the maxiplex bubble as if he was slapping her on the back. "Me, too."

"Well, let's get out there," Dena said, with a massive sigh. "I've got the most hazardous task still ahead of me."

Ramos looked confused. "What? We rousted the bad people, we saved the hostages, and we avoided getting exposed to the outer space toxin. What's left?"

Dena turned her floatchair reluctantly toward the door. "I've got to go say 'thank you' to Sardwell Marin. He's going to gloat, and that'll hurt more than ningustan poisoning."

Airborne All the Way!

⊕

David Drake

Crewgoblin Dumber Than #3 stared with his unusual look of puzzlement as labor goblins unrolled Balloon Prima. He scratched his chain-mail jockstrap and said to Dog Squat, the balloon chief, "I dunno, boss."

Dog Squat rolled her eyes expressively and muttered, "Mana give me strength!" She glanced covertly to see if Roxanne was watching what balloon chiefs had to put up with, but the senior thaumaturge was involved with the team of dragon wranglers bringing the whelp into position in front of the coal pile.

Dog Squat glowered at her four crewgoblins. "Well, what don't you know?" she snarled. "What is there to know? We go up, we throw rocks down. You like to throw rocks, Number Three?"

"I like to bite them," said Dumber Than #1. "Will we be able to bite them, Dog Squat?"

The plateau on which the Balloon Brigade was readying for battle overlooked the enemy on the broad plain below. The hostile command group, pulsing with white mana, had taken its station well to the rear. White battalions were deploying directly from their line of march. Gullies and knolls skewed the rectangles of troops slightly, but the formations were still precise enough to make a goblin's disorderly mind ache.

"But boss," #3 said, "how do we get down again?"

"Getting down's the easy part!" Dog Squat shouted. "Rocks aren't any smarter than you are, and they manage to get down, don't they? Well, not much smarter. Just leave the thinking to me, why don't you?"

"I really like to bite them," #1 repeated. He scraped at a black, gleaming fang with a black, gleaming foreclaw. "After we throw rocks, will we be able to bite them, Dog Squat?"

Dog Squat tried to visualize biting from a balloon. The closest she could come was a sort of ruddy blur that made her head ache worse than sight of the serried, white-clad ranks on the plains below. "No biting unless I tell you!" she said to cover ignorance. "Not even a teeny little bite!"

The large pile of coal was ready for ignition. The metal cover sat on the ground behind for the moment. Instead of forging a simple dome, the smiths had created a gigantic horned helmet. To either side of the coal was a sloped dirt ramp so that labor goblins could carry the helmet over the pile and cap it when the time came.

Balloons Prima and Secundus were unrolled to either side, and the three wranglers had finally gotten their dragon whelp into position in front of the pile. The other unfilled balloons waited their turn in double lines. It was time to start.

"All right, Theobald!" Senior Thaumaturge Roxanne said to the junior thaumaturge accompanying her, a mana specialist. "Get to work and don't waste a lot of time. We're already forty minutes behind schedule. Malfegor will singe the skin off me if we don't launch an attack before noon, and I promise that you won't be around to snicker if that happens."

Roxanne strode over to Dog Squat and her crew. The balloon chief tried to straighten like a human coming to attention; she wobbled dangerously. A goblin's broad shoulders and heavy, fanged skull raised the body's center of gravity too high unless the hips were splayed back and the knuckles kept usefully close to the ground.

"Everything ready here?" Roxanne demanded. The senior thaumaturge in charge of the Balloon Brigade wore a power suit with pinstripes of red, Malfegor's color. Her attaché case was an expensive one made of crimson belly skins, the sexual display markings of little male lizards. Very many little male lizards.

"Yes, sir, one hundred percent!" Dog Squat said. She frowned. She wasn't very good on numbers. "Two hundred percent?" she offered as an alternative.

"Yes, well, you'd better be," Roxanne said as she returned her attention to the dragon-filling.

The dragon whelp was no bigger than a cow. The beast didn't appear to be in either good health or a good humor. Its tail lashed restively despite the attempt of one wrangler to control that end while the other two held the whelp's head steady.

Junior Thaumaturge Theobald stood in front of the whelp with a book in one hand and an athame of red copper in the other. As Theobald intoned, a veil of mana flowed into the whelp from the surrounding rock. The creature's outlines softened.

Purple splotches distorted the generally red fields of force. The whelp shook itself. The wranglers tossed violently, but they all managed to hold on.

Dumber Than #1 bent close to Dog Squat and whispered gratingly in her ear. The balloon chief sighed and said, "Ah, sir?"

Roxanne jumped. A goblin's notion of a quiet voice was one that you couldn't hear in the next valley. "Yes?" the senior thaumaturge said.

"Ah, sir," Dog Squat said, "there's been some discussion regarding biting. Ah, whether we'll be biting the enemy, that is. Ah, that is, will we?"

Roxanne stared at the balloon chief in honest amazement. The four crewgoblins stood behind Dog Squat, scratching themselves but obviously intent on the answer.

"You'll be throwing rocks," Roxanne said, speaking very slowly and distinctly. She tried to make eye contact with each crewgoblin in turn, but a goblin's eyes tend to wander in different directions.

The senior thaumaturge tapped the surface of the plateau with one open-toed, wedge-heeled shoe. "Rocks are like this," she said, "only smaller. The rocks are already in the gondola of your balloon. Do you all understand?"

None of them understood. None of them understood anything.

Dumber Than #3 scratched his jockstrap again. Roxanne winced. "Isn't that uncomfortable to wear?" she said. "I mean, chain mail?"

The crewgoblin nodded vigorously. "Yeah, you can say that again," he said. He continued to scratch.

"But when is she going to tell us about biting?" #1 said to Dog Squat in a steamwhistle whimper.

The dragon whelp farted thunderously. A huge blue flame flung the rearward wrangler thirty feet away with his robes singed off. The veil of inflowing mana ceased as Roxanne spun around.

"Sorry, sorry," Junior Thaumaturge Theobald said nervously as he closed his book. "The mana here is impure. Too much ground water—we must be over an aquifer. But she's full and ready."

"Carry on, then," Roxanne said grimly to the remaining dragon wranglers.

The leading wrangler crooned into the whelp's ear as her partner stroked the scaly throat from the other side. The whelp, shimmering with newfound power, bent toward the pile of coal and burped a puny ball of red fire. Roxanne frowned.

"Come on, girl, you can do it," the wrangler moaned. "Come on, do it for Mommy. Come on, sweetie, come on—"

The dragon whelp stretched out a diamond-clawed forepaw and blasted a double stream of crimson fire from its nostrils. The jets ripped across and into the pile of coal, infusing the flame through every gap and crevice. The wranglers directed the ruby inferno by tugging their charge's head back and forth with long leads.

After nearly three minutes of roaring hellfire, the whelp sank back exhausted. It seemed to have shrunk to half its size of a few moments before. The two normally robed wranglers clucked the beast tiredly to its feet and walked it out of the way. The third wrangler limped alongside. In place of a robe he was wearing a red gonfalon borrowed from a nearby cavalry regiment.

The coal pile glowed like magma trapped deep in the planetary mantle. "Come on!" Roxanne ordered. "Let's not waste this. Get moving and get it capped!"

The capping crew was under the charge of two novice thaumaturges, both of them in their teens. In response to their chirped commands, the four labor goblins lifted the gigantic helmet by means of crosspoles run through sockets at the front and back of the base. They began to shuffle forward, up the earthen ramps built to either side of the pile of coal.

The porters were goblins chosen for brawn rather than brains. The very concept of intellect would have boggled the porters' minds if they'd had any. In order to keep the crews moving in the right direction, the novices projected a line of splayed, clawed footprints in front of the leaders on either ramp to carefully fit his/her feet into.

The goblins on the rear pole set their feet exactly on the same markings. They didn't put any weight down until they were sure the foot was completely within the glowing red lines. The cap's rate of movement was more amoebic than tortoiselike. Nevertheless, it moved. Senior Thaumaturge Roxanne drummed fingers on the side of her attaché case in frustration, but there was no hurrying labor goblins.

The leaders paused when they reached the last pairs of footprints at the ends of the ramps. The porters stood stolidly, apparently oblivious of the heat and fumes from the coal burning beside them.

The novice thaumaturges turned to Roxanne. "Yes!" she shouted. "Cap it! Cap it now!"

The novices ordered, "Drop your poles!" in an uncertain tenor and a throaty contralto. Three of the porters obeyed. The fourth looked around in puzzlement, then dropped his pole also. The helmet clanged down unevenly but still down, over the pile. The metal completely covered the coal, shutting off all outside air.

The horns flaring to the sides of the giant helmet were nozzles. Thick hoses were attached to the ends of horns. The novice thaumaturges clamped the free ends of the hoses into the filler inlets of Balloons Prima and Secundus. Adjusting the hoses was hard work, but the task was too complicated to be entrusted to a goblin.

Roxanne personally checked the connection to Prima while the junior thaumaturge did the same on the other side. "All right," she said to the novice watching anxiously from the top of the ramp where he'd scrambled as soon as he attached his hose. "Open the cock."

The novice twisted a handle shaped like a flying dragon at the tip of the horn, opening the nozzle to gas that made the hose writhe on its way to the belly of Balloon Prima. The senior thaumaturge stepped away as the balloon began to fill.

The balloons were made from an inner layer of sea serpent intestine. The material was impervious to gas and so wonderfully tough that giants set bars of gold between layers of the stuff and hammered the metal into foil.

Prima bulged into life, inflating with gases driven out of the furiously hot coal in the absence of oxygen to sustain further combustion. The four drag ropes tightened in the clawed hands of labor goblins whose job was to keep the balloon on the ground until it had been completely filled with its inlet closed.

"You lot!" Roxanne said to Dog Squat and her crew. "What are you waiting for? Get into your gondola now!"

Dog Squat opened her mouth to explain that she'd been waiting for orders. She forgot what she was going to say before she got the words out. "Dumber Thans," she said instead, "get into the little boat."

The wicker gondola creaked as the five goblins boarded it. The balloon was already full enough to lift off the ground and swing in the coarse steel netting that attached the car to it. A light breeze swept down from Malfegor's aerie, ready to waft the brigade toward the enemy on the plain below.

The floor of the gondola was covered with rocks the size of a goblin's head. Many of the missiles were delightfully jagged. Number 3 patted a piece of chert with a particularly nice point.

Balloon Secundus lifted into sight from the other side of the helmet. It was sausage-shaped, like forty-nine percent of the brigade's equipment. Prima was one of the slight majority of balloons which, when seen from the side, looked like a huge dome with a lesser peak on top. The attachment netting gleamed like chain mail over the pinkish white expanse of sea serpent intestine.

Dog Squat picked up a rock and hefted it. A good, solid chunk of granite. A rock that a goblin could really get into throwing, yep, you betcha. Dog Squat had heard some principals would try to fob their crews off with blocks of limestone that crumbled if you just looked crossways at it, but not good old Malfegor. . . .

"Shut off the gas flow!" Senior Thaumaturge Roxanne called to the novice on the ramp above her. She released the catch on the input. When Prima wobbled, the hose pulled loose, and Roxanne clamped the valve shut.

"Cast off!" she ordered the ground crew.

Three of the goblins dropped their ropes. The fourth, an unusually powerful fellow even for a labor goblin, continued to grip his. His big toes were opposable, and he'd sunk his claws deep into the rock of the plateau.

Balloon Prima lifted at an angle. The gondola was nearly vertical, pointing at the goblin holding the rope.

"Let's go!" Roxanne screamed. "Drop the rope!"

She batted the goblin over the head with her attaché case. He looked at the senior thaumaturge quizzically.

"Let go!" Roxanne repeated. "Don't you understand what I'm saying?"

The goblin blinked. He continued to hold onto both the rope and the ground. Balloon Prima wobbled above him.

Roxanne looked up. Dog Squat peered down at her.

The balloon chief wore a familiar puzzled expression. The crewgoblins were stacked, more or less vertically, on the back of their chief. A gust from the wrong direction and the contents of the gondola would tip out promiscuously.

"You!" the senior thaumaturge said. "Hit this idiot on the head with a rock. A hard rock!"

Dog Squat looked again at the rock she held, decided that it would do, and bashed the handler goblin with it. The victim's eyeballs rolled up. He dropped the rope and fell over on his back.

Balloon Prima shot skyward, righting itself as it rose.

The rope the goblin dropped whipped around Roxanne's waist and dragged her along. The senior thaumaturge weighed scarcely more than any one of the rocks in the bottom of the gondola, so her presence didn't significantly affect the balloon's upward course.

Dog Squat looked over the side of the gondola at Roxanne and blinked. The senior thaumaturge, swinging like a tethered canary, screamed, "Pull me in, you idiot!"

"I didn't know you were coming along, sir," the balloon chief said contritely. She rapped her head hard with her knuckles to help her think. "Or did I?" she added.

"Pull me—" Roxanne said. The rope, kinked rather than knotted about her, started to unwrap. Roxanne grabbed it with both hands. Her attaché case took an obscenely long time to flutter down. At last it smashed into scraps no larger than the original pelts on the rocks below.

Dog Squat tugged the rope in, hand over hand, then plucked the senior thaumaturge from it and lifted her into the gondola. Roxanne's eyes remained shut until she felt throwing stones beneath her feet rather than empty air.

"Are we...?" she said. She looked over the side of the gently swaying gondola. Because of its heavy load, Balloon Prima had only climbed a few hundred feet above the plateau, but the ground continued to slope away as Malfegor's sorcerous breeze pushed them toward the enemy lines.

"Oh, mana," Roxanne said. "Oh mana, mana, mana."

"Boss," said Dumber Than #2, "do you remember when I ate that possum the trolls walked over the week before?"

"Yeah," said Dog Squat. Everybody in the crew remembered that.

"Well, I feel like that again," #2 said.

He did look greenish. His eyeballs did, at least. He was swaying a little more than the gondola itself did, come to think.

"Where did you find a dead possum up here, Number Two?" Dog Squat asked.

"I didn't!" the crewgoblin said with queasy enthusiasm.

He frowned, pounded himself on the head, and added, "I don't think I did, anyways."

"Oh, mana," the senior thaumaturge moaned. "How am I ever going to get down?"

"Getting down is the easy part!" Dumber Than #3 said brightly. "Even rocks manage to get down! You're probably lots smarter than a rock, sir."

Senior Thaumaturge Roxanne took another look over the side of the gondola, then curled into a fetal position in the stern.

"Did you eat a dead possum, too?" #2 asked in what for a goblin was a solicitous tone.

Balloon Prima had continued to drift while the senior thaumaturge considered her position. The battalions of white-clad enemy troops were by now almost directly below. They didn't look the way they ought to. They looked little.

Dog Squat frowned. She wondered if these were really the people she was supposed to drop rocks on.

"Boss, are we in the right place?" #4 asked. The gondola tilted thirty degrees in its harness. All four crewgoblins had leaned over the same side as their chief. "Them guys don't look right."

"They make my head hurt to look at," #3 added. "They're—"

Goblins didn't have a word for "square." Even the attempt to express the concept made lights flash painfully behind the crewgoblin's eyes.

In a fuzzy red flash, Dog Squat gained a philosophy of life: When in doubt, throw rocks. "We throw rocks!" she shouted, suiting her actions to her words.

The goblins hurled rocks down with enthusiasm—so much enthusiasm that Dog Squat had to prevent Dumber Than #1 from tossing Roxanne, whom he'd grabbed by a mistake that nearly became irremediable. When Dog Squat removed the senior thaumaturge from #1's hands, the crewgoblin tried to bite her— probably #1's philosophy of life—until Dog Squat clouted him into a proper attitude of respect.

The gondola pitched violently from side to side because of the repeated shifts in weight. The entire balloon lurched upward since the rocks acted as ballast when they weren't being used for ammunition. The crew of Balloon Prima was having as much fun as goblins could with their clothes on (and a lot more fun than goblins have with their clothes off, as anyone looking at a nude goblin can imagine).

They weren't, however, hitting anybody on the ground, which was increasingly far below.

The tight enemy formations shattered like glass on stone as Balloon Prima drifted toward them. That was the result of fear, not actual damage. The goblins could no more brain individual soldiers a thousand feet below than they could fly without Prima's help.

That didn't matter particularly to Dog Squat and her crew. Throwing rocks was a job worth doing for its own sake; and anyway, the collapse of ordered battalions into complete disorder fitted Dog Squat's sense of rightness. The universe (not as clear a concept as it would have been to, say, a senior thaumaturge; but still, a concept in goblin terms) liked chaos.

White-clad archers well to the side of the balloon's expected course bent their bows in enormous futile efforts. The altitude that made it difficult for the goblins to hit targets on the ground also made it impossible for archers on the ground to reach Balloon Prima. The arrows arcing back to earth did more damage to other white-clad troops than the goblin-flung rocks had done.

Malfegor's breeze continued to drive Balloon Prima in the direction of the enemy command group. The hail of missiles from the gondola stopped.

"Boss?" said #4. "Where are the rocks?"

Dog Squat looked carefully around the floor of the gondola. She even lifted Roxanne, who moaned softly in response.

"There are no rocks," Dog Squat said.

Dumber Than #3 scratched himself. "I thought there was rocks," he said in puzzlement.

"Can we bite them now, Dog Squat?" #1 said.

Dog Squat looked over the side again. She hoped there might be another thaumaturge or somebody else who could tell them what to do.

There wasn't. Dog Squat checked both sides to be sure, however.

The enemy had made preparations against the Balloon Brigade's attack. Two teams of antiballoon ballistas galloped into position between Balloon Prima and the white command group. The crews dismounted and quickly cranked their high-angle weapons into action.

A ball nearly the size of the rocks the goblins had thrown whizzed toward the balloon and burst twenty feet away in a gush of white mana.

"Oooh," said Dog Squat and three of her crewgoblins. The breeze shifted slightly, driving Balloon Prima in the direction of the white blast. Malfegor was hunting the bursts on the assumption that the safest place to be was where the immediately previous shell had gone off.

"Ohhh," said Dumber Than #2, holding his belly with both hands. "The more we shake around, the older the possum gets."

Sure enough, the next antiballoon shell flared close to where Prima would have been if she'd continued on her former course. The breeze jinked back, continuing to blow the balloon toward the command group below.

The hostile artillerists cranked their torsion bows furiously. They were also trying to raise their angle of aim, but Balloon Prima was almost directly overhead and the ballistas couldn't shoot vertically. By the time Prima was in the defenders' sights again, the balloon would be directly over the command group.

Dumber Than #4 nudged Dog Squat and pointed to the tightly curled senior thaumaturge. "Can we throw her now, boss?" the crewgoblin asked. "Seeings as we're, you know, out of rocks?"

Dog Squat pursed her lips, a hideous sight. "No," she decided at last. "Throwing rocks is good. Throwing thaumaturges is not good."

At least she didn't think it was. They ought to throw something, though.

"Can we bite them, then?" said #1.

Dumber Than #2 vomited over the side with great force and volume, much as he'd done after the never-to-be-forgotten (even by a goblin) possum incident.

The huge greenish yellow mass plunged earthward at increasing velocity. It was easier to track than a rock of the same size because it was slightly fluorescent. For a moment Dog Squat thought the bolus was going to hit one of the antiballoon ballistas. Instead, it glopped the ballista's captain, who fell backward into his weapon.

The toppling ballista fired its shell straight up. Though the glowing white ball missed the gondola by a dragon's whisker, it punched through the side of the gasbag above.

The top of the balloon ruptured with a loud bang. The blast of mana expelled and ignited the bag's contents in a puff of varicolored flame—a mixture of hydrogen, carbon monoxide, and methane, all flammable and dazzlingly pretty.

"Oooh!" said all the goblins in delight. Number 2, no longer holding his belly, had a particularly pleased expression.

Ex–Balloon Prima dropped, though not nearly as fast as the rocks thrown earlier. The gasbag had burst, but the steel netting still restrained the tough fabric of sea serpent intestine. The combination made an excellent parachute.

There was wild panic on the ground below. The enemy commanders had realized Prima would land directly on top of them.

Dumber Than #1 looked at the lusciously soft enemy officers, coming closer every moment the air whistled past the gondola. He asked plaintively, "Please, boss, can we bite them?"

Dog Squat glanced at Roxanne—no change there—and made a command decision. "Yes," the balloon chief said decisively. "We will bite them."

Dumber Than #3 scratched himself with the hand that wasn't gripping the edge of the gondola. He gestured toward the senior thaumaturge and said fondly, "Gee, it must be something to be smart enough to plan all this. She's really a genius, ain't she, boss?"

"She sure is," Dog Squat agreed, preparing to jump into the middle of the terrified enemy at the moment of impact.

Senior Thaumaturge Roxanne whimpered softly.

Airborne: The Next Mission

⊕

David Drake

Dog Squat, Balloon Prima's crew chief, tried to straighten and throw her shoulders back the way humans did when they stood to attention. She wasn't very good at it, which was just as well. A goblin's head is a solid mass of bone and the weight would probably have pulled Dog Squat over on her back.

Senior Thaumaturge Roxanne probably wouldn't have noticed anyway. She was talking with—being ordered by—Malfegor himself.

"Mistress Roxanne," Malfegor said, "I'm counting on the Balloon Brigade. Another brilliant attack like the last one could leave us on top of the world."

"Sir!" Roxanne said hesitantly. "I'm proud of our success last time but we were very lucky. We can't expect that sort of luck again."

"Of course not!" agreed Malfegor. "By sheer good luck your Balloon Prima was directly over the enemy command group when you were hit by an enemy bolt. Your forces completely disrupted the enemy."

Actually, Dog Squat thought, *we* massacred *the enemy*. Crewgoblin Dumber Than #1's whole philosophy of Life had been to bite them, and he and his fellows had done that brilliantly in the midst of enemy officers whose plan of defense seemed to be to wait for the goblins' jaws to get tired. The goblins didn't tire before they ran out of enemy officers.

"I can't take much credit for that," Roxanne said. Dog Squat remembered the senior thaumaturge curled up in the belly of the gondola where the rocks had been before they threw them all. She hadn't been good at all at biting the enemy, but that was all right. Dog Squat and her crew could take care of that after Roxanne had done the plotting.

"This time," Malfegor said proudly, "I've added a spill valve to the top of the balloon so that it can be dropped from a thousand feet directly on the enemy commanders. They won't know what hit them!"

"I see that," Roxanne said. "That's a very thoughtful plan, but it may be more thoughtful than goblins can easily execute. I know you don't have much contact with warrior goblins, sir, but I've had a great deal and I can assure you that there's a problem."

"One that I've already solved, Mistress Roxanne," Malfegor said. "You will be in the gondola with your troops!"

Dog Squat didn't remember Roxanne getting a single mouthful that time. "But sir," she said to Malfegor, "I'll be a thousand feet in the air also."

"Yes," Malfegor said. "But it can't be helped, you see."

"Don't worry, Mistress," #3 said in a cheerful bellow. "We'll all be with you."

"I don't see how that will help with gravity!" Roxanne said, noticeably less cheerful.

Dog Squat was trying to figure out what gravity was. It was a concept above her rank. She squinted, and the thaumaturge jumped. Dog Squat meant her expression as friendly, or at least neutral, but someone who had recently watched her obeying her colleague's suggestion that they *Bite 'em* could be forgiven for concern.

"Is gravity the thing about going down?" Dog Squat said, voicing the idea that had rattled out in her mind.

"Yes! You could say that," Roxanne said in a bitter tone. She was staring at Malfegor's back as he walked away. "Down a thousand feet!"

"Don't worry, Mistress," #1 said. "It isn't as hard as it sounds! You'll manage."

All the labor goblins hauling coal had completed their tasks and the dragon wranglers were dragging and prodding their charges to the piles. Senior Thaumaturge Roxanne said, "I'll have plenty of time to figure it out while plunging a thousand feet down to the plain," and gestured over the edge.

Dog Squat followed the movement with her eyes. The blue army was below in rows so neat that they made Dog Squat's head ache. How could people live like that? It wasn't natural!

When Dog Squat turned back, Roxanne had disappeared. If the blue ranks hadn't been so dizzying, Dog Squat would have worried herself into a headache. There wasn't really a lot of time before they had to be aboard Balloon Prima's gondola, ready to drop rocks!

Dragon wranglers hissed spells in the ears of their dragons. Some stroked the scaly necks and whispered encouragement.

One after another the rank of dragons belched sulfurous flames into the waiting coal piles, igniting them instantly. The dragon on the right, serving Balloon Secundus, had a greenish tinge and didn't look healthy. It hadn't flamed. Its wrangler screamed curses at it and punched it in the flank with no result. A labor goblin who wanted to get by the wrangler kicked the dragon in the ribs. The dragon spewed flames—and then farted explosively. The dragon wrangler was at a safe distance, but Senior Thaumaturge Roxanne leaped into sight with her hair on fire.

"There you are, Mistress!" Dog Squat shouted. "I was afraid you were going to get lost!"

The banner of the Balloon Brigade stood on a pole ready to be taken aboard Balloon Prima. Dog Squat grabbed the banner and threw it over the senior thaumaturge. There was a lot of gold thread in the red silk, so it didn't flare up as Dog Squat rubbed out the burning hair. Roxanne screamed and thrashed. She wasn't strong enough to pull free, but to be safe Dog Squat said, "Number One, get the thaumaturge into the balloon and make sure she doesn't get lost."

"I know!" #2 said. "I can sit on her!"

"No!" shrieked Roxanne as #1 carried her to the gondola. "You'll kill me and Malfegor won't like that!"

A senior thaumaturge was a lot smarter than a goblin, even a crew chief like Dog Squat. She was right!

"Don't sit on her, Number Two!" she shouted. "Just make sure she doesn't wander off!"

"I'll help!" #1 said. He handed Roxanne to #4, already in the gondola, pulled the slack tie rope from one of the labor goblins, and wrapped it around the senior thaumaturge. Some of the balloons were already filling, their fires capped and hoses feeding illuminating gas from the coal.

Prima's hose handlers attached the hose of dragon intestine to one of the pair of headers from the metal fire cap. It was getting to be time. Dog Squat followed #1 into the wicker gondola. The basket rocked queasily under the weight of the goblins. Roxanne had sure been right about #2 squashing her if he'd sat on her. That was why it was so good to have a senior thaumaturge like Roxanne in the Balloon Brigade.

Their balloon began to fill and rise, taking up slack in the guy ropes. Roxanne wriggled and began to scream. "Loosen this rope!" she shouted. "You'll squeeze my guts out through my teeth and what will Malfegor say?"

Number 1 moved over to the edge of the gondola. "Hey!" he shouted to the labor goblins. "Stop pulling or I hit you with rocks!"

He looked over at Dog Squat and said, "Is that all right?"

Dog Squat had gotten lost trying to figure out the question Roxanne had asked about what Malfegor would say when the senior thaumaturge's guts squirted out her mouth. It probably depended what direction she was facing when it happened. Number 1 wasn't smart enough to figure out the question, so he just acted.

The labor goblins scattered from the threat and released their end of the guide rope. Roxanne resumed struggling and managed to writhe free of the wrapping. That was good, because in Dog Squat's experience anything Malfegor said to her would be loud and angry.

"That's all right," Dog Squat said. Malfegor looked back toward them as the balloon bobbed half off the ground, but he didn't shout at them.

The balloon drifted over the edge of the escarpment. The labor goblins on another rope let go to avoid being dragged over, as did all the labor goblins on the tie ropes. Prima drifted toward the neat blocks of the blue army, but not as high in the air as she was meant to be. The enemy saw this.

Teams of ground ballista men unlimbered their weapons and began launching bolts from all sides. Blue mana arched into the sky, but instead of losing its energy in its climb to high altitude, it skimmed at low level over the front ranks of its own army and crashed into the ground in bright blue plumes, flinging turf and men in every direction. Couriers, many of them mounted, rushed from the command group on the rear toward the artillerymen.

The shooting stopped. None of the shots had passed close to Balloon Prima.

Malfegor's directed breezes continued to drive Balloon Prima toward the hostile command group. The enemy officers had heard what happened to the white army previously and the stories had lost nothing in the telling. The blue command group began to scatter even before Balloon Prima was overhead.

"We're not very high," #2 said.

"That's all right," said Dog Squat.

"That's all right," said Roxanne. "It's not so far to fall."

"We'll get lots higher after we throw rocks," Dog Squat continued, choosing a delightfully jagged rock from the pile in the bottom of the gondola.

She hurled the rock toward one of the blue regiments and watched with pleasure as the ordered formation broke up, men running in all directions. The balloon shook itself and bobbed up noticeably higher. Roxanne had hopped on the pile of rocks to reach the spill valve, but the motion threw her down. She scrambled up again but when she started to raise her foot to place it on another rock, #2 whisked the rock away, shifted toward the edge of the gondola, and poised to fling it over.

"Hey!" Roxanne shouted. "I was going to climb on that rock!"

"Well, climb on another," #2 said. "This one just called to me."

Roxanne jumped onto the highest remaining stone in the heap of ammunition. She reached up for the spill valve and touched it just as Dog Squat saw what the thaumaturge was doing.

"Not yet, Mistress," the balloon chief said to the senior thaumaturge, and lifted her away from the line. "We still got to be higher."

As she spoke, #2 flung her rock and a moment later #3 flung another. The balloon jolted upward like a bucking horse. It even managed a corkscrew motion as though it were alive.

Roxanne's guts went through a similar series of motions. She reached the side just before she threw up. "Nice try, ma'am," #1 said. "But I think it's best to use rocks for as long as we've got them."

So speaking, #1 picked up the last of the rocks on the floor of the gondola.

They were very high now. If the balloon fell it might flatten against the wicker frame and let them down gently as it had the first time, or it might shift sideways and dive straight for the earth at increasing speed until not even the massive bones of goblins could survive the impact. On the other hand, if they drifted on over they would lose gas slowly and reach the ground at the speed of a slow walk.

"Mistress!" Dog Squat said in a polite bellow. "Are we high enough now?"

"We're high enough," said the senior thaumaturge, "but if we wait we won't hit so hard!"

Dog Squat wasn't interested in qualifiers. She reached up as Roxanne had been trying to do earlier and swiped her clawed hand across the balloon fabric. She missed the spill valve but she tore through the balloon itself easily. The bag of dragon intestine was gas proof, but no match for the thrust of a goblin determined to carry out Malfegor's instructions.

The gas rushed out with a foul odor as the fabric of the bag flattened against the wicker framework. They were dropping as fast as they had the previous time when the bolt of mana had blown a huge hole through the balloon. They'd survived that, no problem.

"We're going to hit!" cried Roxanne as she saw the ground rushing up.

"Yes!" said Dog Squat. "Good news, Number One. It's all right for us to bite them soon!"

And so they did. Turned out thaumaturges didn't bounce too well, though. Next battle, they'd need a new one. Dog Squat hoped Malfegor wouldn't mind...

Goddess of War

A.C. Haskins

"All tracks, this is Arrow Five." The radio in Sergeant First Class Lily Hanover's helmet crackled with the company executive officer's voice. "Buffalo Company reports a minefield vicinity Checkpoint Papa, approximately five-zero-zero meters by one-zero-zero meters running east to west. Give it a wide berth and carry on to Objective Guardian Three."

Lily heard her platoon leader acknowledge the XO's report as she quickly scanned the touchscreen in *Athena*'s command station. Checkpoint Papa was on the western border of their platoon's line of advance, meaning they'd have to adjust course. The minefield popped up on her screen within seconds, its exact location transmitted from the XO's system to every vehicle in the company—his radio call was more of a courtesy than a necessity. She touched an icon on the screen acknowledging the update, then another that prompted the computer to recommend a new route around the obstacle. The new path showed up a few seconds later, flashing bright green; she accepted the recommendation with another tap and then forwarded it to the other three tanks in her platoon.

She keyed the platoon net. "Olympians, this is Athena. Company reports a minefield; we'll have to go around. Anyone have a problem with the recommended route I just pushed?"

"This is Apollo," the commander of her wingman tank answered with his slow Alabama drawl. "Looks a mite bumpy."

"That it does, Apollo," she acknowledged, "but I don't see another option unless Ares cares to request a boundary shift." The new route would require the platoon to drive up and down the steep sides of a series of moraines nonstop for a kilometer and a half. This region of eastern Europe was lousy with the low ridges, deposited millennia ago by the glaciers that covered the area in the last ice age, but the area they now had to cross was the roughest she'd seen yet. It would be slow going.

"Negative, Athena," Lieutenant Kerry rejected her subtle suggestion. "We'll push through."

Lily rolled her eyes. The lieutenant had only joined the platoon a week ago—he hadn't struck her as a bad sort thus far, but he was brand spanking new, fresh from Basic Officer Training. She, on the other hand, was the most experienced tank platoon sergeant in the division and had been kicking Russian ass up and down Ukraine and Belarus for months. But this was the US Army, where rank was everything: regardless of Lily's experience and qualifications, the twenty-two-year-old lieutenant had final say on all life-and-death tactical decisions for the four tanks of Second Platoon, A Company, 1st Battalion, 44th Heavy Armor Regiment. Such was the way of the world.

"Roger, Ares," she acknowledged, her tone conveying no hint of her irritation. She was a professional.

"Let's move out, Olympian Platoon," the lieutenant ordered. "Wedge formation, heavy left. Artemis, you have eyes on the sky."

"Roger, eyes up," Staff Sergeant Beth Jordan called back.

Lily tapped a green button next to the touchscreen, instructing *Athena*'s driving computer to move along the programmed route. The M-39 Griffith tank's sensor suite let it maneuver around obstacles and find the most appropriate line of travel along their route, automatically coordinating with the rest of the platoon's tanks to maintain proper speed and formation. Unlike the human drivers in the old Abrams tanks they'd replaced, a Griff's driver never misunderstood the tank commander's instructions—or fell asleep when the tank stopped for more than thirty seconds, for that matter.

"What fun," her gunner muttered over the intercom.

"You said it," Lily replied, rolling her eyes again.

Artificial intelligence could do most everything these days, to the point that a lot of factories, shipyards, mines, farms, and other so-called low and medium-skilled industries were being replaced with massive automation, and whole swathes of the population back home were finding themselves out of work. But no matter how advanced computers had become, everyone agreed that the moral responsibility of killing a human being rightfully belonged to another human being. By both federal and international law, no computerized decision-making system was allowed to control any process that might involve deliberate lethal force. Griffith tanks could drive themselves, load themselves, and intercept incoming missiles or drones without any human input. They'd even identify potential threats and aim the appropriate weapons automatically, but someone like Specialist Lorelei Chase had to press the trigger before it could do anything that might take a human life.

"You have our sector locked in?" Lily asked her.

"You're really gonna insult me with a question like that, boss?" Lorelei sounded wounded.

"Sorry," Lily chuckled. "It's my job. Now please reply in the affirmative so I can feel better about having asked."

"Fine," the gunner grumbled. "Affirmative, sector locked and sensors are actively scanning. Antimissile and drone countermeasures are on automatic. Sabot in the tube, and an even mix of sabot and HE in the pipeline. Happy?"

"Very." Lily turned to the third woman in the turret. "How about you, Cortez?"

"All good over here, Sergeant," Private Gina Cortez answered in a thick Nicaraguan accent. "Comms up, drone deployed, all sensors and systems optimal."

Modern tanks may drive themselves and load themselves, but the Army had decided that reducing tank crews to fewer than three people presented too great a risk in combat. Cortez's primary job was to maintain and troubleshoot the advanced computational and information systems that ran the tank, but having the Vehicle Systems Tech on board also gave the crew an extra pair of hands for crew-level maintenance and repairs, and meant there was someone who could take over the weapons systems if either the commander or gunner were incapacitated or killed.

"Alright, here we go," Lily said as the tank began climbing up the first moraine.

⊕ ⊕ ⊕

"Missile warning," the soft feminine voice of *Athena*'s computer stated tonelessly, accompanied by the distinctive rapid-fire thumping of the tank's right-side counter-missile gun automatically engaging. A fraction of a second later came the sound of an explosion as the incoming threat was destroyed in flight over a hundred meters short of its target. There were a few loud dings as shrapnel from the missile struck the exterior armor.

"Contact, two o'clock!" the gunner called out. "Tank, stationary, three-one-hundred meters!"

"Contact, front right!" Lily relayed over the platoon net. "Tank, stationary! Engaging!"

"I've got lock," Lorelei told her calmly, indicating *Athena*'s gunnery computer had optimized its calculations and was ready to fire.

Lily glanced at the screen to the right of her command panel, which currently displayed exactly what her gunner was seeing at her own station: the unmistakable outline of a Russian T-30 tank's gun turret peeping over some rocks, a stand of trees to its rear. It almost blended into its surroundings, but *Athena*'s sensors had picked up on the sharp angles of its armor and identified it as an artificial shape that it highlighted for the convenience of its human masters.

"Send it," Lily said, almost nonchalantly.

"On the way!" Lorelei replied as she squeezed the trigger on her control stick.

The main gun boomed, the sound incredibly loud even through the noise-cancelling headsets in their helmets. The cannon's massive breech rocked back in the turret compartment between the command station and the systems tech's position, inches from the guard on which Lily's left knee rested. The autoloader cycled, pushing the next round into the chamber before the gun reset itself. From trigger squeeze to the gun being ready to fire again took just under two seconds. Her nostrils filled with the acrid smell of burned propellant.

"Hit!" Lily said as she saw the enemy tank explode on her monitor. "Good shooting."

She keyed the mic to the platoon net. "One Russky down. Watch out for indirect."

They'd killed the enemy within seconds of identifying it, from well outside its own maximum effective range, but Russian tanks didn't fight alone. There were almost certainly at least two more tanks watching the platoon advance through the rough terrain. Lily wasn't worried about their direct fire weapons; a Griff would shrug off a main gun round from anything more than two kilometers and its active defenses could easily handle guided missiles at anything less than hypersonic speeds. But if the tanks had artillery support, Olympian Platoon could be in for a rough afternoon—they were sitting ducks against a rocket barrage until they made it to the other side of this goddamn moraine system, and the counter-guns only had so much ammo.

"The drone has identified two more tanks," Cortez piped up. "Both out of range."

Lily tapped a button on the screen and it switched from showing the gunner's view to displaying the feed from *Athena*'s drone, which hovered a couple dozen meters above the tank. Yellow boxes highlighted the distinctive shapes of the remainder of the Russian platoon, almost five kilometers away. She watched as they backed out of their positions and began withdrawing.

She keyed the platoon net.

"Ares, this is Athena. Looks like the other two Russkies are bugging out to the northeast. Recommend giving Titan Platoon a heads-up."

"Roger, Athena," Lieutenant Kerry acknowledged. "My drone just IDed them, too. I'll pass it on."

"Arrow Six, this is Ares," she heard him call the company commander a few seconds later. "Sitrep: Olympian Platoon engaged and destroyed one tank—location marked on your screen. Two more tanks identified out of range, currently withdrawing into Titan's sector at speed. Olympians continuing our advance north, keeping an eye out for indirect. Over."

"Roger, Ares," Captain Tupuola replied. "Titan platoon, did you hear that?"

"Apocalypse acknowledges," Titan Platoon's lieutenant answered.

"Roger. Carry on, gents," the company commander said. "Let's try to make it to the objective by 1900. Six, out."

"Ares, this is Arrow Five," the XO jumped in after the commander was done. "No need to worry about indirect. Battalion confirms no artillery positions within twenty klicks. Carry on with as much speed as possible."

"Ares acknowledges," Lieutenant Kerry said.

"Olympians, this is Athena. XO says no arty in range," Lily relayed on the platoon net. "The only thing slowing us down is the terrain."

"Apollo acknowledges. Continuing to move."

"Artemis, roger."

But a minute later, as *Athena* began to climb the next moraine, there was a grinding noise and the tank's forward progress stalled. The computer backed the tank down the slope, and a low alarm tone sounded.

"Error. Right track damaged," the computer stated over the intercom.

"Fucking hell," Lily muttered, then keyed the radio. "Olympians, this is Athena. Looks like I spoke too soon. I've got a damaged track and can't make it up the hill. Stand by; I'm gonna send my tech out to check it."

"Roger, Athena," Lieutenant Kerry replied. "Olympians, halt in place and wait for Athena."

Lily glanced over at Cortez, who was already moving. The tech hit the switch to pop her turret hatch, then pulled herself up and out of the tank. While waiting, Lily looked back over at the drone feed on her secondary screen. The two enemy tanks had disappeared; they were presumably well into Titan Platoon's sector by now.

Cortez stuck her head down through her hatch.

"Bad news, Sergeant. The track is fucked. Looks like a bit of shrapnel from that missile cracked a section, and it broke clean through when we tried to go up the slope."

"Goddammit," Lily shook her head. "Alright, thanks." She keyed her radio. "Ares, this is Athena. We've got a broken track. We've got a spare section on board, but we'll have to replace it and reconnect. It's gonna be a hot minute."

"Copy, Athena," Lieutenant Kerry replied. "We'll stand by. Make it as quick as you can. Olympian Platoon, pull security; I'll let Arrow Six know we're going to be delayed."

She heard him start to call the sitrep up to the company commander as she stripped off her helmet, then she opened her own hatch and climbed onto the turret to take a look for herself. At least the weather was nice. Repairing track was an utter bitch in the rain and mud.

She and Cortez climbed down the turret onto the front slope, then hopped down to the ground. The right track was flat on the ground, the broken section a few feet in front of the tank, the other end dangling skirt armor, exposing the idler wheel. Cortez hadn't exaggerated about the damage to the track; the steel around the cooling tube had twisted and sheared straight through. Lily saw clearly where a chunk had been gouged out of it by the shrapnel. That just was an unlucky hit; it must have struck the track at just the right angle and velocity to cause a critical structural flaw.

At least both sides of the break were easily accessible, so they wouldn't have to move the tank itself. It would take some time and effort to repair, but it was a pretty straightforward process.

"Okay, Cortez," Lily said, her hands on her hips as she contemplated the damaged track. "Go ahead and grab the impact wrench out of the sponson box, and get that spare track section off the railing."

Cortez scrambled back up the turret, and a minute later pushed a heavy section of tank track off the side of the turret, where it fell to the ground with a thump. She then clambered down the front slope with an impact wrench in hand.

"Here you go, Sergeant," she said, handing the power tool to Lily. "I'll go grab the section and bring it over."

"Get the end connector puller and the sledge out while you're at it," Lily instructed. "And we're going to need the track jacks, too."

While Cortez gathered the tools they'd need to fix the track, Lily plugged the impact wrench's cord into an outlet on the tank's hull and began loosening bolts. With only three crew members, there was no standing on ceremony: someone had to stay on the gun and maintain security, and repairing a broken track was at least a two-person job. Everybody worked on a tank crew; rank was irrelevant when shit needed to be done.

After the bolts were removed, she and Cortez pulled off the connectors that held the broken section to the rest of the track and started lining up the replacement. But before they could hook it on, Lily heard her gunner shout. She looked up to see Lorelei's helmeted head sticking out of the turret hatch.

"Hey, boss! Avenger Platoon's dealing with some shit and Arrow Six ordered Ares to head that way and assist! We've been instructed to expedite repairs and make our way to the objective on our own, linking up with the company there no later than 2100!"

"Alright," Lily called back. "Thanks for the update!"

She sighed and contemplated this development.

A lone tank was a sitting duck if they encountered the enemy; the main gun could only engage one target at a time, so multiple vehicles could easily overwhelm them. That's why they had wingman tanks. She was annoyed that the lieutenant hadn't left *Apollo* to watch her back.

But there was nothing to do about it now, and they still had to repair the track either way. She shrugged and unzipped her fire-resistant coveralls and pulled the top down, tying the sleeves around her waist. Her undershirt was already soaked through with sweat, and it wasn't even midafternoon yet.

"Feel free to dress down, Cortez. We've got plenty of heavy lifting to do before we're done here. Might as well be comfortable."

Lily wiped the sweat off her face and got back to work.

"Boss!"

Lily looked up to see Lorelei's helmeted head once again protruding from the hatch.

"XO says Battalion spotted a bird coming in. Looks like a solo Ka-52. Three to four minutes."

"Fuck," Lily muttered, thinking quickly.

"Cortez, throw all this shit under the hull," she instructed, indicating the tools and supplies they were using to repair the track. "We're going to pretend to be dead—Russkies won't waste rounds on a smoking hull, but if they see signs of repair, they might be tempted to go for a gun run, just in case."

Attack helicopters used to be all but a death sentence for a lone tank—their missiles could take out an armored vehicle from well outside a main gun's effective firing range, and their speed made them difficult to hit even if they came close enough. These days it was a more even match: the Griffith's defensive guns negated the long-range threat as long as they had ammo and functioning sensors, but the Alligator was also equipped with a 30mm autocannon that could rip through a tank's top armor like tissue paper. It needed to get close to use the cannon—well within range of *Athena*'s 130mm main gun. But if it came to a head-to-head race, Lorelei would only have time for one or two shots before the Russian strafed them, so it was a dangerous gamble. It was a safer bet to convince them that *Athena* wasn't worth their time and fuel.

She quickly zipped her coveralls, then scrambled back up the hull and dropped into her station. As soon as she had her helmet on, she keyed the mic on the company net.

"Arrow Five, this Athena, do you read?"

"Athena, this is Arrow Five, read you Lima-Charlie," the XO replied.

"Arrow Five, is anyone intercepting that Alligator?"

"Negative, Athena. You're fifteen klicks outside of the battalion air defense envelope and close air support is otherwise engaged. Keep your head down."

"Roger, Arrow Five." She sighed. "We'll let you know if we manage not to die. Athena out."

Cortez dropped back into her station through her hatch on the other side of the turret.

"Everything's out of sight, Sergeant," she said. "Should I pop smoke?"

"Black smoke, two cans, from the launcher," Lily responded, "and get the drone out of the air. Then button your hatch and let's play possum."

"Drone's down," Cortez reported a half minute later. "Popping smoke now."

The tech pressed a series of buttons at her console, and in a moment Lily saw thick black smoke beginning to pour out of the grenade launchers on either side of the turret. Satisfied they'd done what they could to play dead, Lily closed her own turret hatch and settled into her seat. They'd find out one way or the other in a few minutes.

She tapped a button on her commander's view screen and it switched to displaying the feed from the Commander's Independent Viewer, a 360-degree thermal camera on top of the tank. They wouldn't be able to move the gun to track its flight, but with the independent viewer she could lock onto its signature and, should it prove necessary, with a press of another button the turret would swing to aim at the designated target within a fraction of a second.

"Lorelei, you've got prox in the tube, right?"

"Way ahead of you, boss," the gunner answered. "One in the tube, two more in the chute."

High explosives rigged with proximity sensors were standard against aerial threats. Even if the pilot managed to avoid a direct hit, the sensor would detonate the round if it got within twenty meters of the target, sending a cloud of shrapnel into the fuselage, hopefully doing enough damage to the engines and hydraulics to take it out of the air.

"What do you think they're doing out here, Sergeant?" Cortez asked.

"What's that?" Lily replied, pulled from her focus on the screen.

"I mean, don't Russian helicopters usually fly in pairs?" the tech continued. "And an Alligator is an attack helicopter, right? So what's it doing out here with no ground forces to support?"

"I don't know." Lily shrugged. "Probably just reconnaissance, especially on its own. With combat losses and maintenance issues it's not uncommon to see them solo for recon missions."

"If it's doing recon, it's probably not looking to engage, right?" Cortez sounded nervous.

Lorelei snorted. "We can hope. But Russian pilots sometimes get bored. They might decide to shoot up a dead Griff anyway, just for target practice."

"Right," Lily agreed, "which is why we're gonna keep a close eye on them until they're long gone. They come in gun range, we pop 'em."

She realized that this was Private Cortez's first real encounter with an enemy who might well try to kill her—the tech had only joined their crew the previous week, the same day the lieutenant had shown up at the platoon.

"Don't worry, Cortez," she said, trying to sound comforting. "Specialist Chase here is three-and-oh against helicopters. We'll be fine."

"Damn straight," Lorelei said firmly. "If they decide to fuck around, they're gonna find out."

The enemy helicopter had come into view, a bright dot on her monitor, several kilometers northeast of their position and moving west-southwest. Still too far away to lock in as a priority target, but getting closer every second.

"Come on, you Russian bastard," Lily whispered to herself, "just keep on flying. Nothing to see here but burning wreckage... Damn it."

The Russians had changed course south. They weren't coming directly toward *Athena*'s position, but it appeared they'd decided to get a closer look.

Lily watched the dot as it grew larger on her thermals. Soon it was recognizably a helicopter; within a minute she could make out the elongated nose and the distinct double-rotor of a Ka-52. She tapped her screen and a second later the computer highlighted it with a white box. A number popped up indicating its estimated distance from Athena's location: 5,420 and falling. The tank could theoretically engage at 3,500 meters, but it would give the pilot a few seconds to evade and give away the element of surprise. She decided to wait until 2,700—the Russian would need to close within two kilometers before its autocannon could dent Athena's armor, and it flew at around a hundred meters a second during a gun run. That would give Lorelei plenty of time for two solid shots before the enemy could return fire. If both missed, a rain of 30mm rounds would tear the three of them to shreds. Simple as that.

Right now, however, all of that was hypothetical. The chopper was taking a curving path around them, staying outside of four klicks. It was tense—nothing Lily could do but wait. A minute later, they were almost due west, still a little over four klicks and continuing to curve around to the south.

But then their path straightened out; the target on her thermals started to get smaller and smaller as they continued south. Thirty seconds later, the Ka-52 had disappeared from view, hidden by a large stand of trees to the southwest. Lily breathed a sigh of relief and let out a little chuckle.

"Guess they decided we were already dead enough," she said.

"And here I was hoping to get to paint an alligator silhouette on *Athena*'s turret," Lorelei laughed. "Oh well. Maybe next time."

"Let's not count our chickens yet," Lily said. "They can always come back for another look. We'll stay buttoned up for a few minutes, just in case."

She keyed the radio. "Arrow Five, this is Athena."

"Go ahead, Athena. Glad to hear you're still kicking."

"Me too, Five. We lost sight of the 'gator to the southwest. Any chance Battalion's keeping an eye on it?"

"I'll check, Athena. If so I'll push it to your station. Stand by."

"Roger, Five. Standing by."

Thirty seconds later, a red diamond icon appeared on the map on her touchscreen, moving steadily southwest.

"Athena, this is Arrow Five. I've pushed Battalion ADA's tracking data to your system. Do you have it?"

"Affirmative, Five. Thanks much. We'll keep an eye on it and hope it doesn't come back before we can get mobile."

"Roger, Athena. Best of luck. Arrow Five out."

With Lorelei watching to make sure the Russian helicopter wasn't in danger of returning, Lily and Cortez returned to repairing the track.

"Okay," Lily said after they got the new track section attached and bolted on. "We're gonna have to do it sooner or later, so may as well get it over with. We need to release the tension before we can connect the two ends together."

"Roger, Sergeant. What do you need me to do?"

"Oh, it's gonna take both of us. You ever break track before?"

"No, they didn't cover that in the accelerated basic course," Cortez shook her head. "Told us we'd have to learn on the job."

"Yeah, that's what I thought. They're so desperate to get bodies to the front they skip all the fun stuff. Okay, you know what the tensioning arm is, right?"

Cortez nodded. "It's the one connected to the idler wheel, right?"

"Correct. It pushes the wheel into the front of the track, to keep it nice and taut so we don't throw track every time we hit a bump or turn too sharply. Which means that we have to loosen it, or we'll never be able to get the two ends close enough to fit the connectors on. And loosening it is not fun."

"How's that, Sergeant?"

"Tension grease is thick stuff. It doesn't pour out on its own. We're gonna have to open the valve, then whack the hell out of the idler wheel with the sledge for a while until we've forced enough grease out to get the track reconnected."

"No. Seriously, Sergeant?" Cortez's eyebrows went up. "All this tech and no one's come up with a better answer to the problem than 'smash it with a hammer'?"

Lily snorted. "Yeah, you'd think one of those fancy engineers would have thought it through, but I guess they never actually had to break track. Just pretend you're hammering their stupid college-educated faces every time you take a swing—it doesn't make it any less tiring, but it's definitely cathartic."

"Okay, Sergeant," Cortez shrugged. "I'll take the first turn."

"Atta girl."

Together, it took them almost two hours, trading off every few minutes. By the time Lily judged the tensioning arm to have relaxed enough to connect the track, her shoulders, arms, and upper back were screaming.

"Alright," she sighed wearily. "The hard part's over. Now just to pull 'em together, connect, and re-tension. Thank whatever gods may be for hydraulic track jacks."

Twenty minutes later, just as they were closing up the front skirt panel to protect their newly repaired track, Lorelei's voice called down once more.

"Boss, we got trouble!"

"What now?" Lily yelled back.

"Drone's spotted movement to our southeast. You'd better come take a look yourself."

"Cortez," Lily said, turning to the tech, "we're done with the track. Get everything put away as quickly as you can, then get back to your station."

She then scrambled up the hull and dropped into her command station as Lorelei moved back to the gunner's seat.

"What's up?"

"Looks like Russkies sneaking around the flank, boss."

"Did you report it to Arrow?"

"I tried. No response. No answer on the platoon net, either."

"Fuck," Lily swore as she turned her attention to the drone feed.

There was nothing happening at the moment, but the system

automatically stored ten minutes of video at any given time. She backed up to the earliest available and played it at quadruple speed until she saw the movement Lorelei had mentioned.

"Double fuck," she swore again. The monitor showed at least three armored personnel carriers and two tanks moving somewhere to the southeast; they'd disappeared behind an intervisibility line several kilometers away a couple minutes ago and hadn't reappeared. The remains of the tank platoon they'd encountered earlier must have linked up with a mechanized infantry platoon and slipped down the seam between Titan Platoon's sector and Battle-axe Company to their east.

She quickly switched to the map on her other screen and input the enemy's last known location and direction of travel from the drone's camera, then tapped a sequence of buttons. A few—very long—seconds later, the computer spat out what it believed to be their three most likely routes.

"Triple fuck."

The computer assessed that the enemy unit was likely trying to hook around behind Arrow Company and hit them from the rear, targeting the lightly defended headquarters and support assets that the Russians knew would be somewhere behind the front line of maneuver platoons. And the terrain and that minefield to the west meant that all their potential routes involved crossing the same series of moraines Olympian Platoon had crossed earlier that day, straight through *Athena*'s current position.

The computer was usually correct in such assessments.

At least the Ka-52 had apparently gotten far enough away that it no longer showed up on her feed. Small favors.

She keyed her mic.

"Arrow, any Arrow, this is Athena. Do you copy?"

May as well try. But there was no response. It was possible company headquarters was just in a dead zone. But more likely they were already out of range of *Athena*'s radio.

She switched to platoon.

"Olympian, any Olympian, this is Athena. Do you read?"

She sighed. She knew the tank's comms definitely wouldn't have the power to reach Titan Platoon from here, let alone Battalion. They were on their own.

"Alright, here's the situation," she said over the intercom as Cortez dropped through her hatch and put on her helmet. "We've got a bunch of Russians headed our way from behind. *Athena*'s computer thinks they're trying to hit the company trains in the ass. The way I see it, we've got two potential courses of action. We're heavily outgunned, so the smart play is to keep our head down, make our way out of their path, and try to get somewhere that Arrow Five can hear us so we can hopefully warn him in time and give the company time to turn around."

"And the other option, Sergeant?" Cortez asked.

"We," Lily said somberly, "can turn around and fuck up their day."

"You think we could take them on and win?"

"No, I don't." Lily shook her head. "Not really. Five on one is a tall order. But if we could take out two or three of them before they got us, that would be enough to keep them from posing much threat to the XO and the support vehicles. That said, there's a better than even chance it's a suicide mission. I won't order anyone to knowingly sacrifice their life when there's another reasonable option."

"So what do we do?" Cortez asked.

"If we run," Lily answered, "there's no guarantee we'd get in comms range in time to warn anyone. The only way to make sure those Russian bastards can't kill the XO and the support folks is to stop them ourselves. But it has to be a unanimous decision. We all volunteer, knowing exactly what it means, or we don't do it."

"You already know my vote," Lorelei chuckled. "Going out in a blaze of glory is my exact aesthetic."

"Okay." Lily nodded. "Cortez?"

The tech swallowed heavily, but pressed her lips together firmly and did her best to look determined.

"I've got friends with the XO, Sergeant," Cortez said, sounding every bit a nervous teenager, despite her brave front. "I couldn't look myself in the mirror if they got hurt, when we could have stopped it."

Lily nodded again. "Alright. Let's show everyone what *Athena* here can really do when we let her loose."

"I see them, Sergeant. Camera three IDed a probable APC moving into dead space about six klicks south."

"Thanks, Cortez."

The drone was out of the sky—Lily didn't want it giving away their position by hovering overhead, and sending it toward the enemy to reconnoiter would just get it shot down before they learned anything useful. But Cortez had gone out and set up a half dozen portable observation cameras on the ridge of the moraine to their south, which were tied directly to *Athena*'s computer and would act as extensions of her native sensors. They'd turned the tank around and set up on the north slope of the moraine. It wasn't exactly a proper three-tiered fighting position, but it was what they had available.

"Sabot in the tube, two sabots in the chute, followed by HE, boss," Lorelei reported. Depleted uranium sabot rounds were made for killing heavily armored tanks, but they'd want to switch to high explosive for the more lightly armored personnel carriers.

"Thanks. Now we wait," Lily said. "How about some music, Cortez?"

The tech smiled and nodded, then pressed a couple buttons on her station, filling the intercom with the opening riff of an oldie power metal tune from the 2020s.

Lily snorted in amusement.

"That'll do."

Cortez had selected the track listed in the computer as "Olympian Platoon Theme Song." Their previous platoon leader had been a history major who'd specialized in ancient Greece at West Point. Along with decreeing the platoon's tanks would be named after Olympic gods and goddesses, he'd selected Sabaton's "Sparta" as their official song. The story of the outnumbered Spartan warriors at the Battle of Thermopylae seemed especially appropriate given the circumstances.

Fortunately, unlike Xerxes's Persians, the oncoming Russians wouldn't be able to sneak around their position and hit them in the rear. It would be a straight-up fight. And with any luck, Athena would have the element of surprise—the Russians would assume all of the American tanks had continued north. Even if they'd gotten a recon report from that helicopter, they'd just expect a dead hull.

Just as the last notes of the song faded a few minutes later, Cortez piped up.

"Tank in the open, Sergeant. Camera two."

Lily tapped her screen to switch to camera two's feed; she saw a T-30 crest the top of a low rolling hill, then begin to make its way down the slope. The computer highlighted it as a potential target and displayed its estimated range as over four and a half kilometers.

"Welcome to the party, comrade," she muttered. "Now where're your friends?"

"Another contact, Sergeant." Cortez's voice shook slightly. She cleared her throat. "I've got another tank and an APC on camera four."

Lily switched over to that feed. The second tank moved steadily across the terrain, a personnel carrier lagging a hundred meters or so behind. It looked like the two tanks were leading the movement on opposite ends of the line, with the mechanized infantry following in the center. Presumably the other two APCs would be popping into view shortly, too.

"Okay, Lorelei, the tanks are the priority. Once they're in range, if you can take them both out in a single berm drill I'll buy you a beer."

"That'll be refreshing!" The gunner chuckled. "I hear hell's hot, and there's no way I'm going to the other place."

Lily didn't respond, her eyes locked on the camera feeds. The other two APCs appeared in due course, and the map on her command screen showed all five enemy vehicles moving across the open farmland, slowly getting closer. Until they hit the chain of moraines in which Athena was sitting, they would have no real cover to speak of, just minor variations of elevation forming pockets of dead space in which they could hide. *Athena* was badly outnumbered, but this was as perfect a defensive scenario as Lily could imagine—it was a carnival shooting gallery come to life.

"Thirty-five-hundred meters, boss. You want to call it, or should we let them get closer?"

"No need to keep our guests waiting." Lily shrugged. "Left tank first, then right tank."

"Roger," Lorelei replied. "Left target ready, awaiting your movement command."

Lily took a deep breath, held it for a second, then let it out.

"Alright, let's do this," she said, and then tapped a button on her screen commanding the tank to move up the berm into firing position. "Fire as soon as you've got gun lock," she told the gunner as the tank began the short movement up the slope.

"On the way!" Lorelei announced a second later, followed by the deafening boom of the main gun firing. The breech rocked back and the autoloader cycled as the gun reset, ready to fire again. For the second time that day, the turret filled with the smell of burned propellant.

"Hit!" Lily called as she saw the enemy tank explode, its turret popping off entirely to land on the ground next to the hull, flames shooting up where it used to be. But there was no time to celebrate; the gun had already swung over to the other tank.

"Target locked! On the way!"

The gun boomed once again, and before the sabot round made impact, Lily hurriedly mashed the button on the command station that told the tank to reverse back down the slope of the moraine.

"Missile warning," the computer announced as the left-side counter-missile gun engaged the threat. Only one of the APCs had gotten a shot off before they'd retreated behind cover, and *Athena*'s defenses handled it easily.

"Goddammit," Lily said as she watched the camera feed. "One tank destroyed, but the second shot was ineffective. They're still moving."

"Shit," Lorelei muttered. "I must've pulled the trigger before it was really locked. Sorry, boss."

"That's alright, just don't do it again."

The tank was moving at Lily's instructions—once they'd backed down, they'd turned right and were heading a hundred meters away from their first position. It was a bad idea to pop up to shoot at the enemy twice from the same spot.

She continued watching the camera feed as they moved to the next firing position. The enemy tank was charging at full speed toward some low ground, where *Athena*'s gun wouldn't be able to depress enough to engage it without first fully exposing her hull along the crest of the moraine.

Clever, Lily thought to herself. Once down there, the Russians could take their time and find a route to approach *Athena*'s position that didn't expose them to her superior firepower and range until they were close enough to fight back.

Meanwhile, the three APCs had all changed course and were heading northeast as fast as they could go. Lily guessed they were going to try to reach the first moraine and hide behind it, then dismount their infantry to flank her position and swarm her with antitank missiles and rocket-propelled grenades.

"Damn," she muttered. "Why can't we ever get stupid enemies?

"Swap out to HE," she ordered. "We're not going to get a second shot at that tank this time. Focus on the APCs."

"Roger, changing battle carry," Lorelei answered, hitting the gun control that told the autoloader to remove the sabot round in the main gun and replace it with high explosive.

"Alright, let me know when you're ready. We'll only have time for one shot this time, now that they know we're here."

"HE in the tube, ready for movement," the gunner replied a few seconds later.

"Here we go," Lily said, and she once again commanded the tank to climb the slope into a firing position.

"Target locked! On the way!" Lorelei called out a fraction of a second after the gun tube cleared the crest of the slope, and Lily hit the reverse button before the breech had even reset.

"Hit!" she announced as she saw the armored vehicle flipped onto its side from the force of the high-explosive impact.

They'd only been exposed for a second or two, just long enough to fire, and the enemy hadn't managed to launch any missiles this time. She took a second to reassess the situation.

The surviving Russian tank had reached its low ground; it was still visible to the cameras, but *Athena* couldn't engage it without completely exposing herself to enemy fire for several seconds beforehand. And as it worked its way closer, it would move into dead space and disappear from the cameras' field of view, a dangerous proposition. But the bigger risk right now was the group of APCs— if they got their dismounts in position to flank *Athena* down the length of the moraine, they'd be able to send five or six missiles right at her with nowhere to hide. That was a death sentence.

"Okay," Lily said, making up her mind, "we're gonna go after the infantry. Cortez, get that drone in the air and have it keep an eye on that tank from a safe distance. We have to move out and deal with those troops before they can get into position."

"Roger, Sergeant," the tech replied.

Lily quickly plugged a route into the computer and told the tank to execute at max speed. They backed down the slope farther to the valley between moraines, then raced down the length of the moraine as fast as the tank could manage without throwing track. By the time they'd reached the end of the ridge a few minutes later, the two remaining APCs had dropped out of sight from the cameras. *Athena* slowed as they approached the eastern tail of the moraine and began creeping forward, the turret slowly pivoting to clear the corner.

"Contact! Dismounts at five hundred meters!" Lorelei announced.

"Engage with coax," Lily ordered as she saw the troops in question setting up a missile launcher.

"Roger, engaging!" the gunner replied. A moment later came the sharp sound of rapid fire from *Athena*'s coaxial machine gun.

Lily didn't bother watching the rounds impact; the computer had identified two other dismount positions, both of which were also setting up antitank missile positions.

"Cortez, troops on the ridgeline southeast at four-fifty meters!"

"Identified!" the tech replied, no longer sounding nervous.

"Fire and adjust!"

"On the way!" Cortez engaged her own machine gun mounted on the left side of the turret at the troop position. Like the main gun, *Athena* had already aimed it for her and locked in the target, but a human had to pull the trigger.

Meanwhile, Lily wordlessly engaged the third group of dismounts with her own machine gun. For several seconds, *Athena* sprayed death in three directions simultaneously, and three squads of Russian infantry were annihilated by her impossibly accurate computer-controlled fire. When the dust cleared, there was no movement. If any of the enemy had survived, they were keeping their heads down.

"Alright, good shooting," Lily said. "Now let's go kill their taxis."

A quick glance at the drone feed showed the T-30 had made it to the southern slope of the first moraine, but was still working its way around to try to hit *Athena* from the western flank. That gave them time to mop up the two APCs, then head back west to deal with the tank.

We might actually win this after all, she thought. She quickly suppressed that line of thinking—she didn't want to jinx anything by thinking about victory too early. One thing at a time.

The tank drove around the eastern end of the moraine and Lily saw the remaining personnel carriers in the open.

"Target locked," Lorelei said calmly.

"Fire."

"On the way."

The main gun boomed for the fifth time that day and one of the armored vehicles erupted into flames.

Lily didn't even bother reversing behind cover as the autoloader cycled. The remaining APC launched a missile their way, which *Athena's* defensive guns shot out of the sky almost instantly. She then heard the enemy's 25mm rounds impacting with a steady *thunk-thunk-thunk*. Lily wasn't worried—they had no hope of getting through *Athena's* front armor, even at that close range.

"Target locked," Lorelei said, singsong.

"Fire," Lily ordered gleefully.

"On the way."

A second later, the only remaining enemy was the lone T-30 at the other end of the moraine.

"Okay, let's finish this," Lily said with a grim smile.

"New threat, Sergeant!" Cortez said suddenly, looking at her station console.

Lily glanced at her screen and her smile disappeared.

"Fuck."

An icon of a Ka-52 had suddenly appeared on her screen, courtesy of the Battalion air defense feed her computer was still receiving. Probably the same one from earlier, called to assist the Russian ground forces she'd been fighting.

"Alligator, closing quick," she said. "Looking like it's coming in for a gun run. Swap to prox and get ready."

"Roger," Lorelei said as she commanded the autoloader to change ammunition, the carefree singsong gone from her tone.

"That tank is coming our way, too, Sergeant!" Cortez said.

Lily switched to the drone feed and saw she was right—the remaining T-30 was charging down the other side of the moraine; it would be appearing directly behind them in a few minutes. They had two threats rapidly closing on their position, and could only effectively engage one at a time. Proximity rounds were useless against heavy armor, and sabot was too easy for a helicopter to evade.

"Alright," she said after a moment's consideration, "we'll just have to deal with the 'gator and hope that tank commander is too cautious to get around the corner before we can swap back. Lorelei, take the shot as soon as it hits two-seven-hundred."

"Roger," the gunner said.

"And I want you both to know," Lily added somberly, "if this is it, it's been an honor."

"You, too, boss," Lorelei said quietly.

Lily caught Cortez's eyes; the tech looked terrified, but she put on a brave smile. Then she closed her eyes and Lily saw her lips moving in what looked like a silent prayer.

There was nothing else to say.

"Three-five-hundred meters," Lorelei announced a few agonizingly long seconds later. "Three-four-hundred. Three-three—whoa!"

"What the fuck?!" Lily exclaimed, watching the gunner's view on her own screen. The enemy helicopter had just exploded in midair.

"American tank, this is Renegade Five-One," a voice came over her radio, broadcasting on the general NATO net. "Hope you don't mind the assist. No doubt you'd have taken him out yourself, but I was bored and hadn't gotten to shoot anything today."

An F-40 fighter jet with US Air Force markings screamed through the air where the Russian helicopter had been a moment previously.

"This is Renegade Five-Two," another voice called. "Engaging one Russian tank in the open."

A second fighter flew low directly over *Athena*'s position. From inside the tank Lily couldn't hear its guns firing, but she saw the dust clouds from its rounds impacting on her screen, then an explosion followed by billowing black smoke from the other end of the moraine. She switched over to her drone feed and saw the T-30 torn to shreds by the jet's 30mm cannon rounds.

"American tank, this is Renegade Five-One," the first pilot called again. "You good down there? You look awfully lonely."

Lily swallowed and took a deep breath before responding. Mere seconds ago, she'd been convinced she was about to die. Her hand was still shaking with adrenaline.

"Renegade Five-One, this is Athena," she called. "We're very grateful for the assistance. When this is all over, look up Sergeant First Class Lily Hanover, and drinks will be on me!"

"From the looks of it, Athena, you did plenty of work yourself before we got here. Do you need us to let anyone know where you are?"

"This is Athena. We got separated from Arrow Company, 1-44 Armor. I'd be obliged if you could pass on that we'll be late for our rendezvous this evening."

"Will do, Athena. Stay safe, and good hunting. Renegade out."

Lily closed her eyes and took another deep breath.

"Holy shit, that was intense!" Lorelei said with a relieved laugh.

Lily nodded. "That it was." She glanced over at her tech. "You alright, Cortez?"

"I—" the tech started to answer, her voice catching in her throat. She swallowed a couple times before continuing. "I'm okay, Sergeant. I'll be okay."

Lily popped her hatch and stood up on her seat, just breathing in the fresh air for a long moment. It smelled of diesel smoke and burning metal, but there was a breeze, and that was enough.

"You good, boss?" Lorelei asked.

"Yeah," Lily chuckled. "Yeah, I'm good. You know what?"

"What's that?"

"Some days, I fucking love this job."

Barbie and Gator Ken versus the Hurricane

⊕

Joelle Presby

I rolled through the Midtown Tunnel to the Norfolk side. My tank's treads crunched over crash debris. The wall-mounted tunnel lights reflected off bits of plexiglass, and the almost spent road flares burned red in the gutter. I'd been in a hurry to get the lane cleared and left some car bits behind. I took a closer look with my cameras. What had been a piece of fender was now flattened thoroughly enough even non-tanks should have no trouble driving over it.

Cars whipped past me in the other lane on autopilot. The city's emergency override system had them nose to nose going at least 50 mph in the tunnel's second lane, but the passengers inside clutched at baggage and stared at their comm device newsfeeds instead of pressing their faces to the windows to ogle at *Ken*. If I'd needed any more evidence that Hurricane Idalia had the town in a panic, that would do it. Because *Ken* is exceedingly ogle-worthy. Even demilitarized and heavily modified by me, he remains a great lumbering hunk.

He's originally a Gator III–class light tank handed off to civil authorities during the last military drawdown, and maybe he hadn't looked like much with the faded reactive camo paint he'd had when I first got him. But he's a gorgeous dusk gray now. The color's almost regulation except for the extreme shine, and he's adorned with unauthorized but nonetheless exquisite flame-wreathed National Guard Disaster Relief Unit shields on both flanks. The fire art around the shield's transitions from a forward curl of hottest blue all the way through flame's full spectrum to end in trailing orange-red and just a hint of blackest black smoke. And that's just the paint job. The fuel cell drive system redesign is even neater, but...

"Need some help now, Sergeant!" Marjorie Kidd's voice on the radio was tinged with an edge of panic.

"En route, Kidd," I said and picked up speed.

Gator IIIs were built to be all-terrain light tanks, which meant they could move on unpaved roads and go over a few wet ditches. Nobody had intended for them to submerge.

The bottom of the tunnel had almost a foot of standing water. Since the cars whizzing by in the other lane tended to float on anything more than a couple inches, and I didn't have an autodrive connection to instantly correct for any trajectory errors they experienced, it was a problem. The tunnel pumps were running at maximum capacity, but they'd been designed to be turned off and the tunnels closed during severe deluges. We needed this tunnel open for at least an hour more. The autodrive-controlled personal vehicles were being ramped down and through the wet on momentum, then picking speed back up as soon as they regained traction. The very best stunt car drivers could've done it without computer backup, but these were just regular people, so the autodrive systems were in full control.

Thankfully, the heavily populated parts of the Hampton Roads area were a cluster of peninsulas with no true islands, so the older vehicles that couldn't handle a brief hydroplane even with computer assist had been routed elsewhere. Five bridge tunnel monstrosities crosslinked the densely populated zone with its convergence of rivers and ocean bay. They were all as crammed with fleeing vehicles as the Midtown Tunnel was—well, except for the MMMBT, the Monitor-Merrimac Memorial Bridge-Tunnel. That one was a mess I didn't want to even think about. The situation made me want to find the city engineer's house and level it with *Ken*'s main battery.

The swath of water filling the center of the tunnel had puddled deeper in the last hour. *Ken* was heavier than a passenger vehicle. A lot heavier. We could do this. We might even keep traction. We'd better, because I didn't have an autodrive to take over for the hard parts. I kicked up my speed, closed all lower air intakes, and splashed through. Ha! I'd managed to keep us in our own lane without even a wobble. I'd half expected a little bit of float toward the tunnel wall there in the middle.

We clawed on up, and I slowed. We'd need to stop soon, and the momentum on something this big takes a little time to bleed off. I got my air coming in again. *Ken* requires no external oxygen, but I still need to breathe. Someday I might miniaturize an O_2 exchanger for the cabin, but I haven't yet. Instead I've got an old-fashioned scuba air tank strapped next to my driver's seat for if I really need it.

Ken can do a lot, but not everything. Not to take too much credit, but I'd been tinkering with his systems since my unit got him.

Automotive engineering skills don't directly map to military mechanized transport redesign, but a bored engineer is a motivated engineer. I'm the Roanoke Tesla Plant paint R&D girl. It's dull. Watching paint dry dull.

So I play with *Ken*. God bless the National Guard. Every car enthusiast should really have a hobby tank hidden in the backyard garage. Thoughts of the way the HOA busybodies' brains would explode if they knew were driven from my mind by what waited on the Norfolk side of the tunnel.

Corporal Marjorie Kidd's hologram waved me over. A crowd management study said people respond best to rescuers they think are present with them. So we try not to do disembodied voices from loudspeakers. But Captain Wallen isn't willing to put more people in the middle of an evacuation zone than he really has to. So Kidd was actually standing in a guardhouse shower room on the other side of the state with the taps on full instead of being in the pre-hurricane rainfall. Programming code existed to mimic getting soaked without actually being uncomfortable, but I'd been overspending on *Ken*'s mods lately. Wallen had put the remaining budget into top-quality hologram projection instead of splitting it between projection and image modification. He'd gotten his money's worth. Kidd didn't even waver out of focus when I got right up next to her. Water was dripping from her plastered blond hair. Her uniform rain gear was soaked through. I had a failed automotive high-gloss lacquer that would've refreshed the water repellant on her coat and only sort of stank like a dying skunk. I refrained from offering her a pint of the stuff to try out later. It wouldn't have been appreciated.

"I can't! I can't!" the man in the pristine restored Tesla squeaked when a trickle of rainwater from the overflowing gutters lapped at his front tires. "The Midtown's pumps must've failed. I can't take my Rosebud through that!"

Ah. A true classic car would lack any connection to the city's grid, which was how he'd been able to stop and block a full lane of frustrated traffic.

"Sir, sir!" Kidd yelled at him from a speaker at the tunnel mouth. She'd given away her hologram nature trying to get the driver's attention and get him moving into and through the tunnel. Manually driving that car through a tunnel with the rest of the traffic on autodrive wasn't the best idea, but she didn't really know cars and might not have had time to look at the camera feeds for inside the Midtown Tunnel. "The pumps here are good. It was the Monitor-Merrimac where the pumps failed," she said.

Failed. I suppressed a snort. Turned off intentionally by a panicky idiot was not the same thing as failed.

I glanced behind the lovely red Tesla. His lane was full bumper to bumper all the way back around the curve of Hampton Boulevard, and the cars in the other lane whipped on by with none of the little extra spaces the emergency drive system allowed in as traffic density began to ease. We had no time for another tunnel crash. Even with all highway and tunnel lanes reversed for outbound traffic, the Midtown was a major choke point, and all the lanes needed to move.

I jumped down to check out the Tesla problem. "Original restoration?" I asked. "And it's a limited edition 2028, right, the one that used the same lines as the 2008s but not a 2048LE with all the insides changed up?" The pearly red of the car's finish shone even under the darkening gray skies. Very good paint.

"We don't have time for admiring old cars," Kidd said to me with gritted teeth. The fixed traffic cameras couldn't swivel for her, so she actually couldn't have checked the car like I was doing.

"I can't do it!" the man said again, his voice getting a panicked edge to it. I reached under the Tesla and made certain the custom restoration hadn't done anything weird with the chassis. I wanted to tow the whole car and not just a piece of it.

"Sir, please speak in your normal tone of voice," Kidd said. "The way is clear. All pumps are operational."

The woman in the van behind him leaned on her car horn and a half dozen other drivers beat a staccato of angry agreement. Turn signal blinkers flared in a domino effect in the stopped lane as the people tried to take manual control and move into the unblocked lane. The system was able to block most of them, but some few managed to nose into the other lane, forcing the anticollision rules of the city autodrive system to further slow traffic. That aftermarket override was legal in this state, if not helpful in this particular instance.

Kidd lifted her issued bullhorn and bellowed an order for all vehicles to stay in their original lanes and to keep their vehicles slaved to the city autodrive system. Her voice echoed out of all the vehicles' speakers, which earned us glares as whatever the occupants had been trying to listen to was interrupted. The cars did comply, but I couldn't tell if it was because the people in the remaining stopped cars were civic-minded or if they just didn't have the override.

I hooked my tow chain to the Tesla's chassis. "Get in the tank," I told the man. "I'm not sure if water intrusion backflow would short Rosebud out at the bottom or not, but we've still gotta clear the lane. The pumps are keeping up enough for recent vehicle models that can connect to city control, but a classic needs a little more help than that."

Kidd shot me a concerned look. "Sergeant, I know you've figured out driving backward, but towing, too? Thought you'd push it out of the lane."

"Tell Captain Wallen this'll be faster. I've got to get *Ken* back through the tunnel anyway unless I'm sheltering him on this side somewhere."

Kidd nodded. "Good luck, Sergeant."

The man blinked in surprise at having a solution chosen for him and proved to have more sense than I'd come to expect from stressed and panicked people by climbing onto the tank. While he snapped a selfie with *Ken*, I made sure his Rosebud was in neutral and gave Kidd a cheery wave. "Clearing lane one, again," I called out to her.

A second quick check around Rosebud confirmed it was precisely the restoration princess it looked to be, and no obstructions would prevent a safe tow.

"I'm Ford," the man called out from the top of *Ken*. "Henry Ford the Tesla driver," he added with a smirk. Well, at least his name was going to be easy to remember. "Thanks for saving my car," he continued.

That was no sure thing. I wasn't sure it'd start again on the other side of the tunnel. The rain had slowed to only spit occasional fat droplets. *Ken* would smell like wet dog, but the drizzle wasn't enough to damage the tank interior. Ford's hair started to mat, and the man brushed frantically at it while ducking farther into the tank. I snorted. There was a reason I liked my tough *Ken* more than most people.

"I know Rosebud is not as important as people, of course, but I got stuck," Ford called out from inside the tank.

"Yeah," I acknowledged. I'd have him through the tunnel and out of my tank again soon enough.

I climbed back into *Ken* and started us rolling smoothly in reverse back through the tunnel. The powerful pumps had lowered the bottom water level down to only inches now, thanks to the break in the rain. Still, the backward driving could get a bit tricky with the extra pushes the water could give us. We splashed through the wet at the very bottom of the tunnel, and arched back up to sunlight with only a few seconds of the Tesla floating during *Ken*'s point of least traction. Momentum had carried us through without any side drift into the very full other lane. I allowed myself a grin.

Ken's treads pulverized another piece of road debris, and I nudged the driving lever to keep us in our lane.

Ford pulled out his personal comm and turned on a video news weather report as if driving a tank backward while towing a car were a nothing job that required no focus. As a former combat vehicle, *Ken* had no autodrive, and absolutely no remote override capability. Even military contractors hadn't been able to convince the government to do that.

The talking heads on Ford's news show spoke with breathless pronouncements about the hurried evacuation efforts. Idalia was disappointing them by remaining only a Category II hurricane. "Well, at least it's not a three," Ford said with the resignation of man whose house was about to lose its roof and get filled with only four feet of mixed seawater and sewage rather than eight. The reporters' vulture-like interest remained high. A local news show well inland had managed to corner some early evacuees. The two men and a woman interviewed seemed to take tearful delight in their fifteen minutes of fame. Until the questions got to pets, that is. Then the woman made an offhand comment about no provisions having been made for the animals.

"They better not have left their pets behind." My passenger swore at his screen but used unusually mild epithets.

I agreed with him about the animals. I would've said it much more crudely, but I try not to curse in uniform while a member of the general public who may or may not be live-streaming his evacuation experience sits in the cab with me.

"I got the family out on one of the evac ferries yesterday," he said. Yup, sure sounded like he was talking to an audience of more than just me. "Got the cats out this morning. I'd never leave a pet behind. I can't believe some people. Anyway. The cats went into hiding, you see, and I had a devil of a time finding an open grocery store to get some tuna to lure them back." He continued without needing encouragement or interaction from me. "I was going to take Rosebud to one of the raised parking garages and shelter-in-place after. Since I'm a volunteer firefighter, you know." He blushed. "But, ah, I've been too busy to do shifts in a couple of years, so they didn't have me on the active list. So I couldn't get a parking spot at the MacArthur North parking garage, and the MacArthur South was all full up. So I thought I'd just drive Rosebud out. Come to find out after six hours in line last night for the Hampton Roads Bridge-Tunnel that the water level there was too high for Rosebud, so I got in line here for the Midtown Tunnel even though the chatter is that, once I got over to Portsmouth and wanted to take the freeway route north, the Monitor-Merrimac Bridge Tunnel might not open again before Idalia hits, so I'll have to take a west-and-southwest evac route rather than my planned highway route through the MMMBT—that's the Monitor-Merrimac Memorial Bridge-Tunnel—after getting through the Midtown Tunnel, thanks to this tank driver here." He finally took a breath.

Spelling all those things out with the extra details? He was definitely talking to an audience.

My radio chirped. "Yup, Sergeant Barbie here," I said. "Almost through clearing lane one."

"Hey, her shirt says, 'B. Ommerowie . . . ' um, something." Ford, like most people, couldn't pronounce Oumarou. I didn't bother to help him out. "They ought to be calling her by her last name. Big O., who won the Heisman last year, had the same name. And his cousin Johnny O. got that seat in our state assembly last year."

"Stop talking," I said.

"But they should call . . ."

"Stop." I leveled a glare at him, and he finally snapped his mouth shut. I was well aware that some famous and semi-famous people shared my last name. And nobody called them by it either. I was good with Sergeant Barbie. I'd been with the Guard long enough and met enough active duty types to know the nickname could've been a lot worse.

"Barbie here," I said. "Had some local static, sir, say again, over." Captain Wallen would know that meant a member of the public was present, and I'd just shut him up. We don't use strict communications protocols in our unit, but we do have a working set of unit specific codes to report things we need to share but don't want broadcast out of context on the local news.

"Gotcha," Wallen said. "We just got a bunch of reports about some chic animal-boarding center being abandoned without anybody evacuating the pets. I need you back on the Norfolk side for a dog rescue."

"All based on some comments from a pet store receptionist interviewed by Roanoke Channel Four?" I asked.

"Glory be, really?" That meant he thought it was shit intel, but he had to pretend it wasn't. Captain Wallen's grimace wasn't visible on the audio-only channel, but I'd worked with him long enough that I could see it. "Yes, Mayor, yes, Lieutenant Governor," he said without keying the transmission off, "I'm about to have someone on the ground check it out. Yes, I understand that your constituents are very concerned."

Ford flashed a smile at his comm and said, "I'm staying for the dog rescue." He turned to me. "Seriously. I found a place three-point-eight miles from here and still open where I can pick up some dog chow. Do you think half big dog and half small dog mix? What about puppy chow?" He held up a hand even though I hadn't agreed. "Don't worry about it. I'll just get whatever they have left."

I counted to ten in my head. "Mr. Ford, your car may or may not start. If it doesn't, I've got to radio for a state trooper or convince a random vehicle to let you take an empty seat on out of here."

"Rosebud will start." Ford blinked at me. "I live in Norfolk. Of course I have her whole underside water sealed. I get it refreshed every six months. I just didn't want the upholstery ruined if water came into the interior through the ventilation system."

"The upholstery," I said and crunched out of the active lane. I took down a section of guardrail. Oops. Rosebud's narrower body followed through without a scratch. I bled *Ken*'s momentum off with a curving tight turn at the gravel edges of the little side lot. A big sign overhead read EMERGENCY VEHICLES ONLY. Normally I'd have slowed before the turn and avoided damaging the guardrail, but I wanted everyone behind us moving at top speed.

I nosed *Ken* to a stop. I did some calculations in my head, guessing at the number of cars backed up waiting to clear the tunnel, assuming no further delays . . . I tapped a few buttons to pull up some info from the video cameras on the major roads to help estimate how many cars were still coming through and to check if the emergency system had them quite up to 80 mph yet. They'd be doing 120 once they got through to I-480, but traction in standing water was shit. I did the math and suppressed a few curses.

They'd be getting out ahead of the storm, but Midtown wasn't going to be empty soon enough. I was going to have to crawl *Ken* across the bottom of the Elizabeth River again. I'd tested that out last year during drill in non-storm conditions, and it did work, but tanks were really, really not supposed to have to do stuff like this. Whatever happened to blowing things up with a main turret? Assuming, that is, I ever officially got any ammo to try out or was able to reinstall the targeting computer from one of the other tank hulks. Of course if it were known that I had a functional gun, I'd have to accept an actual tank crew instead of driving around alone and unafraid as my one-woman, all-terrain wrecking ball.

"Ford," I said. "Out of the tank. Show me that you can really turn Rosebud on without turning yourself into a charcoaled and smoky former car nut."

"We prefer the term car fanatic," he said. But he was moving.

I unhooked my tow cable and stepped well back as he got into the gleaming old Tesla and demonstrated the car was on with a few headlight flashes. He started to turn Rosebud toward the fast flow of cars exiting the tunnel.

"No way, Ford! You're taking the back way." I pointed at the narrow parallel tracks of gravel leading out an anonymous waterfront side street.

"That adds eight minutes to my route to the pet supply store," Ford complained. "You could be back with the dogs and I'd miss it if I go the long way. You'll have to stop traffic anyway to go back through the tunnel."

I wasn't going to get to use the tunnel. I suppressed my shiver, not wanting to have it caught on camera. "You aren't coming back with puppy chow unless you want the state police to impound Rosebud and chain her to the cleats here right next to the last tunnel wreck."

"Harsh," Ford said. But he was holding up his comm for a good camera angle and had a slight smile on his face. Sometimes I hate humans. Why can't everybody be more like a reliable tank?

A thought hit me. "Your cats. Where are they? Tell me you didn't leave them in a cat carrier in the back of that Tesla to maybe get electrocuted if your wetproofing failed during the tow."

Ford flipped his comm down, genuinely hurt. "Of course not. I dropped them off at the boat Muddy Paws had going out. They'd chartered a ferry for pet evacuations and were getting everything two-footed, four-footed, and no-footed out of the storm path. They even told me that a police officer had cut the locks for them at a certain competitor kennel to get some dogs out that idiots had left behind. Not exactly breaking and entering when a police officer helped, but of course I won't stream that. People can get all shitty with the insurance and liability claims." He double-checked his comm. "Good: off. Can't curse on the feed or they give you an NSFW label and you lose all the under-eighteen viewers who don't know how to log in under an adult's access."

I pointed at the gravel path leading out to Seaboard Avenue. "Get."

He drove off and managed to squeal his tires on the turn onto pavement despite going no more than 15 mph.

I stowed the tow chain and re-entered my tank. I had really been hoping I could stay on the Portsmouth side until after the storm passed. The police car fleet and ambulances had streamed past more than an hour ago. The Portsmouth Naval Hospital complex had a new Deltec II building the emergency responders were using for shelter on this side. It was compact, wind-resistant, three-stories, and extremely well engineered. It'd do just fine in the storm. The rebuilt MacArthur Center and associated parking garages were only Deltec I and had more stories. Since the lower floors would flood, they needed the height but the upper levels would be battered by higher winds and more debris.

"Captain, this is Barbie," I said. "New intel. Local reports some Samaritans with the pet supply and boarding co Muddy Paws may have the dogs." Samaritans was our code for do-gooders who weren't entirely following the expected social norms of who was expected to do what. I left out all mention of police involvement and of breaking and entering.

"Roger that," said Wallen. "Got new tasking anyway. Need you to check on a Lily Sunset—again on Norfolk side."

I pulled my hatch shut and dogged it tight. I had *Ken* rolling down the soft incline toward Seaboard Avenue and the water as Wallen kept talking.

"I'm working on the exact address. This is for a city's civil engineer."

I paused. "The one who shut off the pumps and closed Monitor-Merrimac early, and will be directly responsible for a lot of deaths if any further screwups slow the evacuation?" I asked. "The same civil engineer who told the city to turn off the pumps for the Monitor-Merrimac Bridge-Tunnel while the evacuation was still in progress, and about fifty thousand people without access to personal boats still needed to drive through that bridge-tunnel?"

"Uh, negative." The rustle of pages meant Wallen was checking something in his unofficial personal logbook. "Believe that guy's been removed for cause, so this would be the newly promoted former underling who's in a wet suit inside the MMMBT's tunnel right now."

"Shit." The word slipped out. I did not compound it with my demands to know what possible useful thing anybody thought they could do in the tunnel now. Three days ago, sure. Even last night, if there were extra pumps that could be brought online, they might have been able to drain the thing and reopen it as an evacuation route. Now it had to be too late.

"You'd be going even if Lily were a relative of that, ah, citizen," Wallen said.

We probably shouldn't have chosen "citizen" as code for "asshole." It'd make sense, though, if Lily were the former city engineer's mom. Assholes do tend to breed true.

Some background babble that might be one of the dignitaries included a fair bit of cursing people who insisted on sheltering-in-place until just before storm landfall and then screamed for the city to evacuate them. They didn't sound particularly politician-like at the moment, but maybe they were imagining the police and EMS funerals that they'd be asked to speak at after this.

"Just remember," Wallen said, "you need to be back at the MacArthur Center North Parking Garage on at least the fourth level before the storm makes landfall. Oh, and secondary mission if you have time: we've got an ambulance boat on Fairfax Canal that needs a tow. They were responding to a driver in need of assistance. Somebody's classic car was floating in figure eights and they tried to save it instead of just bailing out the driver. Ambulance boat got stuck on a lawn. They think it's stuck and not actually hull damaged. They want to have it in service for post-Idalia relief ops, but it won't be if they can't get it to cover before the storm hits."

"Got it. Two missions. The engineer's Lily is primary. Ambulance boat tow is secondary. Going under." I had rolled up right to the bank of the Elizabeth River. *Ken* could do this, but I was going to be blind getting across. Lily Sunset better be the world's sweetest grandma who'd only stayed behind because her fifteen cats needed to be saved from the storm too, and she'd had some trouble rounding them up. And why the fuck couldn't somebody on the other side check on Lily?

"I asked up the chain about other responders," Wallen said. We'd worked together long enough that the officer was excellent at guessing my questions and he took to heart all the directives about keeping the troops on the ground fully informed about other available resources. "You're all we've got that can handle the terrain. I've got no backup for you."

If I'd had a crystal ball earlier, I could've stayed on the Norfolk side and had some Portsmouth wrecker truck come through to tow out Rosebud. But no, that would have involved a wait and those critical minutes were making a difference in how many of the last-second evacuees got entirely clear of the storm or ended up sheltering in freeway underpasses later when the hurricane spun off its usual mess of nuisance tornadoes.

"Hey, remember," Captain Wallen said. "If *Ken* gets stuck; if there's new debris washed across the route; if the ramps we put in have been dislodged; if you can't get through for any reason, you bail out like we practiced. Do not wait down there for a crane. It won't be coming. You hear me, Sergeant?"

Like hell I'd bail on *Ken*. I didn't answer him. I'd already signed off for submerging. And what do you say to that sort of commentary anyway? For that worst crossing attempt we'd done, the crane had torn one of *Ken*'s treads, and I'd woken up in a bed at Norfolk General. But they had gotten us out, and if I'd rammed through once more that time, *Ken* would've gotten us out on his own. It was operator error that I'd passed out from oxygen deprivation before I'd figured a way through crawling around blind on the river bottom. Tankers historically used to drive around pretty close to blind in combat conditions with just a narrow slit to see through. And the whole Gator line from the first has been able to move while hermetically sealed to harden it against chemical and biological attack. What I'd done with *Ken* wasn't that extreme of a modification.

"She's going to fucking drive that tank across the Elizabeth River?" a new voice said. Captain Wallen had left the radio transmitting again. He probably thought it'd be encouraging for me, or something.

"Absolutely, Governor," the Norfolk mayor said. "They do it all the time."

Once. We'd done it successfully once. And I'd gotten stuck seven other times including the last two times we'd tried it. Lily Sunset better be worth this, and I hoped that ambulance boat crew had the sense to find the most survivable nearby house and break a window or whatever it took to get themselves into a shelter if I couldn't reach them in time. If Lily was an ornery sheltering-in-place, mind-changing, ah, citizen who'd chosen an unsurvivable shelter, she could be tough to move.

The countdown clock for Idalia's upcoming landfall clicked ever downward.

Ken's treads crunched over to the ramp. Three minutes. The ramp we'd installed on this side wedged between two wharf-side buildings and pointed due east instead of straight at the opposite bank. If I turned correctly immediately off the ramp and crawled across the river bottom on a straight line course to the opposite ramp, I should be resurfacing at Plump Point Park right behind Norfolk General Hospital's neurology building within three minutes. If not, if I had to wiggle in a zigzag back and forth, guessing and second-guessing about where that second ramp had gotten to, I had about an hour and a half of air. That'd be eighty-seven minutes of knowing I'd never before managed to find that second ramp or rediscover the first ramp after missing the goal on the first shot across. I could and had found riverbanks with high rock seawalls that even *Ken* couldn't climb. I could open the hatch against water pressure, let the river pour in, and let that brackish water fill the entire cabin. After the water pressure equalized, I could swim up, still breathing just fine with my scuba tank, and I'd get out.

But *Ken* was waterproofed only from the outside. Water in the cabin would seep from there into every nook and cranny of *Ken*'s electronics and electrical systems. He had no protection against threats from inside himself. He'd be only a paperweight after that. His chassis and treads would be spare parts for some other tank with all the tweaks that made him dead on the bottom of the Elizabeth River. If I swam up with my air tank, surfaced, and found a part of the seawall where I could climb out, I'd be fine. Sure, I'd have to still find a shelter, but there'd be enough to choose from and people tended to open their doors in welcome for a woman in uniform. Only *Ken* would be dead. They might not even rent the crane to get *Ken* out after the storm passed. Call it a burial at sea, maybe.

I wiped my sweating hands on my uniform pants. I could do this. I had do it. *Ken* had done it. We just needed to do it again. Perfectly. With no backup.

I put on my breath mask and tested my air, and rigged *Ken* for dive. The four external cameras gave me a 360-degree surround-view of the ramp and the Portsmouth commercial waterfront behind me.

The cameras had no ability to angle up and of course I had no headlights, but at least I wasn't squinting at a collection of finely aligned prisms and trying to peer through a little slit visor.

Ken rolled down the ramp into the water. I didn't hear the water lap and splash against *Ken*'s sides as we sunk into the Elizabeth River, but the view from the front and then the side cameras fogged and dimmed to a murky gray. By the time water covered my rear camera, the front view was solid gray. I'd be blind until halfway up the second ramp.

My aftermarket gyrocompass was the only reason this had worked that once. It gave me true compass headings while submerged without *Ken*'s magnetic field distorting it. We reached the bottom of the ramp. I gave *Ken* a gentle turn to a heading of 047. I tried to ignore the monitors but didn't turn them off. The billows of river mud churned up by *Ken*'s treads built optical illusion structures in the inky grayish brown nothingness. I had just under half a mile of bottom to cross at an easy 10 mph.

We tilted gently downward. The gyrocompass heading stayed steady. I rolled *Ken* onward. Something crunched under us. We'd shifted slightly north to 045. I hissed a curse at myself and angled back to 049. I counted out a guesstimate of twenty seconds off course and returned us to 047.

Two minutes and two seconds in, *Ken* stopped moving. I revved up the power, and we continued to not move. Something blocked our forward path. We were at least a tenth of a mile from Plum Point Park. I closed my eyes. This was either a big new wreck, or it was something that'd always been here, but I'd not run into before. I stared at my map, knowing I had to make a choice fast. If I let *Ken* stay still long enough, we'd sink too deeply into river-bottom mud for even his tank treads to get us moving again.

I hoped the obstacle was new and small. I'd go backward and then slightly north to get around. That way, if my earlier off-course northerly drift had been longer than I'd thought, I could work my way south and more south and, I prayed, find the ramp out.

I backed *Ken*. He moved. Five seconds back. Stop. Forward turning to 045. Hard stop at five seconds. Shit. This was a big obstacle. North again. Backing for five along bearing 227 in the straight-line reverse of bearing 047. Forward at 045. Hard stop. But

Ken twisted as he stopped. There was a corner on this obstacle, and we'd found it. I cut power. We were pointed 097. *Ken*'s left tread had been clear of the obstruction and kept moving while the right side ground against an immovable something. I stared at the map and did a quick measurement. There was a high seawall for the piece of land just south of Plum Point Park. I was almost certain that that was what we'd been ramming into.

Well, at least if I had to abandon *Ken*, I'd be close to our intended destination.

Wait, no. I didn't have to keep guessing! I could make just one last guess. If I was right about where I was, I had an exact point for my current location. I had the last pre-storm satellite image enlarged into a detailed map with my two ramps marked, and—there—I had the corner seawall that *Ken*'s right tread might be rolling ineffectually against. I drew the line to my target. I needed an 039 course for 0.11 miles from here to the second ramp. After I'd drifted too far north, I must've overcorrected south. Hope bloomed inside me; I might still be able to get *Ken* out.

I pulled back from the corner for just a half second, turned to 039, and headed north-northeast. *Ken* scraped against the seawall corner as we passed it. Just over a tenth of a mile to go at ten miles per hour meant a smidge under forty seconds to the ramp at our 10 mph crawl. My clock counted down. At thirty-nine seconds, *Ken*'s nose lifted. I slammed on the brakes. The ramp wasn't wide. I shifted backward and forward bare seconds of movement at a time. Gator tanks do not corner well. It took us an eighteen-point turn to get from an 039 bearing to an 047 one. But the front of *Ken*'s treads still found the base of the ramp, and we powered up it without falling off a side.

The monitors cleared to show the beautiful storm-grayed skies, sodden unkempt city park green space, and the cracked old walking path of Plum Point Park. I spat out my regulator, cracked open the hatch to get my cabin air speedily refreshed, and rigged *Ken* for normal operation.

"Barbie and *Ken*, checking in at Plum Point," I radioed Captain Wallen.

"Took her long enough," the mayor said, and Captain Wallen cut the transmission before whatever other snark the politicians had to say could come through.

Corporal Marjorie Kidd appeared at the head of the ramp. *Ken*'s speakers crackled with her voice. "Thank God, Sergeant! Captain Wallen was going crazy looking for a crane operator company who'd let him do a remote operation to rescue you, but none of the ones he browbeat into giving him control codes could reach to this side of the river. We used a crane boat last time, and it was evacuated weeks ago."

Huh. So much for nobody coming to get me out. We didn't have microphones on the ramp to catch any of my responses, so I only gave the camera a turret wave. "Address on Lily received," I reported back in to Captain Wallen.

"Go, go, go," Kidd said. "Winds are picking up faster than the models predicted."

We crunched directly over empty streets, soaked lawns, and the lacy patchwork of canals that made up the Norfolk water transportation grid. In a row of old houses, I found my address for Lily. The ambulance boat crew struggled on a neighboring lawn. They'd procured a heavy rope from somewhere and with one end of the line wrapped around a tree, they were trying to pull their boat back into the canal by main force. The winds knocked over two of the four EMTs. It wasn't going well.

I popped open *Ken*'s top and almost got my head lopped off by a piece of tree better described as trunk than branch. I pulled the hatch almost entirely closed and peered out more carefully. Taking a hint from Kidd's style, I used my bullhorn.

"Lily Sunset, this is Virginia National Guard Disaster Relief Unit Six. We have received a call that you require assistance. Please respond."

Silence from the house. I was going to have to go knock on the door and maybe get my skull cracked by another tree.

Four thumps hit against *Ken*'s side. The crew of the ambulance boat had dashed the hundred meters to shelter on *Ken*'s leeside. I opened the hatch wider. No reason for them to wait outside.

Four blessedly lean EMTs sporting bruises and scratches wedged themselves into *Ken*'s cabin and clumped together to give me space at the controls. Like me, they had their names embroidered on their shirts.

"Lily needs to be shot, not evacuated," B. Haven said.

"Hardly the plant's fault that its gardener is an egotistical asshole with no concern for human life," G. Whittaker said.

"Thanks for the rescue." P. Doyle gave me a nod.

"I just wish we weren't going to lose Betsy," P. Gold said.

"Lily is a plant, not a person. And my orders to help her evac are some sort of bullshit," I translated. I got four nods. "Who is Betsy?"

They blushed. "The boat." P. Gold sighed. "I couldn't keep her steady during the swells while Doyle and Haven were trying to figure out which lily was the prize-winning sunset lily that the overly connected asshole pretending to be a civil engineer wanted dug up and saved."

"I really think if we could just pull *Betsy* back into the canal, the mud lawn's soft enough that she ought to slide back without major hull damage," B. Haven said. "We can still get back to the boat lift at MacArthur North."

P. Doyle turned to me. "Would you help pull? With five together maybe we can shift her." He looked at my slim shoulders with more doubt than hope.

I snorted. "*Ken* will rescue your *Betsy*." I patted the side of the tank cabin and their eyes lit with understanding. I gave them the tow cable to attach.

As Doyle and Whittaker got *Betsy* hooked up, Haven tried to explain that they had a collection of code phrases for stuff they need to share with dispatch but didn't care to hear repeated on local news channels, and a "classic car rescue" meant . . . I waved away the details, I got it. This lily belonged to the citizen who'd closed the MMMBT early. The assistant who was trying to make sure a pump system subjected to an emergency override shutdown would still restart after the storm didn't own it.

"Backup only comes after the tunnels get pumped. We're going to be on our own for a fair bit after Idalia's gone through, and *Betsy*'s a tough boat. She can do it, but, um, only if we can get her unstuck," Haven summarized.

I grinned. "Don't you worry. *Ken* will save you."

We pulled *Betsy* free in one easy tug. Before Haven and Gold left, I pointed at the front of the house where a raised decorative planter stood in a position of honor in the front landscaping. Whatever plants (lilies or otherwise) had been there, the wind had already ripped all leaves from the bare earth. "Are you absolutely certain that this is the citizen's—I mean, asshole's—house?"

"One hundred percent," B. Haven said. P. Gold nodded in confident agreement.

I turned *Ken*'s turret at the stone planter and fired. It's amazing how much damage pulverized stone can do to a house when a tank round hurls it through the front façade. The round itself kept going through interior walls, through the back siding, and out into the gentle waves beyond. "Gotta love waterfront property," I said.

Haven grinned. Gold stared. Haven pointed at my comm unit. "We're on channel sixteen for the return transit." He and Gold ran to their boat.

I adjusted my settings in time to hear the all-stations emergency coordination channel crackle on. P. Doyle's voice from the ambulance boat *Betsy* reported, "High winds from Idalia kicking up excessive debris. Ambulance Unit One-Two returning to shelter. Gratitude to National Guard for assistance above and beyond. I wish we had tanks. Over."

Dispatch answered, "You aren't getting a tank, Doyle. You'd shoot something. How's the classic car? Over."

"Unable to locate at this time," Doyle said. "Unit One-Two, out."

Ken saw *Betsy* home, steady and reliable just like the gentleman tank he was.

Jeanne d'Architonnerre

⊕

G. Scott Huggins

Even inside the armor of the *tartaruga* that she was preparing for battle, Gia could hear the bellowing of the Florentine leaders. Them, and the crunching thunder of the siege guns.

"This is your army? You are trusting the fate of the Republic to a blind man and a crippled girl?" shouted Soderini.

"It's better than trusting the mercy of that son-of-a-whore Borgia and His Profanity Julius II!" hissed back Machiavelli.

Gia inspected the turret. Bearings, greased. Springs and gun-track, polished to a shine. She snapped the slats of the viewports up and down on their hinges. She saw the Florentine militia wavering in their ranks, the dust and smoke where mortar stones had fallen, and finally, the sour, square face of *Gonfaloniere* Soderini, red jowls flapping.

"You call him profane!" he cried. "But you're the one dealing with a sorcerer!"

"Well, if he can conjure up a spine for your militia, then he is no wizard, but a worker of miracles and therefore a saint!" growled General Machiavelli. His smooth face was a saturnine mask. Gia was not fooled. The man's rage was hotter than the copper of the *architonnerre*. And that shone with heat, steam venting from its valve.

"They're *your* militia!" roared Soderini. "You trained them! You led them! You led us all—to this!"

"And you refused to let me train them more," Machiavelli went

141

on, implacably. "You and the rest, so worried that I might declare myself a prince that they are now—as I warned you!—unable to save us from the devils beating at Prato's gates!"

Gia snorted. At least she and her fellow *tartaruga* crews had drilled. They'd had to learn the machines inside-out.

"Have faith," said a voice with an odd accent. French? A short man in blue uniform under a breastplate stepped into view. "Gaston de Foix comes from victory over Spain at Ravenna, and though wounded, he rides to your aid. But he cannot retake Prato if it has already fallen, and Prato is the key to Firenze. Better to fight now than beg Christ's mercy from the black hearts of Pope Julius II or Borgia."

At that name, rage mounted in Gia's belly, spreading even to the legs she could not otherwise feel. She looked at the Florentines with disgust: they'd wanted to wait like princesses for some dashing French officer to ride to their rescue without having to fight. She'd never had any such illusions. She looked down into the belly of the *tartaruga*.

"Carlo, are we loaded?"

"*Si, donna.*" The squat man gestured to the long trough of cast-iron balls.

"Gun breech?"

He grinned. "Smooth as a whore's passage."

"Don't talk dirty about my baby, Carlo. Gun barrel?"

"Hotter than Borgia's soul in Hell."

Gia listened to the Florentines' cursing and said, "I think it's time for a valve test, don't you?"

Carlo's smile turned wolfish. "*Si, Donna.*"

Gia looked out, making sure that the gleaming muzzle was turned well away from the arguing lords. The general's hand was drifting slowly toward the hilt of a large dirk at his belt.

"Lock breech."

"Locked and empty."

Gia reached over and slammed the valve shut. The steam hissing through the turret vent cut off. Boiling water rushed through its siphon tube and hit the barrel of the gun, heated by its cage of coals. It flashed instantly into steam.

The copper barrel loosed a jet of vapor with a roar that silenced the shouting Florentines. Slamming the lever back, Gia unhooked a rope and lowered the chair-sized cart on which she sat. It settled to the deck of the war machine on its two wheels next to Carlos's station. With a yank on the wheels, she propelled herself past the *tartaruga*'s tiller and off the ramp.

She looked back at it. It still looked a bit like a turtle's ovoid shell. But the upper third of it, where she sat, could swivel, and the protruding copper barrel along with it. Its hull was sloping, laminated wood backed with thin iron plate, and lined inside with sheets of linothorax armor, tougher than boiled leather. Now there were . . . clay pots, bolted to its sides? What had her master been doing?

Twirling her cart again, she pushed herself around the hull of the war machine until she sat before the pale-faced Florentines.

She glared at them and then looked right and left at the other four *tartarughe*. Five. Five of the machines were all they had. Without taking her eyes from the two men before her, she called out, "Gunners! Vent your guns!"

Irregularly, the copper barrels snarled and spat steam.

"We are ready, *signiore*," said Gia. "Are you?"

"This is madness," muttered Soderini, looking at her with disgust.

"No, *signor Gonfaloniere*, madness would be to surrender," said a new voice. It came from a white-bearded man who steadied himself on the *tartaruga*'s sloping hull. "You cannot make peace with Borgia," he said. "And if you hide here, he will grind your walls to dust."

The men, pale before, went white as milk. But Machiavelli's voice was steady. "We are counting on you, Captain da Vinci, to lead this charge. Can you?"

Without turning his face away from them, da Vinci said, "Giovanna, the blast you loosed over my head means this old turtle is *quite* ready?"

"Yes, master," she said, her guts curdling. He'd been right there?

"My arrangements are also complete. *Signor* Machiavelli?"

"The men of Firenze stand ready," said the general, jaw tightening. "And will outfight paid robbers and the conscripts of princes." He wheeled and shouted at them. "Men of Firenze! If Prato falls, so falls the Republic! Today, you are Horatius before the gates! If we hide, the devil Borgia will loose the fires of Hell upon us and we shall deserve to be consigned to them! Shall we cower, or shall we fight?"

A ragged cheer rose from the Florentine militia. Some men brandished their arquebuses and pikes, while others shuddered at the crunch of falling stones. "Form your ranks!"

The men shuffled past. Some looked down at Gia. In their faces, she saw pity, disgust, and not a few signs of warding from the *malocchio*, the Evil Eye. She turned her cart and felt her mentor grip the wooden handle at its back. "Let us make ready to lead them, Giovanna," he said.

Gia threw the brass lever on the side of her cart. The clockwork rattled to life beneath her dead legs and it lurched forward, pulling him along. Adjusting the gears, she guided it into the belly of the *tartaruga*. Then she pulled it back into place in the turret until the pulley locked. Her master ran his fingers over the tiller and gearing levers below.

"Is everything in place, Captain da Vinci?"

He tilted his face upward. His ruined eye sockets stared through her, and his smile was gentle but grim. "I may be the 'captain,' but you must direct us. Oh—light a slow-match." Her master was fumbling with a network of cords she hadn't seen before.

"Why?" Their weapons did not need them. Nevertheless, she held a match to the coals of the *architonnerre*. It lit.

"Because now everything is in place to face Cesare Borgia and his pope. Even old Leonardo da Vinci."

"It's very pretty, sir," she'd said, holding the confection of wood and paper in her callused hands. It looked like cakes she had once seen being carried to the palazzo. The gossamer paper icing hung over its delicate, wooden basket.

The old man smiled down at her. She saw that smile when people bothered to look at her: pity. Sometimes followed by coins. Keep him talking. "What is it?"

"Just a toy," he chuckled. "For now." He reached for it, but Gia twitched out of reach. It was risky, but he didn't look the type to cuff or kick a crippled beggar girl.

"Now? What later?"

He smiled. "What if I told you that if I could make it big enough, a man standing in the basket could spin this screw and it would carry him into the sky like a bird?"

She laughed. But the thing had fluttered gracefully down from his balcony, three floors above the streets of Milano. A kind of flight. "Would not a man whirled about like that be sick?"

He grinned and plucked the model from her hand. "One of many problems to solve: for when the screw is spun, the basket spins the other way." He laid a grosso coin before her.

"Then use two screws," Gia said.

He blinked and looked at her. "What?"

"If one screw turns the basket the other way, can't you add a second screw? Going the other way? Then the basket wouldn't spin at all, because it would try to spin both ways at once." She thought a moment. "Of course, you'd need another man to spin the other screw, I suppose."

Now the man was staring at her. "Who are you, girl?"

She shrugged. "Maledetta." She eyed him suspiciously. Of all the stares she'd endured, no one had ever looked at her like that. "Giovanna da Mirabello, really. But Father calls me Maledetta." Accursed. She gestured at her useless legs, thin and twisted beneath her. Wrapped in sackcloth to protect them from cuts as she dragged them home each night, swinging them between her arms.

"Tell me, Giovanna," he said. "Do you think your father would be interested in an apprenticeship?"

"For my brothers?" Gia said. "Yes, signor."

"Not your brothers," said the man. "For you."

Gia gaped, "But I am just a lame girl! How can I do anything but beg when I cannot even walk?"

"Well," said the man, handing her back his toy, "it can't be more difficult than fixing this, can it?"

Footsteps pounded on the ramp, and a man hurtled past da Vinci and squeezed in beside Carlo's bulk. "*Excusez-moi, mes amis,*" he said. It was the young French officer.

"What are you doing here?" said Gia. "Get out, we're about to move!"

"*Exactement,*" said the officer, grinning at her. "And I must be here. Henri Fitzmorton. The Duc de Nemours has charged me to see these wonders in action, and *Signor* da Vinci says that you, even more than he, are responsible for them, Mademoiselle...Jeanne, I believe?"

"My name is Giovanna." So he was a Scot? Scotland and France had often aided each other against the English.

"But of course, it is just that French is a habit. So this...is your work."

"It is not!" she said, color rising to her face. "Master, what have you told this man?"

"The simple truth," da Vinci said, blandly. "This armored chariot, this *tartaruga* is due to Giovanna. Without her, it would not exist."

"Master, that is not true: they were all your drawings! And you cannot come with us: the *tartaruga* has but three places. Carlo must load, I must direct, and my master must steer and keep us moving. And you must go."

Fitzmorton gave her a broad grin. "My duty, Mademoiselle Jeanne, I am not large, and can crouch on the deck out of your way. And—since I see you have built-in firing slits—who knows? I may make myself useful after all." At this, he produced a pair of pistols, inlaid with ivory and fashioned with a mechanism that drew a gasp from Gia's lips.

"What is it, my dear?"

"He has your pistols, master. The wheellock."

"A copy?" her master said. "Or mine? Oh. *Gaspard* Fitzmorton?"

"I am honored," said the man, "to carry the pistols you yourself made for my father, *Signor* da Vinci."

Gia bent over her workbench, assembling the intricate gunlock that her master had laid out, piece by piece. The metal edges, cut smooth as the purest water.

"Giovanna!" Leonardo called, from the main room of the workshop. "Come here, and bring me the flechette case."

"Coming, master." She tripped the lever on her three-wheeled cart. With a steady clicking as the clockwork unwound, she rode it over to the end of the room and took the heavy cylinder from the shelf. Then she reversed the gears and released the brake.

Her back and hands no longer ached from having to drag herself about the streets of Milano. In just a year, so much change! Hand on the tiller, she aimed as best she could for the door. Almost as an afterthought, she grabbed the little wheel off her own workbench—her own workbench!—laying it beside her.

"Master, I . . ." she began, and then fell silent, eyes wide in shock.

Her master was not alone in the workshop. Five men stood there: four soldiers in red-green-gold livery, and, standing before them, a man of middle height with a long, sallow face and a neat beard. Cesare Borgia, Duke of Milano.

With a shaking hand, Gia steered over to Leonardo. The lord of the city looked at her twisted legs with distaste. "Signior da Vinci, what is this? Surely my patronage is not so stingy that you must rely on crippled beggar girls as assistants?"

The chill she felt at this denunciation was dispelled by her master's quiet laughter. "Allow me, my lord, to show you what we have devised for your cannon."

"Cannon?" The man's eyes lit. Then glared. "We?"

Da Vinci shrugged. "Giovanna had a most interesting suggestion, which I believe has merit." He indicated a scroll laid out on the table. "This mortar: it will fire solid shot, but it was too difficult to fuse explosive shells so that they would burst among their targets. My lead flechettes also were impractical: their very sharpness made them unsuitable for use in cannon. However, when my apprentice saw them, she suggested . . . this." Da Vinci took from her the squat cylinder bound with thin cord. It was made like a puzzle, of wooded wedges. And between the wedges protruded a dozen thick, pointed, iron spikes.

"What is this? Some kind of canister shot?"

"A longer-range canister shot, it is to be hoped."

"With a wooden shell?"

"It is bound with a simple cord," said da Vinci, "and flies into splinters as it leaves the gun barrel. But it has served its purpose, throwing the flechettes—for they have fins as an arrow. If you elevate your guns, they should fly at least twice the distance of canister shot, giving you twice as long to defend your cities."

Borgia took it. "Intriguing." His voice was calm, but his eyes were greedy. "We shall make trial of it. What is that?" he said, looking over at the next table. Another drawing lay there, in the master's sure, strong strokes. "A cart . . . surely those are not cannon around the edge of it?"

Da Vinci sighed. "An idle dream only, my lord. Unfortunately for me, Giovanna discovered that it is impossible."

"*And she is the last word on what is impossible, is she?*" asked the duke, a cold look in his eye.

Unable to contain herself, Gia said, "*Not impossible, my lord. Only impossible as drawn there. It requires eight men to turn the wheels, and they are too narrow. Besides, the bottom of the cart would catch on the rocks . . .*" She trailed off as her master raised a gentle hand to stop her torrent of words beneath Borgia's cold stare.

"*My lord, do not allow the immobility of Giovanna's legs to blind you to the quickness of her mind,*" said da Vinci, softly. "*Consider her cart, which moves without recourse to horses or the strength of men. I designed it; but she, who lives her life on wheels, has brought to light problems—and thus, solutions—that older eyes, with their eyes on loftier goals, miss.*"

Borgia sniffed. "*You built her wheels?*" This is how you spend my patronage? *The message was clear.*

"*And she improved them. As she improved the flechettes. She has an uncanny knack for bringing together disparate elements, Giovanna.*"

"*So long as she learns when to keep silent.*" Borgia sniffed. "*These mechanical carts: can they carry food or guns, for an army?*"

"*Not yet,*" said da Vinci. "*But we make progress from day to day.*"

"*Then perhaps less work on toys, and more on useful things. Good day,* signor."

"*Master, I am sorry . . .*" she started, when the duke had left.

Her master turned a kind but frustrated smile on her. "*I suppose it was partly my fault, to call you out here. The duke does not like being addressed by 'lesser men.'*"

"*And I am but half a woman.*"

"*You are more than enough,*" said her master, "*but I beg that you will allow me to decide what the duke should know of our labors. Some things I am willing to build for him. Others*"—he rolled up the scroll bearing the tartaruga *tightly, handing it to her*—"*should have been put safely away. Let us make sure he does not see your improvements.*" Gia nodded. "*Now tell me: Are you finished with the wheellock for* Monsieur Fitzmorton's *pistols?*"

"*Not quite, but nearly.*"

"*Good girl: I will inspect your work after supper.*"

"*Master . . .*" With a shy smile, Gia brought out the wheel. It was *awkwardly put together, with the axle held on either side by a wooden flange. The flanges met in a loop where they joined in an offset pivot.*

"What have we here?"

"A wheel: look, if you place it on a surface, then the wheel always trails. It turns from side to side, or forward and back, without having to drag its frame around."

Her master's eyes glowed. "Placed correctly ... you would create a pivot. A fast pivot for a wheeled cannon. Or ..." He looked at the scroll in his hand. "Perhaps more than a cannon."

Gia grinned, threw her cart in gear and awkwardly steered it around the benches. She was glad to be out of Borgia's sight. Quite apart from his slurs at her—she got those from everybody except her master—Borgia made her feel cold. Like a dead thing that he had not bothered to bury.

Later, she would remember the feeling as a premonition.

"Carlo," da Vinci said quietly, but firmly. "Shut the door." With the pull of a rope, the ramp shut, and they were sealed in the stifling belly of the war machine.

"Locked and loaded," called Carlo. Outside, Gia heard Machiavelli shouting at his men to form ranks. The shaken men formed into columns behind the *tartarughe*. Another hammering crunch slammed through the plaza, and a section of wall beside the gate buckled.

"They have to get the gates open *now*!" snapped Gia. If the thick, iron-bound gates were smashed, the wreckage would make the narrow passage completely impassable.

"*Monsieur* Fitzmorton," said da Vinci. "Do you see that mouthpiece beside you?"

"What, this one hammered into the side?"

"Sound 'advance,' please."

Gingerly, the man put his lips to the mouthpiece and blew a series of rising notes.

Slowly, far too slowly, the gates were cranked aside. Smoke hung like white thunderclouds over the enemy a mile distant. Now there was nothing to do but meet them. Nothing to trust but the name of da Vinci. "We're clear! Go!"

Below, her master released the tension on the two huge drive springs beneath the deck. Gears spun, and the *tartaruga* lurched forward. A new spurt of smoke went up from the clinging bank of fog and Gia clenched her teeth on the scream she felt building in her throat. This was the most dangerous moment. The war machines were in tight column. If Borgia's mortar hit just right, the heavy stone ball would shatter them like a *bocce* ball cast among pottery pins.

But much faster than this and they would outrun their infantry. And run their mainsprings out of power before they were halfway across the field.

The stone ball hit with a deafening crunch, leaving a dent like the fist of God twenty feet to the right of the gate. Bricks avalanched to the ground. But they were through the gate, and turning south across the fields. The wide, cylindrical drive-wheels, wrapped in layers of thick, studded leather, drove them sturdily forward, but she had doubts about her four smaller pivot-wheels mounted before and behind. They wobbled, and the car shimmied, but there was nothing to be done now. Gia heard the cries of the infantry as their officers lined them up behind the war-cars. She looked left and right from her cupola.

To the right, two more war cars pulled into place abreast of her, their infantry quick-marching to keep up. To the left . . .

One of the cars was spinning toward the Fiume River in a long loop. Her heart sank. *Jammed tiller, or worse, gear failure.* If it was that, they'd never untangle it in time. The other car on the left was hesitating. "Don't bother about what you can't fix!" she screamed through the slit. "Form your line!"

The notes of a trumpet cut through the noise. It was Fitzmorton, sounding "rally." Slowly, the hesitant war-car caught up. But a fifth of their armor was gone, its infantry column unscreened. At least it was on the left, where the Fiume protected them from being flanked.

The papal artillery and infantry stretched out in a thin red line, crawling closer, minute by minute. Mortars belched. Half a mile to go. She picked out the gleam of metal on a barrel. "Sound 'halt'!"

Fitzmorton obediently blew the trumpet, and the levers rattled to slow the machine.

"Sound 'aim'!" The other *tartaruga*-commanders would be picking their targets.

"Five marks starboard!" she called.

"Five marks starboard!" Carlo echoed, shoving with all his might at the cupola's tiller. Her platform and the *architonnerre* rotated on their greased rails. Now she heaved at the steam-gun's elevation. One. Two. Three clicks.

"Firing!" she cried, and slammed the lever home.

The steam cannon roared, and the whole car rocked back as it drove forth a hundred pounds of solid shot. Gia saw puffs of dust as her shot bounded across the fields, heard the roars of the other guns. A ragged cheer went up from the Florentine militia behind them. Had she hit something? At this distance, it was hard to tell.

The *architonnerre* had not the power of the cannon Borgia commanded, to say nothing of his great mortars that hammered at Prato's walls. It had two overwhelming advantages as the war-car's main weapon, though: it required no stores of explosive gunpowder, nor the precious time to measure it out, or to wait for the barrel to cool.

"Load roundshot!" Gia shouted. "Advance!"

Carlo spun the interrupted screw forward of the steam chamber, placed another ball in the breech, and shot it home again. "Locked and loaded!" The car jerked forward again. But suddenly Borgia's infantry was crawling nearer much faster: they were on the march. Their long line was sweeping around to their right. *They're flanking us.* Now, all depended on speed. "Sound 'charge.'"

"Charge?" said Fitzmorton. "At this distance? Your infantry will be exhausted and shot down like dogs!"

"They only have to charge until we stop to shoot." She saw his bafflement. "Just trust me, *Monsieur*. Charge!"

Fitzmorton blew the trumpet. "I hope the springs hold." Da Vinci's mutter was almost too soft to hear. The *tartaruga* accelerated to the speed of a sprinting man.

"Is this possible?" Fitzmorton stared out the window at the terrain flashing by.

Borgia's cannon fired. "Down!" Gia yelled. She threw herself flat against the cupola deck just as the leaden arrows struck like a hailstorm.

"What was that?" asked Fitzmorton.

Three lead points protruded through the linothorax of her cupola.

"They're using your flechettes," she said, grimly.

"But we knew he would," da Vinci replied, as cool and smooth as polished steel. "Has the armor held?"

"None made it completely through. I think some were deflected. Your sloping armor worked." Another hail of flechettes struck. Here and there, cries went up from the Florentine infantry that sheltered behind the war-cars, but it was nothing compared to the death that slashed through the unsheltered men on the left. Their screams tore at her ears.

"Sound 'halt'!"

The trumpet sounded and the war-car slowed. Now they had closed to perhaps a furlong, and she could see the enemy frantically reloading beneath Borgia's hated banner. Was he there? Was God so good?

"Three marks port!" Carlo grunted, and the *architonnere*'s sight bracketed the artillery crew. Gia dropped elevation one notch. "Firing!"

Steam roared and this time she saw the ball smash the gun's carriage. Its bronze barrel leapt up and crashed to the earth. Around her she heard the Florentine infantry shouting. They were deploying into line!

"No, not yet, not yet!" she screamed. What was that idiot Machiavelli doing? They were still in range of the papal canister shot!

Then she scanned the horizon and her stomach curdled.

Machiavelli had no choice. The papal cavalry was charging from the tree line. They overtook the infantry. To her right, the Florentines formed their ranks, refusing the flank. Her war-car's charge was done.

"Suppress the canister!"

"What?" Fitzmorton's face was nearly in hers, looking out the viewport beside her.

"Stop watching the battle! You're in charge of this battery, *non*? That cavalry is leaving firing lanes for Borgia's guns. Suppress the canister, or our men die!"

Gia nodded jerkily. The other war-cars had fired, but she wasn't sure what they'd hit. "Load hot shot!"

Carlo shoved Fitzmorton aside, and the man swore as his arm brushed the barrel. With blacksmith's gloves, he seized one of the glowing balls that lay caged beside the steam cannon's boiler and shoved it into the breech.

Gia scanned the enemy artillery line for a target . . . there!

"Seven marks starboard!" She wheeled around, ratcheting the gun. Fitzmorton helped Carlo spin the turret. "Firing!"

The heated shot plunged into the stacked barrels of gunpowder, and touched it off: a toadstool of rotting smoke and fire rose over the papal lines. A cheer went up from the Florentines. "Reload!" screamed Gia. The other *tartarughe* were doing their work. One fired, ripping a bloody hole in the line of infantry.

"Here come the horsemen!" shouted Fitzmorton.

"Carlo! The organ!"

"*Si, donna!*" The big man fumbled at the fore of the car.

"What, are you going to play them a tune?" Fitzmorton demanded.

"Giovanna!" da Vinci snapped.

Oh, God, I'm falling apart. "Pivot forty-five degrees port!" she replied.

"*Thank* you," said the old man. He yanked at levers. A glance to the side—the car on her right was turning toward her, as planned. Suddenly, a great fist struck them in the side, and the whole *tartaruga* rocked. There was the sound of rending wood, but the linothorax shell merely bulged inward. *One more hit there, though . . .* They were turning too slowly.

The thunder of horses' hooves shook the car through the very ground. The matchlocks of the Florentine infantry fired a ragged volley, but it was far too early, and only a few horsemen fell. "Bearing!" shouted da Vinci. Lances snapped downward for the kill.

"Fire!" Carlo yanked his lanyard and eleven wheellocks spun. The front of the war-cars spat a hail of lead. The short-barreled muskets ripple-fired. Their partner *tartaruga* had done the same, and the papal cavalry went down beneath enfilading point-blank fire. But it wasn't over. Carlo reached forward and ratcheted the bank of muskets sixty degrees backward . . . revealing a *second* row of muskets. He fired again. The rending crash of gunfire blended with the screams of men and horses as smoke filled the car. Gia's eyes stung, and she wept unbidden tears.

⊕ ⊕ ⊕

"Yes," da Vinci had said, eyes sparkling as she spun her cart, weaving between the workshop tables. "A great improvement, and one we can adapt."

"Thank you, master."

The door crashed open, and Borgia stepped through.

"So, you are leaving us, Master da Vinci? After all of my patronage?"

Gia stifled a shriek. More frightened than she had ever been in her life, she clutched her cart. Through the windows, she saw a score of the duke's men surrounding the house.

Six more big men entered behind Borgia. At a signal, two of them strode forward and seized da Vinci.

"What is the meaning of this? How have I offended my lord? I am a free man and merely return to Firenze, the city of my heart."

Her master was frightened, too. And that was the most terrifying thing of all.

An ugly light shone in the duke's eyes. "Oh, of course. But my dear Leonardo, you have been so useful to me. Your canister-darts. Your mortars. Your maps. I'm really not sure I can do without them."

"I am sorry, my lord, but my mind is quite made up."

"Your mind is made up," repeated Borgia. "Yes, that marvelous mind of yours. That concerns me a great deal. For if it goes elsewhere, then who knows where its deadly fruits might next appear? In the artillery of the king of France perhaps? Among the infantry of Venezia? Or even"—his face darkened—"in the hands of my most gracious lord, His Holiness Julius II?"

Gia's blood thundered in her ears. It was known throughout Italy that Borgia and the pope hated each other, and that Cesare alone had escaped Julius's purge of the Church from what he had described as "Borgia filth."

And Cesare had maintained his place only by dint of the armed might that made him too powerful to dismiss, and too dangerous a rebel. Armed might made possible by the devices of Leonardo da Vinci of Milano. And Gia had helped him.

"My lord," said her master, with a haughty dignity that almost masked his fear, "I have commissions in Firenze, from the Church, from many noble houses. For paintings. Nothing more." He gestured to the sketches and half-finished canvasses standing about. "I have done *enough in the service of the sword. I wish to dedicate my life from here on to works of beauty. So that God may forgive me for the part I played in war."*

"So that God may forgive you?" shouted Borgia, stepping forward and grabbing her master by the beard so that he cried out. It had been the wrong thing to say. "You will not buy that forgiveness from Julius with paint, old fool! No, the only coin that buys remission of sin for you is blood and iron."

Da Vinci gasped. "What will you do, my lord? Will you murder me?"

"No," said Borgia. "Death? For trying to run out on me and sell the secrets of my defeat to the highest bidder?"

"I was not—" But Borgia cuffed him to silence. Gia screamed. At a gesture from Borgia, one of his men stepped forward. He must have kicked her cart, because the next thing she knew, she was on the floor, the world spinning through a star-filled night sky. Her useless legs trailed behind her, and she struggled to her hands. She tasted blood. Her cart spun lazily on its side, wheels turning.

"No, you shall live." Borgia turned away, and his men held her master up, though he sagged in their arms. When he turned back, he held in his right hand a poniard not more than four inches long, a spike of steel. "You enjoy the company of beggars," Borgia said, again wrapping his left hand in her master's beard. "So be one." And he struck twice. Once in each eye.

Never after that night could Gia remember whose screams had been higher—her master's, or her own.

Through her tears and the smoke Gia watched the shattered cavalry stagger off the field, or thrash in death upon it. Through the screams of men and horses, she dimly heard a voice crying, "Stand! Stand, for the love of God and of Firenze!"

The arquebusiers had used the time the *tartarughe* had bought them and managed to reload their weapons. Now the papal infantry was nearing, their lines wavering. They had seen what the war-cars had done. Their officers screamed at them to advance, beating them with the flats of swords. "Advance and starboard turn, master!" Gia called, coughing. "Carlo! Load me a round!" But her loader was cursing and coughing himself in the confines of the war-car, and yanking at the "organ" barrels, wrestling the third and last set into position for a shot.

"I have it!" gasped Fitzmorton. Whipping off his jacket, he wrapped it around his hands and worked the *architonnere's* action, slamming a new ball home. The nose of the *tartaruga* came around and Gia caught sight of an officer.

"*Basta!*" she shouted. The war-car halted. "Firing. Carlo, shoot!"

The ripple-fire of the last set of organ barrels blended with roar of steam and the crackle of Florentine musketry. All outside was thick fog. "Advance!" she coughed. Her master's breathing was labored, but the *tartaruga* rattled into blind motion. A dozen feet. A score, and then they emerged from the smoke.

On their right, the papal envelopment was still proceeding. The Florentine infantry was falling back, and as she watched, the enemy fired a single cannon: it looked like they'd been desperate enough to lay one of their mortars flat.

The massive stone ball bounded across the field, and slammed into the leftmost *tartaruga*, crushing its armor. A cloud of scalding steam went up as its gun ruptured, and agonized screams joined the sound of shattered wood. Gia gasped out a prayer.

But before her, the papal infantry fled, leaving the wreckage of shattered men behind. And behind the rout stood the now-riotous standard of House Borgia: red, gold, green, blue, silver—an amalgamation of all his conquests and alliances. Beneath it, a tiny figure on horseback waved his sword. Borgia recognized his danger, and was frantically sending his personal guard to fill the hole she had created. Sending them to crush her.

She was not afraid. She had been crushed by far worse than this.

"Giovanna!" Her master's voice was rough with thirst and thick with sleep. "Wine!"

She dragged herself along the short passage, just as she used to when she begged. She would not use her cart for this. It was too loud.

At the door to his bedchamber, she stopped, and blinked away tears. Her master was filthy, hair matted and stained. His face swung from side to side. Where his bright, brown eyes had been, only scar tissue remained. He stank of sour sweat and wine.

She steeled herself. "No."

"What? What's that?"

"No. There's no more wine. You drank it all."

"All?" He pulled himself upright. "I can't have. Not all; I sent you just last Saturday—"

"To buy wine. But I didn't. You've had enough wine."

He flushed red, staggering to his feet. "What are you . . . ? You didn't? How dare you! Damn you, girl! I'm in pain!"

"Your eyes are as healed as they're going to be!" she shouted. "There's no infection, and whether they pain you or not, you're turning into a drunkard."

"Then let me be a drunkard!" da Vinci howled. "What else have I to do? I will never paint again. Never read again, draw again!" His voice wavered into madness. "I live in a blank fog, and I might as well die!" He flung out his arms and cursed as his left arm slammed into the shutter of the window. "What is there left to me to do?" he groaned.

When he had subsided enough to hear her, Gia said, as gently as she could, "Come to the workshop and see."

"The workshop? And see?" he snarled. "Do you mock me now in my own house? Maledetta! After I took you in, gave you everything you are, taught you everything I could? I can hardly find the workshop, much less do anything in it!"

Every word hurt, hearing them from the master she loved. She took a deep breath. "Take three steps forward and stretch out your hand."

"You direct me like a child now? I should beat you. Who is the master here?"

"I am, as long as you are behaving like a child," she said. Sudden fury struck her. "Do you think you are the only one to be hurt? To face a life with no future? Stop whining and step forward!"

Her master's mouth worked, but he stumbled forward and reached out. "What is this?" he asked, fingers wrapping around frayed fibers.

"The end of a rope that leads to your workbench. You still have fingers. Follow it now, or you will never taste wine again. Unless you sit outside and become the beggar I was for it. The floor is clear, but don't step on me."

Gia crawled before his faltering steps as he walked to the bench, taking the rope hand over hand. He felt for the stool and sat down. "Now that I am here, what would you have me do?"

"Reach out. There is a shallow box in front of you."

He did so. The pieces within rattled. "What is it?" he asked.

"Find it out yourself. With your fingers. Gently."

"Wheels, springs . . ." His voice rose in frustration. ". . . This is a hammer." He paused. "The parts of my wheellock. And?"

"Assemble it," she said. "Your fingers will remember."

"And how would you know, eh?" he demanded. "You never needed legs to draw, to design."

"I did it blindfolded five times last night," she said. "Keep the pieces in the frame." She'd invented the frame to keep herself from knocking pieces skittering across the workbench, or off of it. He fumbled and cursed as she climbed onto her cart, and from the cart to the opposite side of the bench. But at last he held up the mechanism. "I think . . ." he said, fingers working it. "I think it's together. Properly." A touch of wonder was in his voice.

"It is," she said. "Now, try this." She lifted the larger square frame and placed it before him. "What do you feel?"

Her master reached in and said, "It's blocky, whatever it is. Wood. The top, why does it turn like this? It lifts off?" He followed its contours with his fingers. "This tube is metal." He leaned down, sniffed. "Copper. This cage. It's . . ." His voice rose. "It's the architonnerre. *Archimedes's steam cannon. You made a model? Then this is . . . the new* tartaruga. *And it comes apart. My God, it's like a drawing. A drawing I can feel. My drawing. But you've done something to the wheels."*

"Yes, master, I—"

"Sssh!" He waved her to silence. "It's extraordinary. You . . . two wheels . . . four of those swivel-wheels you constructed for your cart. Two of the spring drives. I can't feel the gearing. One drive for each wheel? You carved this. Assembled it. For me?"

She placed her rough hand on his and he grasped it convulsively. "For both of us," she said. "And this will be for Firenze. Or Venezia."

"Or anyone else," he grated, "who will send it against that bastard Cesare Borgia."

It had taken long years to create the *tartaruga*. Years for her to carve models, for da Vinci to channel the genius that would have created paintings of holiness and beauty back into weapons of war and revenge. And now the bastard who had forced him to it, who had taken his easy kindness, his laughter from him, was going to pay.

The Florentine infantry about her were reforming. Reloading. Their right wing was hidden, nor could she count on Machiavelli to hold it. Borgia was advancing? She would meet him. "Full power!" she shouted. "Thirty degrees starboard! Sound 'advance.' And reload!"

Fitzmorton's ragged bugle and Carlo's staccato coughing as he slammed a round home and frantically reloaded the organ barrels ran counterpoint to her pounding blood. Borgia was not going to win.

The *tartaruga* picked up speed, shuddering. "Giovanna—" Her master coughed. "We cannot maintain this speed much further. How goes the battle?"

"We are chasing Borgia. Not much farther!"

Fitzmorton looked out the slit. "You're sending us into a bloody infantry countercharge! Slow down!" He turned to da Vinci. "Sir, stop us, for the love of Christ!"

"No," said Gia, "their muskets can't hurt us!"

"*Nom d'un chien!* They don't need muskets! They can crawl all over us and pry us out of this barrel oven!"

"Giovanna?" asked da Vinci. She peered out at the swelling mass of soldiery, a scant hundred yards away, and behind them, Borgia's banner.

"No! We can take him!" Musket balls slammed against their front like deadly hail, but none penetrated.

Fitzmorton lunged for da Vinci's control levers. Da Vinci fought him. Carlo turned and effortlessly dragged the French officer back by his collar.

"Please, sir," he said to da Vinci, "this is madness!"

Da Vinci turned empty eye sockets in Fitzmorton's direction and grinned, a fey rictus. Fitzmorton shuddered and the *tartaruga*'s designer said, "I'm afraid I trust her madness more than your sanity, my friend. You see, you are sitting in one of its greatest results."

"We have to punch through," Gia told Fitzmorton. "Our right is being surrounded. This is our chance to end him!" He wasn't escaping. Not if it killed her.

Fitzmorton twisted out of Carlo's grasp. "But you've left our own infantry behind! We'll be overwhelmed! Look!"

Out the left port, Fitzmorton's grim prophecy was coming to pass. Red-green-gold uniforms piled onto their sister *tartaruga*, climbing up its slopes. It slowed, and still more men leapt on. They thrust muskets through its viewports and fired. It stopped.

And now the mass of men was upon them.

Gia panicked. "Firing!" she screamed.

"No, Giovanna," shouted da Vinci. "We must stop to shoot!" But she had already closed the valve.

The *architonnerre* leapt from its mount like a live thing, under the stresses of its own firing and the rattling of the *tartaruga*. Braces snapped, and a jet of steam spouted. Carlo screamed as it caught him across the chest. The copper barrel belched, and the steam-driven round *splashed* men aside like bags of blood. Scalding vapors hit those in the front ranks that had escaped the deadly ball, and they shrieked like the damned. For an instant, Gia's heart leapt as she saw Borgia's standard, not fifty yards away, waver and fall.

But the steam-gun was wrecked. Carlo was down, crying out in pain, and the thud of boots echoed on their hull as the *tartaruga* slowed. Stopped. Just before her vision was completely obscured, she saw Cesare Borgia rise from the ground.

Oh, God. Fitzmorton was right. I've doomed us all.

"What do I do?" snapped Fitzmorton. "Donna! Carlo is down! How does this work?" He stood over the organ rack. "I think he loaded it!"

"The lever," she shouted, pointing. "Turn the rack and pull the lanyard!"

A musket barrel was thrust into the cabin, but Fitzmorton reached up and fired his pistol. There was a shriek, and the barrel vanished. The hull resounded under the blows of feet and rifle butts.

"Giovanna. Giovanna!" Her master. He was holding up a thick, braided fuse tied into his network of cords. More fuses. "The match! Light this. Quickly."

"What . . . ?"

"Do it!"

She grabbed the slow-match and the fuse caught. With agonizing slowness, it burned down to the others. They caught, and their burning ends crawled toward the edge of the hull.

Fitzmorton yanked the organ-lanyard, but fewer than half the barrels fired. Then light and a blessed breath of cool air as the rear ramp was hauled down. Fitzmorton yelled defiance and lunged backward, loosing his last pistol round. The first papal soldier fell with a hole through his nose.

And then the whole world shuddered with explosions. Gia saw stars.

When her vision returned, the world was quiet, except for the fading screams of men.

She looked down. Fitzmorton staggered up. Her master sat half-stunned on the springs. The car was moving forward again, slowly. "I take it they worked?" he asked, with a bemused smile.

"What were they?" Gia asked, dumbly. "Those jars. The ones you were working with . . . ?"

"We did have extra gunpowder," her master said. "And all this scrap iron around the place. I always thought you were too critical of my original idea to have guns all around the hull. So I made mines. And I was right."

She patted his hand. "You were indeed. We have broken Borgia's . . ." She peered out the window, at the running figures. *There.* Cesare Borgia. He was running, too. Limping.

"Master, push us forward. Turn twenty degrees starboard."

Fitzmorton stared at her. "What are you doing? We have no more weapons!"

"Oh, yes we do," said Gia, grimly. "All the power you've got." The tottering man swelled in her viewport. He turned just before they hit. The *tartaruga* shuddered to a halt.

"Giovanna? What have we hit?"

Gia ignored her master. Releasing the rope that bound her cart in place, she lowered it to the deck. With the strength of her arms, she forced the wheels forward. Down the ramp, out and around the blasted, dented hull of her war-car. Around to the front where Cesare Borgia lay pinned beneath its wheels.

He looked up. "Save me," he muttered. Then he knew her. "You." His face whitened in horror. "How can you be here? In battle?"

"You put me here," she whispered to him. "When you blinded Leonardo da Vinci to keep yourself safe from his weapons? You made *me*. And he and I? We made *this*."

She heard steps behind her. It was Fitzmorton. She looked back at him. "Is that my master's pistol, *Monsieur* Fitzmorton? Reloaded?"

"It is."

"May I borrow it?"

"It would be an honor, *donna*."

She took it from him and aimed. "A last gift from my master," she said, "who is a more merciful man than you."

Her shot cut off Borgia's scream.

Then she turned back to Fitzmorton. A thunder of hooves approached. "Are we quite lost?"

But he was smiling. "No, *donna*, I believe we are saved." Passing through the gunsmoke befogging the plain, riding under a French banner, was Machiavelli, accompanied by a squadron of cavalry.

"*Madame* Jeanne da Vinci," Fitzmorton said, "please be made known to Gaston de Foix, Duc de Nemours and commander of the armies of King Louis XII."

The young man dismounted, and to her astonishment, knelt. "I understand that I have you to thank for preserving the cities of Prato and Florence against the forces of"—he looked over at the corpse—"Borgia." At her shock, he smiled. "We of France are somewhat used to owing our salvation to unlikely young ladies of your name. One might even believe that our Lord"—he flicked his eyes heavenward—"was making sport of us."

Machiavelli was helping her master and Carlo out of the wreckage. "*Signior* da Vinci," he was saying, "along with *Signior* de Foix, you have saved Firenze and all of Italy this day. Had you not pressed your attack, we would have been crushed. A bitter victory, but sweeter than defeat."

Gia exchanged glances with Fitzmorton. "I . . . I nearly killed us all," she stammered.

"The difference between courage and foolishness is sometimes the breadth of a hair," he said.

"Indeed it is," said de Foix, looking over to where Machiavelli was still heaping praises on da Vinci, overriding her master's attempts to speak. "Don't worry, *Jeanne d'Architonnerre*. We will correct him in time. Accompany us back to Prato. Such a victory calls for a feast."

Gia gestured to her cart. "Sir, my cart will hardly take me all the way back to town."

"True enough," said de Foix, and before she knew what was happening, he had swept her up in his arms and was astride his horse with her. "Let me give you a better view, and while we ride, you shall tell me of the part you played."

As they rode back to Prato, Gia discovered that riding a horse between the arms of a dashing French officer was surprisingly easy to get used to.

Operation Dad Liberation

⊕

Lydia Sherrer and David Sherrer

"Okay, Nigel. We're doing this."

Holo Steele dropped into the command seat of the T52-Maggert hybrid urban tank and flipped on its ready switch.

"It is 0352 hours, young lady. You should be in bed," the tank's AI said, its tone somehow expressing displeasure despite its limited modulation range. "What are you doing in my unit, and, more importantly, where is your father?"

"Headed to Hell's Gate Penal Outpost."

"Captain Steele was assigned guard duty? Why was my command roster not updated?"

"Not as a guard, Nigel. As a *prisoner*," Holo gritted out, flipping more switches, then pausing to glare at the HUD readout of her dad's tank.

"Oh. That is unfortunate."

"No, duh, genius. His charges are sealed, all they told me was he was tried in an emergency court for treason. Which is stupid, because Dad is a die-hard loyalist. There's been some mistake, I'm positive. But no one who goes into that hellhole ever comes back. That's why we're gonna break him out."

" . . . apologies, Miss Steele, my auditory processing software must have malfunctioned. It just informed me you intend to break your father out of prison?"

"Yup!" Holo said, then folded herself in half and wiggled, trying

165

to reach behind the command console. "We're gonna intercept the penal transport."

"Ah ... I see."

Holo's lips twitched. She'd always liked talking to her dad's tank. It had what might, in very loose terms, be considered a sense of humor—something completely lacking in other Maggert units. Her dad blamed it on a software glitch, yet had never reported it or made the slightest effort to correct it. It'd made for many an enjoyable evening spent playing in the rear compartment of the tank's domed body while her dad performed maintenance in the cockpit. Of course, that'd been when she was much smaller, so everything had seemed bigger inside Nigel's hull. Now, at sixteen, she had filled out considerably and things were tighter.

As she maneuvered in the small space, her bulky coveralls caught on something. She withdrew, unzipped them to her navel, and tied the sleeves around her waist, then tried again. The skintight fabric of her standard-issue tank top slid past whatever had poked her before, and she could finally reach the rear panel of the console.

"How did you even get in the hangar?" Nigel demanded.

"Convinced the security system I was a food dispenser bot."

"You look nothing like a food dispenser."

Holo rolled her eyes. "Well spotted, Sherlock. That's why I brought a food dispenser bot with me. It's not my fault the security system is too trusting. Maybe it has a soft spot for food dispensers."

"Regardless, I regret to inform you that this inadvisable and entirely illegal course of action will not be possible as my governor circuit—"

"Got it!" Holo said triumphantly, though she couldn't punch her fist into the air since she was still folded like a pretzel, elbow deep in Nigel's hardware.

"Whiskey Tango Foxtrot," muttered Nigel, sounding just like her dad whenever she used to beat him at checkers. "Unhand my internal circuitry at once, Miss Holo, or I will be forced to— What is that in your hand?"

"Your governor circuit chip," Holo said brightly, squeezing her way over to the hatch.

"I—that—Get back here, young lady."

"This'll just take a sec," she assured the AI, then opened the hatch and peeked out to make sure the coast was clear and her accomplice was still sitting where she'd left it.

It was the work of a few furtive minutes, then she was back and sliding into the command seat, reaching for the tank commander's helmet on its rack above the command console. Behind it was the family photo her dad kept wedged there, old enough that her mother was still in it. The sight made her throat constrict.

"Do not put that helmet on, Miss Steele. Just because you have cut off central authority tracking and control does not mean you can override—What are you doing?"

"Overriding your deactivation status orders," Holo said, her fingers flying across the command console's input screen. "Dad isn't nearly as sneaky with his passwords as he thinks he is."

"How do you even—"

"Training manuals."

"Those training modules are only accessible by approved military personnel."

"Not the simulators, the paper ones."

"Paper?"

"Yeah, the ones from before. Some of the details are out of date, and the paper is getting moldy and faded, but they're still pretty interesting. I found a whole storage unit full of them after"—Holo swallowed—"after Mom died and Dad got me my apprentice janitor job so I wouldn't be shipped off to trade school."

"I see. And did any of your manuals cover the City-State of New Terminus' Unified Code of Military Regulations and Penal Justice?"

"Nope!" Holo said with a grin, and tapped the activation button for her new command line. "Now stop grousing and let's get out of here. We're on a deadline."

"This is most irregular—"

"Not listening—"

"Your father—"

"Still not listening—also, start your grav-lift generators already."

"Absolutely not. Your father will remove my safety protocols and make my grav capacitors melt me from the inside out if I let you get into trouble."

"I'll come to your funeral," she assured the AI, searching for the manual activation button, which had been moved from its original location listed in the manual she'd memorized. When she couldn't find it, she switched back to the input console and started typing more lines of code, hoping the command she was piecing together would compute.

"Tanks do not have funerals," Nigel pointed out.

"I'll throw you one, I promise . . . aaand you can stop griping, because I just assigned myself as your new tank commander."

There was a moment of charged silence.

"Nigel?"

"Why is that food dispenser bot over there shooting bags of Cheetos at me?"

"Oh, that's Larry. I modified his access port to make room for your larger governor circuit. He thinks he's a tank now."

"You did *what*?"

"Nobody will even know you're gone."

"Until they notice the highly aggressive food dispenser attempting to storm the access hatch."

"Nah, Larry's pretty chill. Now, will you *please* start your grav lift so we can get out of here and save Dad? If we don't hurry, we won't catch the transport before it arrives at the outpost and then I'll never be able to break him out."

More silence.

"These mission parameters you inputted are extremely vague—"

Holo clapped her hands over her mouth to muffle her screech of joy. "You'll help?"

"—and could you really not come up with a better mission designator than 'Operation Dad Liberation'? It ruins our operational security."

"Oh, it'll be fine, Mr. Grumpypants. You won't be filing any official logs anyway. So, we're gonna do this?"

As if in answer, the command helmet's HUD lit up and the exterior feeds appeared alongside scrolling status reports from the various tank systems.

"I will carry out my mission," Nigel said, sounding as stiff as an AI could be, "which, by the way, will *not* involve putting you in danger, so don't even think about trying anything stupid. Tank commander training requires hours of intensive simulation exercises. It cannot be learned from a pile of dusty manuals. So keep your sticky fingers to yourself and let me do the driving."

"Sounds good to me," Holo said, getting comfortable in the command seat, its memory pads molded over long use to her father's larger frame. "As long as I get my dad back, I don't care."

"Yes . . . we will discuss that *if* we manage to leave this facility in one piece. You may have given me orders to exit the hangar, but the security system will not be so complacent about letting an unauthorized T52-Maggert tank exit its area of responsibility."

Holo smirked and produced Larry's purloined governor circuit with a flourish. "That's why you won't *be* a tank. You'll be an innocent little food dispenser bot, going on a stroll."

"I cannot believe I agreed to this," Nigel stated in as gloomy a tone as it could manage.

"Oh, come on, it'll be fun," Holo chirped, and got to work.

The Waste was vast, filling up the miles of dead land between islands of artificial and mechanized life that humanity had fought tooth and nail to keep running. After the war destroyed eighty percent of life on Earth, those who remained had to carve out a new reality for themselves in the permanently changed landscape. At least, that's what the educational holographs said. But it'd happened so long ago most people didn't even care—well, except her mom. That was probably why they'd put Mrs. Steele in charge of record preservation. Growing up, Holo had watched more holographs than most kids even knew existed. Her mom had even given her a nickname, Holo Girl, because she was so obsessed with learning new things.

That had all ended when her mom had died and her dad had gotten reassigned to perimeter duty. The systems were older and technology clunkier than in the city interior, where the important people lived. To be fair, conditions were a lot harsher at the perimeter, with residual radiation and all the Waste's crazy weather blasting corrosive materials against the perimeter defenses. Maybe that's why there'd been a storage unit full of paper manuals at their facility, because paper didn't glitch out the way holograph players did when their components got corroded.

Whatever the reason, Holo had been happy to take what she could get.

Being on the perimeter had other benefits too. Instead of a dozen inner-city checkpoints to get past, all they had to do was convince the hangar security system to let them out, then roll across the deserted assembly yard to the massive walls surrounding the city. Their access gate, much smaller than the massive entry points for merchant convoys elsewhere, was built to keep things out, not in. Nobody in their right mind went outside the city unless they were in heavily fortified convoys. There was nothing out there but the skeletal bones of civilization and roving bands of bloodthirsty raiders. So, the security system was unfazed by a food dispenser requesting to be let out. A patrolman might have questioned it, but Holo knew the facility from top to bottom, including the patrolmen's routes and schedules. The howling wind whipping up massive clouds of dust over everything helped too.

Just to be safe, they ditched the bot's governor circuit as soon as they were out of sight of the city walls. Using the tank's infrared optics and hover-capable grav-lift system, Nigel was able to maneuver across the broken terrain while Holo pored over every map they had of the area.

"So, there's no working track direct from New Terminus to the outpost?" she asked.

"No. The old east-west track was destroyed when the Red Rift opened up along the southern end of the Blue Ridge Mountains. The surviving track goes southwest to the Columbus nexus, then northwest to the mines and the penal outpost."

"Okay. Since you're better at math, what's the average speed of an old smoke train, and can we beat it if we cut straight west?"

"Distance from New Terminus directly to the outpost is approximately one hundred and fifty miles, while the penal transport will have to travel over two hundred and fifty miles, with one stop to refuel and change tracks. Average speed—"

"Okay, okay, this isn't math class, Nigel, geez. Can you just tell me?"

"Yes, we can 'beat' it—"

"Whew, that's a relief—"

"—if I do not experience any malfunctions, we do not encounter any obstacles, and we do not slow for any reason, including fighting our way past the raider-controlled bridge over the Red Rift."

Nigel highlighted the location in Holo's helmet display.

"Uhhh, okay? We can do that, too, right? You blow them to kingdom come and I'll flip them the bird as we sail past?"

"You do remember from your 'manuals' that my railgun cannot be operated while the grav lift is engaged, correct? I do not have the energy capacity to run both simultaneously, therefore I must switch to quadruped mode to remain mobile while firing my railgun."

"Errr..."

"Depending on what kind of blockade the raiders have in place, I may be able to ram it, assuming it is sufficiently softened with grenade fire beforehand. There is also my Gatling gun for direct engagement, if necessary."

"Okay, that's good."

"But you will have to operate them."

"What? Why?"

"Because you removed my governor circuit that controls all automated access to my firing systems."

"Aw, crap," Holo groaned. "I forgot about that." She yanked the helmet off, grabbed a few tools from the maintenance compartment behind the command seat, and scrunched herself into the space behind the command console.

"I hope your manuals covered my weapons systems," Nigel said, switching to the cockpit speakers, "because without my governor circuit—"

"Nah, nah, I cah fiss dis," Holo said around the penlight between her teeth. After a bit more poking around, she hauled herself out and back into the command seat. "All I have to do is find the right adaptor to connect the two circuit ends and voilà! That will reconnect your automated access lines."

"And you have such an adaptor with you?"

"Well, no. But I bet there's one around here somewhere." She glared around the cockpit, one eye squinted and mouth scrunched to the side as she mentally shifted through dozens of systems manuals and tried to remember what nonessential piece of equipment might have the part she needed.

"You have approximately thirty minutes to find out, then I will need to give you a briefing to ensure you have the working knowledge to fire my weapons without killing yourself. If you are injured in any way, Captain Steele will—"

"Rip out your innards and leave you to the salvage crews?"

"Most likely."

"Don't worry about it. I'll fix it."

She did not, in fact, fix it.

"Ugh, I'm so close, Nigel! Just a few more minutes?"

"You have been stating that for ten minutes, Miss Steele. We are approximately fifteen minutes out from the Red Rift, and if you do not get your head out from behind my console and man my weapons, I might as well drive us directly into the rift. It would be a quicker death than what the raiders will do to us."

"Okay, okay, fine."

Holo stored her tools and the latest adaptor she'd been testing. Who knew there would be so many different kinds? But she was close, she was sure of it. She knew what to look for now.

Nigel's weapon systems, on the other hand . . .

She glanced nervously at the controls that folded up out of the console at Nigel's command.

"Are you sure about this? I know how this stuff works on paper, but I've never shot a weapon before. Will they be shooting back? What if I . . . I mean, what if I . . . k-kill someone?"

"Miss Steele, you hijacked a combat vehicle capable of firing rounds over three thousand kilometers per second that will shred anything in its path for miles. What did you expect?"

"I—I guess I didn't. Expect anything, I mean. I just . . . acted." She sniffed and rubbed her nose with the back of a grimy hand. "What else was I supposed to do? He's my dad . . ."

She fell silent, staring at her hands, and for a moment only the hum of the grav generator below and the howl of the wind outside was audible.

"Unfortunately, I do not have the proper software to answer existential questions. However, you may have guessed that Captain Steele does not conduct the monthly wipe and reset of my adaptive memory that maintenance protocol requires—"

"Ah-ha! So *that's* why you have a sense of humor."

"—therefore I can tell you from long observation that survival requires hard choices, and your father would be proud of you for being reluctant to make this one."

"Wh-what?" Holo said, head coming up.

"I have been assigned to your father for many years. He speaks of you frequently."

"He does?"

"Very frequently."

"Wow..."

"Too frequently."

"Yeah, yeah, okay. I get it."

"The question remains: Do you wish to rescue Captain Steele?"

Holo's expression hardened and she clenched her hands in her lap. "Yes."

"Then put your hands on the controls and pay attention."

Nobody knew what had caused the Red Rift, only that it had formed about at the same time as the war. There were stories of a weaponized seismic device, though others blamed the nuclear explosions. To Holo, it was simply one more hazard in a world that had been turned on its head, then hit with a few hundred megatons of explosives, just for kicks and giggles.

Holo had never set foot outside New Terminus, but she had watched every bit of footage on the Waste that she could find. So, she knew the story of the miles-long crack in the earth and the long-ago effort to bridge it, followed by the inevitable fighting over who controlled it. After it fell into raider hands during a particularly violent period of unrest, its structural integrity was thrown into doubt. Calls to recapture it withered and died as New Terminus' resources were shifted to securing the old rail lines instead. And so it sat, fought over by various raider groups and changing hands every couple of years. Nigel had no data on its condition, they only had the desperate hope that, if raiders were fighting over it, it was still passable.

"Eyes on the target, Miss Steele. And remember what I told you about rate of fire."

"Yeah, yeah, I remember," Holo muttered behind her command helmet visor. It was possible to monitor everything using HUDs on the main command console, but Nigel had decided the command helmet would work better for her because he could control what it showed and she was less likely to be distracted in a critical moment by superfluous readouts.

"You have checked that your safety harness is secure?" Nigel asked.

"Yes, *Mom*. It's as secure as it was the last three times you asked."

"You are not used to combat situations, Miss Steele. I am merely taking extra precautions to ensure all safety protocols are being followed. If you are injured, your father will—"

"Drop you in a vat of burning acid?"

"If he could acquire such a thing, I do not doubt he would attempt it."

"Well, it's secure, so you can stop worrying."

"I am not worrying, I am performing redundant safety checks."

"Redundant being the key word here," Holo muttered, eyes glued to her visor display.

Despite the harsh wind and low visibility, Holo still wished she could pop the hatch and look at the giant, black slash in the earth that they were approaching. There were no trees or structures to block the view, just dead earth, then blackness. The filtered and reconstructed infrared view in her visor didn't do it justice by far, even if it was much more useful in identifying signs of life.

They had little intel and few expectations about the raiders' defenses. What little information New Terminus maintained suggested there was an encampment on each side of the rift, though the encampments were constantly destroyed and rebuilt. So the good news was, whatever barriers the raiders might have erected should be easily destroyed by something as hefty as a T52-Maggert. The bad news was that the raiders were probably alert for attack, expecting it to come from rival groups.

Their only hope, then, lay in the element of surprise. If they stopped or got bogged down, they'd be swarmed by raiders. Fortunately, the darkness and wind effectively made them invisible. Even if their lookouts had stolen infrared optics, Nigel's infrared signature was shielded by its adaptive armor, so hopefully no one would spot them until the grenades started dropping. Nigel was confident they could take the near side by surprise and get onto the bridge. The problem would be with whatever lay on the other side, and how quickly the raiders could mobilize.

Holo resisted the urge to fidget as the distance to target counted down and shapes became visibly clustered around the black gash in the distance.

"I count three road barriers erected prior to the bridge. None of them appear to be permanent structures, simply burned-out vehicles piled with debris. The bridge itself is secured with a locked gate. Unfortunately, I do detect several guards at each barrier as well as several patrolling the gate."

Holo swore.

"Language, young lady. Captain Steele would not approve."

"He can disapprove all he wants, as long as he's alive," she shot back, gut twisting itself in knots as she tried to steady her hands.

"Select the three barriers as targets and prepare to fire, Miss Steele. Your targeting system will do the aiming, but the timing is up to you. Wait for my mark."

The T52-Maggert sped through the darkness at nearly sixty miles per hour, though Nigel would slow to about forty to actually ram the barriers. Holo's job was simply to press a button when Nigel told her, releasing each barrage of grenades to break up the barriers and trip any booby-traps.

Despite her coveralls being tied around her waist and the tank's cooling unit being turned up, she still felt sticky with nervous sweat.

"Prepare to launch the first barrage in ten, nine, eight . . ."

As Nigel counted down, Holo's fingers tightened on the weapons array, her eyes fixed on the gray shape of the first barrier in her sights. She tried not to think about the two bright orange figures on either side of it, huddled down at their guard posts.

"Fire."

Holo squeezed her trigger finger, and the night erupted in noise and fire.

"Second barrier targeted, prepare to fire."

She couldn't see anything even though the optics system did its best to filter out the raging static of heat from the blast. Fortunately, the targeting system already had the locations of the other two barriers locked in.

"Fire."

The tank vibrated this time from the blast's concussion, and a second later it jerked and shuddered as it made it through the first barrier with a screech of protesting metal.

"Third barrier targeted. Fire."

Seconds after the third round of grenades exploded and the

teeth-rattling *whump* of it had washed over her, she noticed an arrhythmic *ping-ping-ping*.

"Uh, what is that, Nigel?"

"We are under fire. Brace yourself, we're approaching the gate."

Holo just had time to tense before the view of the metal gate filled her visor and a screeching crash vibrated through her ears and bones.

They were through.

Darkness surrounded them on every side as the guideposts of the bridge whipped past one by one. Holo had a brief vision of herself hanging out Nigel's hatch, staring down into the abyss. Then Nigel's voice brought her back.

"Ready for rapid targeting and fire, Miss Steele. You will have seconds to clear the barriers once we ram the second gate on the far side of the bridge."

Holo swallowed, wiped her sweaty hands on her coveralls, and got ready. The *ping-ping-ping* of small-arms fire continued erratically, and she hoped her dad wouldn't strangle her for getting his beloved tank all marked up. She prayed that was the worst damage they got.

Almost immediately, her prayer was rejected.

"We're on their own godforsaken bridge! *Why are they lobbing grenades at us?!*"

"Raiders are not known for their intelligence, Miss Steele. Perhaps the opposite side is controlled by a faction less concerned with the integrity of the bridge."

The whole tank lurched as something exploded behind them, and Holo got the feeling they wouldn't be traveling back the same way they had come.

Then the far gate was in front of them and Holo barely had time to refocus before Nigel was giving rapid commands that she did her best to follow. She was pretty sure her grenades missed the barriers this time, because there were significantly larger lurches each time Nigel rammed one of them. But then they were through and the smoke and fire, screams, and rattle of old-style machine guns were behind them.

That is, at least, until a high-pitched whistling zipped overhead and an explosion in front of them made Nigel veer wildly off course.

"Grenade bolas," the AI said calmly while Holo's brain did a few incoherently screaming laps around her skull.

Another went whistling past and Holo switched to the rear view to see two ancient trucks roaring after them, their beds filled with angry raiders waving various weapons in their direction.

"Ooops."

"Do not be alarmed, Miss Steele. We will soon outpace them and draw out of range. In the meantime, switch to the Gatling gun controls and target the lead truck."

Holo's hands shook with adrenaline as she tried to remember the correct buttons and commands, but soon she had her targeting reticle up and locked. She hesitated, sure she could see faces on the glowing orange-and-red figures clinging to the trucks as they swerved and bumped after them.

Then she thought of her father, and pulled the trigger.

The rapid *rat-tat-tat-tat* of the Gatling gun filled her ears while the heat signature of the bullets left little streaks and explosions of color where they impacted. The trucks behind them started swerving in response, and Holo couldn't tell if she was actually hitting anything. Suddenly, the lead vehicle jerked violently to one side and hit some sort of obstacle that sent it spinning off into the darkness.

"Well done, Miss Steele."

The whistling of another bola grew louder and then an ominous *thump-clunk* sounded just behind the exterior hatch.

"What was that, Nigel?"

"It appears that an unexploded grenade bola has wrapped around my antenna array."

"*What?*" Holo yanked off her helmet and slapped the release for her safety restraint.

"Miss Steele, return to your seat this instant. We will not be harmed if it detonates."

"But your antenna will be disabled and we'll never rescue my dad!" Holo yelled as she scrambled out of the command chair, heading for the hatch.

"Do not open that hatch. It is most likely a dud and poses no danger. You could be hit by a stray bullet. Miss Steele—"

Holo was sure Nigel regretted the limited range of his voice modulator, because if the AI could have been screaming at her, it would have been.

She didn't have time to care.

In seconds she had the hatch open and was hanging halfway out, fingers tugging at the greasy chain wrapped around the tank's antenna array while dust, sand, and bullets whipped past. She could barely see, but her fingers told her the bola was only loosely caught on the array. If she could just—

A shot whizzed past her ear and another dinged off the tank's hull inches from her hand. Then the chain slid free beneath her grip and slithered off the smooth curve of the tank's hull. She dropped back down into the compartment, yanking the hatch closed after her. An explosion sounded behind them, but Holo was too busy coughing on dust and trying to rub sand out of her eyes to care.

"It is fortunate for you that tanks are incapable of heart attacks, young lady. Now get your posterior back in the command seat where it belongs. If this is what your father has to deal with every day..." the AI trailed off in a mutter.

Holo managed a few chuckles between coughs. "Nah... he's not around... enough to... worry about it."

"Well, then let us ensure he will be in the future. It seems your clinically insane and death-defying stunt has paid off. That grenade bola disabled the second truck, and we are now in the clear. Congratulations, Miss Steele. You have survived your first combat engagement. Captain Steele would be proud. Or horrified. I am unsure which."

Holo grabbed her water canister, then collapsed into the command chair, limbs shaking and eyes burning. She took a swig of water.

"Remind me to put on goggles next time," she croaked.

"There will be no next time."

Holo grinned. "Says you."

"I am confident Captain Steele will be in agreement."

"You're no fun."

"You can have fun after we retrieve Captain Steele and you are safely—and permanently—exiled from my unit."

"Awww, and here I thought you were starting to like me."

"Like a parasite."

"Now that's just insulting."

"Focus, Miss Steele, if you please. You still have my circuit to repair, and I must evaluate the damage and log an after-action report for Captain Steele."

"What? You're not going to tell him about me hanging out the hatch, are you? Because I deserve a medal for that, not a write-up."

"My after-action reports are thorough and precise."

Holo slapped her hands over her face and groaned. "He's going to kill me."

Nigel parked himself behind a pile of rubble several hundred yards from the railway. They were about thirty minutes ahead of the penal transport, and the outline of Hell's Gate Penal Outpost was visible in the distance via Nigel's infrared optics. The outpost was built to house the worst "criminals" of New Terminus, which conveniently included political opponents, social outcasts, and other undesirables that the ruling class of the city state wanted to disappear. The inmates were free labor for the Hell's Gate mine, the only significant source of iron ore on the entire continent outside the Great Lakes Conglomerate. Luckily for New Terminus, they were the only city-state close enough to exert control over the mine. The next closest, New Alamo, was too busy protecting its own resources to bother.

Its protections included a large perimeter wall with automated defenses and a gated checkpoint where the rail line entered, then another wall around the outpost itself. Since the rail line was the only reliable means of travel and supply for the outpost, the train itself was heavily outfitted with autocannons and protected by security bots that didn't mind the residual radiation of the Waste.

This was both good and bad, in Holo's opinion. Good, because she hated the thought of hurting any more people, and the guards would most certainly object to her breaking out one of their prisoners. Bad, because security bots were destructive in the extreme. She'd seen holographs of what they could do to desperate and foolhardy raiders.

"This plan is untenable. You have no sidearm and your father's combat harness armor is not adequate protection against security bots."

"I know, Nigel, but what choice do I have? Sure, you could blow up the tracks and stop the train, maybe even take out any bots that come after you. But we can't shoot the train and risk Dad getting hurt. Besides, he'll be in restraints. Unless I sneak on while you're creating a diversion, there's no way to get him out of there."

"Then we will find another way."

"There *is* no other way! Come on, we've been arguing about this since we crossed the Red Rift and you haven't come up with anything better."

"Captain Steele would never allow me to put you in danger—"

"Yes, yes, I know, you've said that a hundred times. But it doesn't matter—I don't matter, okay! N-not without him. He's all I have left, Nigel."

"You *do* matter, Miss Steele. You matter more to Captain Steele than anything else in the world, even his own life."

"That's a load of crap," Holo bit out. Her eyes were burning and she wished there was somewhere she could stomp off to. Somewhere to hide. But there wasn't, so she folded her arms across her chest and tucked her chin down so she didn't have to look at Nigel's displays. "He cares more about you and his career than he does about me. Ever since Mom died he hardly ever comes home. Even when he is home, he barely talks to me. He only smiles when he's around you, doing maintenance. Why do you think I was always sneaking on board? He's all I have left, and if I can't save him then I don't want to be left alone again. I . . . I can't take that."

"I see . . . While I am not equipped to analyze human mental or emotional states, I do know that Captain Steele regularly tells me how much he loves you."

Holo lifted her head and sniffed. "H-he does?"

"He has also stated that, the older you get, the more you look like your mother. One might conclude from this statement, combined with your description of his avoidant behavior, that the sight of you brings back painful memories. Perhaps he has not been the ideal parent. But if there is one thing I have ample evidence of, it is his love for you."

"Wh-what do you mean, 'evidence'?"

"Before every mission, Captain Steele records a short message for you, in case he does not return. He never deletes these messages and I believe they are the reason he avoids performing the required monthly memory wipe. I can play his most recent one for you, if you wish."

Holo nodded mutely, then watched, wide-eyed, as her father's face appeared in front of her on the command console's main display. The sight of his square jaw, slightly crooked nose, and warm brown eyes made her tear up all over again.

"Hi, sweetie. I . . ." He paused, grimaced, and ran a hand over his buzz cut. "I don't have much time. There's so much I want to say, but . . . Well, I love you is the most important, so I'll say that first. I love you so much. And I'm sorry I haven't spent more time with you. I know I missed dinner again last night, but I had to have a . . . a talk with Captain Roffman. I'm really worried about him. I think he's mixed up in some bad stuff, but we've worked together for years and I'm just not ready to abandon him, so I . . ." Another pause and massive sigh. "Well, maybe it was foolish but I confronted him and now I'm not sure where we stand. He seemed receptive, but . . . I just don't know. That's why I didn't come home last night. I know it doesn't make up for all the times I've been away, but I promise as soon as our protective detail is over, the first thing I'll do is take you out for noodles, okay? Remember how much we used to love doing that with . . . with Mom?" The captain choked up and looked away from the camera. When he looked back, his eyes were glistening. "I love you, Holo Girl, and I'll see you soon."

There was a long silence after the image of Captain Steele disappeared.

"Miss Steele?"

"I-I'm fine, Nigel."

"The state of your face would suggest otherwise, at least by human standards."

"Oh, shut up."

"So, you see, your father does care, and that is why—"

"Wait!"

"—yes?"

"What's going on with Captain Roffman? He's that tall blond guy I see Dad with sometimes, right?"

"Yes, he is the leader of Captain Steele's squad."

"What is Roffman mixed up in? Surely you know, right?"

"I am sorry, Miss Steele, but Captain Steele never spoke of it within my sensor range."

"Okay, but what if . . . He said he confronted Roffman about something, and the next day he's accused of treason and rushed through an emergency trial? If that doesn't stink I don't know what does. What was Dad's mission? What happened that day?"

"He was assigned escort duty to the trade delegation from the Great Lakes Conglomerate. His squad was ordered to exit the city and meet the convoy at the border of our area of control, then accompany them into the city."

"Okay, so what happened?"

". . . Apologies, Miss Steele, but I seem to have encountered an error."

Holo leaned forward, desperation building in her chest. "What do you mean, 'an error'?"

"I mean my logs of that particular day have been wiped. I cannot access them."

The teen's eyes narrowed. "Can't access them, huh? Not if I have anything to do about it." She scrubbed her eyes with the back of a hand, dried it on her coveralls, then brought up the command console input and got to work. If there was one thing she'd learned in all those dusty manuals, it was that data was never as gone as you wanted it to be. Whoever had mucked about in Nigel's logs had erased roughly half a day, from the start of her father's mission to when the unit was returned to the hangar. What they'd failed to realize was that deleting data did not remove it from the hard drive, it only removed the point of access. Data wasn't gone until it was overwritten. So, all she had to do was run a re-indexing protocol to find and reestablish access to the data.

"Done!" Holo threw her hands in the air, grinning like a maniac. She tasted hope, and it was sweet. "Take a look now. Time's ticking, so can you just review the logs super-duper fast and tell me what happened?"

"I have already done so while you were speaking, Miss Steele. It appears your father witnessed an assassination attempt on the visiting delegates and was accused of perpetrating the attack."

"Whaaat? That's insane! He didn't do it, right?"

"Certainly not. I did not fire a single shot. But the unit next to me did."

Holo gasped, eyes widening. "Roffman! It was Roffman, wasn't it?"

"My external optics and sensors have irrefutable data that his unit was the one who fired the shot."

"No wonder Roffman had you shut down and wiped your logs. I'm gonna get that piece of slime," Holo growled.

"Might I remind you that you still do not have a sidearm? You will not be 'getting' anyone. Besides, we have all the evidence we need to exonerate your father. We can simply present the data to the outpost warden and—"

"Are you kidding me? He won't listen to us. We have to break my dad out before they put him in that hellhole, *then* we can worry about uncovering Roffman's conspiracy. And I don't need a sidearm. A good-sized spanner to the balls will 'get' anyone, no matter how big of a gun they have."

"Slow down, young lady. You will defeat no one with a piece of maintenance equipment. We have very little time, so here is what we are going to do..."

As Nigel began to explain, he was already moving toward the train tracks at top speed, racing to reach the automated checkpoint before the prison transport came within sight.

The AI's plan wasn't as exciting as blowing up train tracks or shooting security bots with a railgun, but it had a much higher probability of getting all three of them out alive, so Holo agreed to it.

They reached the checkpoint with barely fifteen minutes to spare and got right to work.

Though Captain Steele had been stripped of his security clearances, no one had bothered downgrading his unit's access because, of course, units did not act independently of their commanders. Thus, the checkpoint's automated security system didn't bat an eye at the query to access its command hub by one of New Terminus' official patrol units. Patrols didn't usually range so far out, but New Terminus had good reason to want all equipment connected to the penal outpost accessible by its own security units.

What Holo had to do next, though, required physical access. So, outfitted in her dad's too-large combat gear and command helmet, she scrambled out of her tank's hatch. Nigel had parked by the checkpoint station, and she popped up the ladder to the command hub's door. The security system obligingly let her in, and it was the work of moments to plug her command helmet into its hub's network using a standard adaptor cable from her dad's maintenance kit.

Once the helmet was plugged in, Nigel had access to the entire system.

Holo watched over Nigel's virtual shoulder as they checked the penal transport manifest and noted her dad's location on the transport. She gasped in surprise and pointed out another familiar name to Nigel, and they upgraded their plan accordingly. Then Nigel added a routine inspection to the transport's schedule, using the security system's authorization code. Finally, Nigel hopped onto the station's long-distance antenna to connect to New Terminus' record system, since the tank's own signal wasn't strong enough to make it through the clouds of dust and sand.

The funny thing about virtual systems was that there were always bits and pieces of programming that survived the updates and redesigns. Holo was able to use a command backdoor from one of her manuals, a backdoor that had been lost and forgotten in the chaos of humanity's scramble to preserve as much of the prewar system as possible. Soon she had Nigel in the city-state's penal records. He updated the necessary files while she covered his tracks in the system logs. She barely had time to back out of the system, unplug her helmet, and get into place on the inspection platform before the penal transport came into sight. The platform stood a few dozen yards from the massive armored and spiked gate blocking the tracks. It wouldn't open until the inspection was complete and logged with the automated security system.

Sweat was gathering on her forehead and, well, everywhere else as Holo stood on the platform, trying not to shiver with nerves.

"Stand up straight, Miss Steele," said Nigel's voice in her helmet. The tank's optics could see her clearly from where it was parked, grav lift shut down and quadrapeds deployed, just in case the rail gun was needed. "You look like a whipped dog, cowering like that, and are making me reconsider the wisdom of allowing you outside my hull. You must at least *try* to appear competent and in charge, otherwise you will be shot and I will be melted into scrap."

"Hey! You try standing up here in the wind and the dark with only a blacked-out helmet visor between you and discovery, followed by certain death. I'm a janitor, not a soldier."

"Well, you are the smartest, bravest, most resourceful janitor I have ever met."

"Did you just compliment me? Who are you and what have you done with Nigel?"

"Apologies, Miss Steele. I was attempting to use Captain Steele's past words to bolster your resolve."

"Oh . . . does my dad really say those things about me?"

But Nigel didn't answer because the penal transport was completing its approach, its front lights blinding as it slowed and finally halted with its lead car in front of the platform. The train consisted of only the engine and three cars: security, prisoner transport, and supply storage in the rear. The entire transport was heavily reinforced with armor plating and the top and sides bristled with weaponry.

At her entry query, the door to the lead car opened and she hurried in before she could second-guess herself. Their plan would work, or it wouldn't. Either way, she had to try.

Inside, the car was sparse and utilitarian, with a central console housing the command hub and power capsules for the security system, a rack of weapons and security supplies on the far wall, and a row of fold-down seats for guards and civilian passengers along the wall to her right. The seats were empty but for one disturbingly familiar man in a similar combat suit to hers. He rose as she entered, a confused scowl on his face, but she ignored him, turning instead to the security bot standing at attention by the door. It demanded her credentials and authorization in the flat, mechanical tone ubiquitous to security bots, while a second and third bot looked on from their post on either side of the door to the train engine. Half a dozen more bots stood at attention in front of the weapons rack, silent and immobile until something triggered their mission parameters of guarding the train and its cargo.

"There's been a change in manifest orders," she said gruffly to the bot, pitching her voice as low as she could. "Send an update request and check it against your current roster." She didn't expect the bot to obey her, but all she had to do was delay long enough for her tank's AI to connect wirelessly to the bot's AI and push the universal update command that forced any unit to do a scan for soft updates to its system. Any moment, now, it would start an information download, and then—

"Hey, who are you and what are you doing?" said an angry voice behind her. "There was no inspection stop scheduled for this transport. This is a special prisoner delivery with orders to report directly to the warden."

Holo didn't reply. It was all she could do not to bounce on the balls of her feet as nervous adrenaline coursed through her body.

Come on . . . come on . . .

"Command received, update commencing." Nigel's voice in her ear sent a shock of sweet relief through her, but they weren't in the clear yet.

"Hey! I'm talking to you, soldier! What is your designation? Who do you report to?" The angry words got closer accompanied by the stomp of boots.

"Download, fifty precent complete," Nigel said.

Holo tightened her grip, muscles tense and at the ready.

A large hand gripped her shoulder and spun her around, and she came face-to-face with Captain Roffman.

"Download, seventy-five percent complete."

The man's brow furrowed as he took in her blacked-out visor and ill-fitting uniform, then his eyes dropped to her shoulder, and they widened in alarm.

Oops. She'd forgotten to cover her dad's name patch.

"This is for my dad, you slimeball," Holo hissed, acting before Roffman could draw his sidearm. She swung the large spanner she'd been hiding against her baggy pants up toward his groin with as much righteous fury as she could manage. It connected with a satisfying thud, and Holo grinned inside her helmet as Captain Roffman's eyes rolled up in the back of his head and he slowly keeled to the side, crumpling with a groan.

"Download complete," Nigel informed her.

"Freeze, detainee," intoned the security bot rather unnecessarily as it honed in on the man whose biometric information had just replaced her dad's in the bot's prisoner profile. "Do not attempt escape, or you will be fired upon."

Holo shuffled hastily out of the bot's way, but couldn't resist a parting whisper-shout to the unfortunate Roffman on the ground. "That's what you get for being stupid enough to personally deliver the guy you framed."

She watched with silent glee as the bot mechanically flipped the groaning captain over, cuffed his hands behind his back, and hauled him to his feet. Of course, Roffman's legs weren't exactly working, so the bot ended up dragging its captive down the length of the car, heading for the prisoner transport. Holo followed silently, almost tiptoeing as she tried to make herself as small and innocent-looking as possible. The other bots ignored her, since her presence fell outside their mission parameters, and unless she did something aggressive or against regulation to catch the first bot's attention, it wouldn't mind little ol' her . . .

Heart in her throat, Holo followed the bot to the next compartment. She nearly sobbed in relief to see her father, clad in convict gray, slumped over in his seat with head drooping and hands manacled behind him to a solid steel bar. At their entrance, his head came up and his bleary eyes focused on them. They widened, but Holo frantically shook her head in warning, hoping her dad wouldn't say anything. Two more bots stood on either side of the lone prisoner, and they angled their heads toward the entering bot, probably communicating on their own private channel.

"Citizen Steele, you are free to go," said the bot holding a limp Roffman. "Please exit the transport immediately." It triggered the release of her dad's cuffs and barely gave him enough time to scramble out of the seat before hauling the still-groaning Roffman into it and manacling him in place. The door to the car slid open, presumably at the bot's command, and Holo scrambled to her dad's side, helping him up and to the car door before the bot changed its mind. It was a good six feet to the dusty ground outside, but Holo didn't care. She couldn't scramble out fast enough. Before she knew it both her and her dad were lying in the dirt with the transport's door closing above them.

"Holo? What? How?"

"Not now, Dad! Let's get out of here!"

She hauled him to his feet and they made a dash for Nigel's protective hull as metal groaned and the railway security gate over the tracks slowly started to open.

The moment Holo pulled the hatch shut behind her, Nigel engaged its grav lift and they were on the move.

"Nigel, what in the nine circles of hell is going on?" Captain Steele demanded as he braced himself against the tank's swaying movement.

"Apologies, Captain Steele. I was hijacked."

"You were *what*?"

"Don't yell at Nigel, Dad. I kidnapped him and forced him to go along."

"Kidnapped? Nigel, full status report, now!"

"Ah, yes, about that, Captain Steele. Unfortunately, my tank commander would need to authorize that order for me to comply."

"Oh, yeah, and I made myself his tank commander."

"*You what?*"

"And the raider damage is totally not my fault. It was Nigel's idea to ram through their barricades."

"*Raiders?!*"

"Calm down, Dad. I'm safe, you're safe, we're all safe. Let's just get you back to New Terminus and clear your name, and then you can yell at me all you want, okay?"

The captain's head swiveled back and forth as he glared at Holo and his tank's command console in turn.

"If it makes you feel any better, Captain Steele, Miss Steele has just successfully completed her first combat mission, designated Operation Dad Liberation. I have graded her performance along standard evaluation parameters and her average score falls within a qualified rating. In fact, she scored higher on initiative and ingenuity under fire than you did in your last evaluation."

For a moment there was only silence.

Then Captain Steele started laughing. His disbelieving barks quickly intensified until he was laughing so hard he had to grab the edge of the command chair for support—which was about when his hiccuping sobs started. Before Holo knew what was happening, her dad had wrapped a strong arm around her shoulders and pulled her into a desperate hug as he laughed and sobbed over her. It wasn't long before she was laughing and crying, too, face pressed against his chest and both arms clutching him like she would never let go.

And maybe, this time, she wouldn't. After all, she was the tank commander, now.

"Come on, Nigel. Let's go home," she said, her words muffled against her dad's gray coveralls.

"With pleasure, Tank Commander."

"I'm never going to live this down, am I?" asked Captain Steele, his voice thick with emotion.

"—nope."

"—I am afraid not, sir."

"Well, as long as I have my Holo Girl to hold it over my head, then I don't care."

"Good, because I plan to guilt-trip you with it until you're old and wrinkly. Just think how many noodle dinners I'll get out of this!"

Captain Steele groaned, but there was a smile on his face and joy in his eyes as he did.

Between a Knight and a Hard Place

⊕

Philip Wohlrab

The sky was alive with sheets of orange lighting, particularly in the northwest, but occasionally branching farther south and east. Sister Mary Catherine de Buenaventura watched the fiery sky with equal parts awe and dread. Awe for the sheer beauty and dread for what it presaged. The seasons were never quite right after the Great Global War, and the fields were not ready for harvest.

"God, give these people one more week of good weather. In your infinite mercy allow this harvest to come to its full fruition. Amen."

The prayer was barely off her lips when she heard a squeal from a girl emerging from the wheat field. The wheat had obscured the child's view. She had not seen the sister sitting comfortably in her commander's cupola. The girl's initial cry of alarm turned to delight as she recognized a woman sitting atop the armored vehicle. Sister Mary Catherine watched the girl run up the low rise to her tank.

"What are you doing in there?" the girl asked.

"Well, this is my tank, and this is where I sit in it. What is your name?"

The girl's bright blue eyes grew wider as she stared up at the sister. Behind her a mature voice called out.

"Victoria, where have you gone? It's time to wash up for dinner." A woman emerged from the wheat field where the girl had come from. She too glanced up at Mary Catherine and then quickly crossed to the child. She reached out, taking hold of the girl, and began to guide her toward a big Mission house that was a short distance away. "Don't bother the sister, Victoria. Come along."

Mary Catherine chuckled to herself at the small byplay and then turned her gaze back to the distance. The smell of the wheat field was fading, to be replaced by the ozone tang of the coming storm. *Yes, this is a place worth defending.*

High Priestess Mahphion smiled in anticipation of the night's coming pleasures. She stood behind a great stone altar with her retinue of priestesses and priests. Mahphion gazed at five young girls dancing inside a large chalk ring. The girls wore nothing, though four of them were covered from head to toe in blue paint with a grimacing skull detailed onto their faces. The fifth girl was decorated in red body paint with golden symbols and runes covering her chest and belly. They danced, unaware of their surroundings and in rhythm to the drums.

Mahphion was tall and lithe, her face covered by a porcelain mask that once would have been called Venetian. Half black and half white, the mask was inlaid with colorful jewels and capped by an elaborate headdress. It was simultaneously beautiful and grotesque, just as Mahphion herself was.

Her priestesses were similarly adorned, though less elaborately while two priests to either side were stripped to the waist and wore only a loincloth and plague mask. Unlike Mahphion, who stood rigidly, these priests and priestesses swayed to the drums. Swirling in the breeze around them was a heady scent of incense and roasting meats.

Four large bonfires surrounded the altar aligning to the cardinal points on the compass. Around each, Mahphion's followers danced and reveled. The sky was alive with the light from the fires and the orange bolts of lightning. An occasional slash would strike the ground with a great peal of thunder but the revelers didn't care, intoxicated as they were on the festivities.

"The gods old and new are watching," rasped Mahphion. Firelight cast a sheen across a jagged scar over her throat. "They take notice of us and these coming sacrifices. The omens and portents are so very good."

At her side her favorite daughter and priestess nodded and said, "It is time."

Analise lifted her heavy ritual dagger up, signaling the other three priestesses who then moved forward to catch the blue painted girls. Once done they guided each to a large scaffold erected in line with the western bonfire. Four men expertly hung the girls upside down so that they dangled waist height off the ground. The priestesses then placed a large clay bowl under each respective girl.

"Oh, great and terrible gods, look! Look here now, I beseech thee! I offer these sacrifices as tribute. Grant us your favors and deliver us victory in our next conquest!"

After Mahphion's invocation she signaled to her four priestesses, who in turn slashed the throat of their sacrifices. Blood poured from the terrible wounds down into the clay bowls and the girls' bodies shook with their death throes, but none of them had cried out. The last girl, painted red, continued to dance in her circle, seemingly oblivious to the butchery just a few short paces away.

Mahphion moved to the final girl's side and guided her to the altar, gently laying her upon it. The girl's eyes gazed into the spirit world. They never fixated on the high priestess. Mahphion raised her ceremonial dagger, calling on the gods again to grant her victory. The crowd roared their approvals at the deaths and brayed for further blood. Mahphion smiled and felt alive with the power of the gods. She slammed her dagger down into the girl's throat. The sacrifice arched her back as the knife was driven home. She emitted a gurgling sound from the gaping wound.

Mahphion waited until the blood stopped spraying from the dying girl's throat. She then expertly used the knife to open the torso. She quickly extracted the heart and liver from the corpse and placed each into a bowl. The other priestesses rejoined her at the altar and began to implore the gods for victory while Mahphion took up the girl's heart. She carefully examined it, looking for any defect in shape or tone. Seeing none, she smiled behind her mask, for that too was a good omen. Stepping back from the altar, she held the heart aloft for all to see and turned to one of the fires near the altar. The high priestess threw the heart into the flames.

The warband went wild with cruel delight. At each of the bonfires a pole was lifted over the flames. On top of the pole was a screaming victim taken from their last raid, and now consigned to the fires as additional sacrifices. The shrieks of horror and pain were quickly drowned out by the cheering warband.

Mahphion took up the last bowl containing the liver. According to the gods old and new this was the organ that housed the spirit. Mahphion lifted the liver from the bowl and carefully examined it. Turning the organ over in her hands she found ... *something*. Hissing, she investigated further. Within the fatty liver tissue, she found a black tumor the size of a golf ball. Screaming in rage, she cast the liver aside. Mahphion seized up her dagger and immediately turned to Analise. She plunged the dagger into her daughter's chest. The warband knew something was wrong and gave out a great, despairing cry.

"Gods and goddesses, forgive me! I give to you my own daughter in recompense for this great shame. Forgive this unworthy offering!" screamed out Mahphion.

Analise fell to the ground, twitching. She did not die well. Thunder split the sky, accompanied by a great slash of blue lightning, so very different from the orange that had previously lit the night.

The village of El Haza wasn't big. Mary Catherine lifted herself up in the commander's hatch to scan around the village main square. Her tank wasn't very large, a mere twelve tons combat loaded. It was based on a much older design yet still retained the Scorpion name, though now it had a better gun with superior armor protection. Despite the relatively small size of the tank, it still seemed to crowd the central plaza of El Haza. The villagers opened shuttered windows to look out at the procession of tanks and infantrymen in their trucks. Many crossed themselves while a few slammed their shutters shut.

Did they think there would be more of us? wondered Mary Catherine.

El Haza wasn't far from the Mission of San Felipe de Jesus and was an outlier settlement in the north. It was a poor village that eked out a living by ranching on the grazing lands that surrounded it. Still, its tenants were faithful to the church and when they had requested help, the Archbishopric of Turcoya had sent aid. That aid was Sister Mary Catherine's twelve tanks and Knight Companion Nicolais's company of Hospitaller riflemen.

But what does the enemy bring? Tanks would be rare for a warband though not unheard of. Most likely raiders in trucks or even horseback. But what are their numbers? How well equipped are they? The only news has been that they are fierce and leave few survivors to flee ahead of them.

"Driver, bring us to a halt just past the fountain."

"Yes, ma'am," answered Novitiate Daphne.

"Gella, keep an eye out while I go talk to the village leaders." This was said to Sister Gella deVere, the tank's gunner.

Once the tank stopped Mary Catherine climbed down and headed toward a small group of men clustered at the entrance of the village chapel. In addition to an old priest, the sister could see three other older men, all looking sick with worry. As she approached them, she could tell they were not reassured. Instead, they looked confused at seeing a woman wearing a habit and tanker coveralls.

"Father, gentlemen." Mary Catherine nodded to them politely. "I am Sister Captain de Buenaventura of the Sisters of Saint Anastasia. I have been sent here to render aid along with Knight Companion Nicolais of the Hospitallers." Here she nodded toward the infantry commander as he walked up to the group removing his helmet. He was dressed in the black battle garb of the Knights Hospitallers.

"Surely you have brought more troops than this!" exclaimed one of the village headmen. He was old and, though animated in his dismay, he was clearly frail.

"I am sorry, sir. We are who the Archbishopric had to send. Do you have a local militia?" asked Mary Catherine.

"A few of us form a town watch but, Sister—we would not be much help against what is coming. We lack anything heavier than some old bolt action rifles and locally made muzzle loaders." The speaker appeared to be in his mid-fifties with the look of someone who had spent a life doing hard manual labor. "My name is Rodrigo Montoya, and I am the *alcalde* of El Haza. This is Father Diego, *Señor* Mendoza and *Señor* Williams," Rodrigo said, indicating each man in turn.

"It is a pleasure to meet you, Alcalde. I wish it were under other circumstances."

"Thank you, Sister. We do not mean to be rude, but we did expect a larger force." As the man spoke, his left eye twitched in apparent nervousness. "You see, we understand from the survivors from across the Rio Mattashaw, the great river north of us, that there is a very large warband numbering in the thousands. They are pagans of the worst kind."

"I understand your concern. Do you have any information on what this warband is equipped with?" asked Mary Catherine.

"There are only a handful of survivors and most of them fled before they could really see much other than fire and destruction in the distance. One person did report vehicles, but they didn't see much."

"What is the lay of the land here? Are there any naturally defensible areas, difficult terrain, or the like between your village and the river?" asked Nicolais.

"Some low ridges, Brother, but mostly this is open country between us and the river, which is some twenty miles to the north."

"Alcalde, prepare to move the townspeople back to the Mission at San Felipe," said Mary Catherine.

"I . . . as you wish it, Sister. I understand, but it is so very hard to think we must abandon this place, our homes."

With this the group broke up. Nicolais and Mary Catherine walked to the northern edge of the village to gauge the land beyond it.

"There is a promising low ridge there for my tanks to go hull down and make some improvised fighting positions, but if these people truly have heavy weapons my twelve tanks won't be enough."

Nicolais sighed heavily as he, too, glanced at the ridgeline. "I am afraid you're right, Sister. My only real hope for defending this place is that the survivors didn't have accurate numbers or misperceived what they saw."

Mahphion sat upon her throne on top of the "tank" known as *Monster*. The vehicle had started life in the distant past as a dump truck for a city that had once been known as Colorado Springs. Everything other than the engine and chassis had been removed over the years and, through a series of warlords, *Monster* had grown into what it was today.

The vehicle was twenty feet long, and nearly as tall. Its broad wheelbase and weight gave *Monster* stability over difficult terrain.

Heavy armor plates had been welded over the chassis, making an improvised fighting compartment behind the driver's station. The fighting compartment had four positions to each side a rifleman could fire from. On top of the compartment and over the driver's station a 106mm recoilless rifle was mounted.

Behind this was Mahphion's throne. Her elaborate seat of power was decorated with various human and animal skulls along with fetishes to individual gods or goddesses. The whole thing was painted in a riotous palette of colors to include blues, greens, yellows, and reds.

Mahphion's new second priestess, Skofiv, leaned into her ear. "My Lady, the Master of the Riders reports his vehicles are ready. The First Spears report they are prepared for the assault."

"Good. We won't bother with the mortars or rockets. Order our battlewagons forward and we will take this village as we have done previously—with speed and violence. Save the heavy weapons for the true prize, the Catolics behind the walls," Mahphion ordered. Liquid brown eyes burning with fury, she leaped to her feet. Extending her arms above her head, she began pumping them up and down. Around her, the roar of diesel engines and the shouts of hundreds of voices rose to the heavens as one. Forty-five vehicles of different types, most old pickup trucks, surged toward the village of El Haza.

The leading trucks got to just over a mile away from the ridge when twelve puffs of flame and smoke shot out from the ridge. Three of the vehicles exploded outright while another slewed to a stop, its crew killed by fragments. Green and orange tracers danced out from the ridgeline, walking toward one of the armored trucks and spalling off its armor. In response every vehicle in Mahphion's warband opened fire with a mixture of machine guns, recoilless rifles, and autocannons. Most of the gunfire was wildly inaccurate, but the defenders on the ridge seemed to pause in their shooting for a moment.

"This is far heavier resistance than we expected, My Lady. Could the Catolics have had time to get help?"

"Hmmm . . . they must have, but no matter. If the help is here, it probably means their big farmstead is undefended. Have the gunners use a round of rockets and a couple of mortars on the ridge, then order the Spears forward."

Skofiv stood up behind Mahphion and took a red and a white flag up in her hands, then began to move them in a precise way to a signalman who was back with the mortars and rocket launchers. The signalman responded and a minute later four rocket batteries each launched a dozen 82mm rockets toward the distant ridge. Within another minute a score of 81mm mortars threw their bombs at the distant ridge as well.

WHAM! WHAM! WHAM! WHAM! WHAM!

"What in the hell was that?" shouted Gella from her gunner's station. The tank rocked from the force of the explosions around it. Through her headset Mary Catherine could hear the startled cries of the other tank crews. One of the voices rose into a bloodcurdling scream that abruptly cut off. Scanning through her commander's periscope, Mary Catherine could see one of her Scorpions was smoking. Hatches suddenly blew open with great gouts of flame as the rounds in the turret cooked off. Fire and smoke also poured from the 76mm gun tube. She knew that no one would have escaped that conflagration.

"May the Lord bless and keep you, Sister Helen, and your crew." Mary Catherine whispered the prayer while turning her attention back to the view in front of her vehicle. "Gunner, technical, six hundred meters!"

"Acquired," responded Gella.

"FIRE!"

"ON THE WAY!"

The low-velocity 76mm gun on the Scorpion wasn't as powerful as a battle tank's main gun, but it still caused the little tank to rock back on its suspension. As the shell casing ejected from the breech of the gun, Mary Catherine reached back and fed another high-explosive shell into the breech. The stink of cordite filled the turret, cloying in Mary Catherine's and Gella's noses. Gella scanned through her day sights, looking to see if the target was destroyed. Disappointed at seeing it still moving, she reacquired and fired a second time without needing a command to do so. This time the HE round found its mark. The pickup truck tore apart, shredding the heavy machine gun crew and incinerating the driver.

Mary Catherine noted the destruction but didn't dwell on it. Not only did she assist in fighting her own tank, but ensured her ten remaining tanks were doing their parts as well. She watched as one of the Hospitaller heavy weapons teams shouldered a recoilless gun and fired a high-explosive squash head, or HESH, round at one of the more heavily armored technicals bounding toward them. The round was briefly visible as it exited the gun tube before streaking toward the enemy vehicle, only to bounce off the front glacis. The technical must have spotted the flash of the weapon. It turned a pair of 23mm cannons on the heavy weapons team, who quickly dissolved into a welter of gore under repeated impacts from the cannon rounds.

"Daphne, displace left fifty meters."

"Yes, ma'am." Daphne's voice sounded muffled through the headset. The diesel engine that powered the Scorpion tank sat to the right of the driver's compartment and could sometimes overpower the mic on her headset. The Scorpion jerked backward, causing Mary Catherine to bang her helmet on the hatch coaming. She was distracted by the sight of ten eighteen-wheelers chugging to a stop about five hundred meters from the ridge. The cab of the first one exploded from tank fire, but the armored trailer survived. To Mary Catherine's horror, the back doors opened and scores of armed individuals boiled out of each trailer. They fanned out to either side of the trucks before dropping to the ground and bringing fire on the ridge.

"Gunner, infantry in the open, six hundred meters."

"Acquired."

"FIRE!"

"ON THE WAY!"

The little Scorpion bucked again and another HE round spat downrange toward a group of fighters who were just a little bit too clustered. The shell burst among the group, tossing them like rag dolls through the air. Mary Catherine slammed another into the breech before turning back to her periscopes. She saw another of her tanks get hit with autocannon fire, shredding the front glacis of the tank before walking up it into the turret and punching visible holes into it. The commander's hatch was thrown open and she observed Sister Ellen pop out of the hatch, missing her right arm from the elbow down. The sister fell out of the hatch, hitting the ground hard.

No one else emerged from the tank. Smoke poured through the hatch, followed by the first hint of flames. A Hospitaller trooper ran to the fallen nun and applied a tourniquet to the mangled arm. He then pulled the sister to cover.

"Gunner, independent fire."

"Roger, ma'am."

The tank rocked back again and the technical that had destroyed Sister Ellen's tank blew apart. The heretical fighters to the front of the Scorpion jumped up in groups of two or three in bounding rushes while the rest of them provided cover fire. Here the Hospitallers, with their light and medium machine guns, were able to do some work, bowling several knots over with accurate fire. A pair of 60mm mortar bombs fell beside the middle eighteen-wheeler, causing it to catch fire and killing several fighters near it.

"Sister Mary Catherine, this is Nicolais. We are not going to be able to hold this ridge much longer as the enemy is flanking us to our right and left. I suggest we withdraw to the Mission at San Felipe."

Nicolais's voice wasn't rushed, and despite the gravity of their predicament he was calm.

"I concur. Have your troops bound back to their vehicles while we cover your withdrawal. We will rendezvous south of El Haza and move back to the Mission."

Mahphion sensed the change in fire from the ridgeline, noticing less and less small-arms fire. Her own vehicle was still too far back for the recoilless rifle to be effective, though it fired a desultory shot toward the ridge. To her front she could see thirteen of her battlewagons either on fire or out of commission. She debated with herself whether she should order another round of rockets to fire at the ridge but decided against it.

After all, they are so damn hard to make, and we haven't visited the Makers and Shapers in a while. After the Catolics are destroyed, I will have to rectify it. We need more weapons to keep the supplying the war band, and we will need more fuel soon, she rationalized.

"My Lady, it appears the enemy is disengaging. Should I order our reserves forward?" Skofiv asked. Mahphion turned to Skofiv, considering her suggestion for a moment.

"No . . . no, I think we shall hold off. We do have this village to plunder, and the Catolics were too weak to stop us. If they stand and fight at their great farmstead, we will kill them and give them to our gods there. If they run, then we don't have to waste the ammunition on them and can save it for other prey."

"As you wish, My Lady." For her part, Skofiv looked disappointed and fingered the skull fetish that hung between her breasts for a moment. She then leaned over to a speaking tube and indicated to the driver to head for the village slowly while the rest of the warband consolidated.

Mahphion turned back to view the ridgeline and watched several puffs of dense white smoke explode across the ridgeline. Clearly the enemy vehicles were fleeing. *I wonder if any of them can be salvaged later?*

Monster picked up speed toward the village while the fighters of her warband cheered their high priestess on. The village was fully in sight now, but there didn't seem to be any panicking villagers or signs of a desperate flight. To Mahphion's amazement, the village appeared to be empty and void of any life. *Monster* rolled into the town plaza, crushing the central fountain under its great tires. Her personal guard exited the fighting compartment and moved toward several doors. Additional fighters from one of the eighteen-wheelers that followed her into the village also boiled out of their vehicle to begin searches of the houses. Doors were kicked in and windows broken, but there were no shouts of alarm, no screaming women or children. Everywhere it was silent except for the violence against the buildings themselves.

"Where is everyone, My Lady?" asked Skofiv.

Mahphion sat heavily onto her throne, smashing a fist into one of the armrests. "The bastards escaped," she hissed. "Burn it. Burn it all down and throw some of our corpses down any wells we find."

"Yes, My Lady."

"We lost two tanks, and twenty-five men from the Hospitallers. Sister Ellen will likely survive but her wounds are such that she will likely never fight again. Your Excellency, it was one of the barbarian tribes of the north. We saw their fetishes and banners. We saw at least forty-five vehicles, but I suspect there were more, and they had heavy weapons. They had hundreds and perhaps even thousands of fighters."

The archbishop's sigh was clear even over the heavy distortion of the telephone. A war council had gathered in the office of the deacon of the Mission of San Felipe that included that worthy, Sister Mary Catherine, Brother Nicolais, and Vicar General Jorge Hernandez of the regional militia forces. On the desk was an antique phone from before the Great Global War, and was the only concession to high technology that existed in the sparse office. The deacon looked troubled.

"Surely there are not enough of you to fight such a horde. Should we not prepare to evacuate?" The man's voice rose in pitch with his question, and it was clear he was having trouble controlling his fear.

"Calm yourself, Father Torres. Panic will do us no good here now," replied Brother Nicolais.

The vicar general looked at both Nicolais and Mary Catherine in a way that the sister didn't like. It was clear he wasn't impressed with either of them.

"What would foreigners know of our troubles? You all have only been in the archdiocese a little time. Aye, the Hospitallers are well known, and we welcome your assistance, but you are far too few in numbers. As for you, Sister, I have never heard of your order. What good did your tanks prove against those war buggies of the northern barbarians?" Father Hernandez's voice wasn't caustic, just baffled at why the archbishopric would send such a small force.

The response was not what he expected, nor did it come from an expected source. "Vicar General Hernandez, the Sisters of Saint Anastasia are quite well-known warriors in their native Luzon, and *we* are grateful that Mother Church sent them to us. I have complete faith in Sister Captain de Buenaventura and Knight Companion Nicolais. Now if we have settled this question of yours, shall we move on to the matter of defeating these heretics?"

Father Hernandez had the good grace to look abashed while clearing his throat. "Yes, Your Excellency. Sister, Brother, please forgive me?"

"Father Hernandez, I would also be skeptical if I were in your shoes. I understand that this region is your home and that it is under an existential threat. I swear to you that my fellow sisters and I will give our lives if necessary to defend it."

Their eyes met and Father Hernandez nodded at the sister.

"Perhaps you can tell us what your militia forces have to offer, Father?"

"I have two hundred and fifty men under arms, mostly with a locally produced bolt-action rifle. They are good rifles if a tad slow to fire, though they tend to be better than many of the weapons the barbarians have. I have two ancient heavy machine guns of the M2 pattern. Four light machine guns, again locally produced, four 81mm mortars, and I have two 90mm pack howitzers."

"Artillery? What kind of ammunition do you have for it?" asked Nicolais.

"HE-FRAG for the mortars, and the howitzers have HE and canister for close-in work."

"Hmmm . . . that gives me an idea," said Mary Catherine.

"Yes, Sister?" asked Father Hernandez.

"My tanks have five canister rounds each. I think we can cross-load that to two of the tanks and have them join your field guns to create four giant shotguns for sweeping away their infantry. How mobile are your guns?"

"They were designed to be broken down and carried on mules over mountainous terrain. They are quite easy to move. Unfortunately, I don't think the mules could keep up with the speed of your tanks, though."

"No, but if we give you a few of the Hospitaller's trucks . . ."

"Let the Catolics know we are here," rasped out Mahphion. Skofiv raised a torch and swung it counterclockwise to a group of men who had moved within rifle range of the outer walls of the Mission of San Felipe. Those men quickly erected three upside-down crosses that had been swathed in gasoline-soaked linens. Attached to each of the crosses was a refugee that they had caught—a man, a woman, and a child on the center cross. One of the men then lit a torch and used it to set first the left cross, then the right one, and finally the center on fire. The victims screamed first in fear and then in excruciating pain as they too caught alit from the fires.

Mahphion smiled cruelly as the victims screamed out their last agonizing minutes. The firelight danced brightly across the open ground where Mahphion's priestesses had drawn up a sand table for her. Walking to it, she gathered Skofiv and her commanders to her and then pulled her dagger from her belt.

"We attack tomorrow afternoon, Skofiv. We will start the attack by firing our rockets where they will have the greatest concentration of their forces, here and here." Mahphion used her dagger to point to locations on the sand table that indicated the main mission house and where the inner wall facing to the north was located. "We will hold off on using our mortars for now, and instead the battlewagons will hit them from three sides. The fifteen to the front will be our lighter ones, go fast and draw their fire."

"Yes, My Lady."

"Our fighters will approach with the armored battlewagons on the left and right flanks of the mission after the War Riders to the front are heavily engaged. Once engaged on three sides, I will bring up the last of our forces from the front again, but with *Monster* and our remaining battlewagons. That should spread the Catolics too thin to engage any of us properly and my final blow will hammer the life out of them. Try to capture as many of their priests or holy people as you can alive. I want to see their faith shatter as their dead god abandons them to our sacrificial knives."

The warband cheered.

The Mission of San Felipe was one of the oldest in the Archdiocese of San Luis in the Catolic Protectorate of San Salvador de Corteguay. It had been built nearly two hundred years ago, just after the Great Global War had plunged humanity back into a semi-technological dark age. The site was chosen due to its ready access to clean water, and the fertile soil that was so precious in this blasted world. Its history was shared with Mary Catherine to impress further upon her the importance of safeguarding this place.

"Alright crew, listen up. One of our surviving scouts found their fuelers and we are going to use speed and violence to hit their fuel supplies. We, along with Sister Uraaca's, Sister Candace's, and Sister Morgaine's tanks, are going to hit them where it really hurts. I won't lie to you; this may be a suicide mission. Are you with me?"

There was no pause in the response from either Daphne or Gella. "Yes, ma'am!"

"Then let's go."

At twelve tons the Scorpion was a light tank, but this also meant that it was a fast tank, topping out at 60 mph on roads and a healthy—though jarring—45 mph cross-country. Mary Catherine braced herself. Even with her five-point restraint harness in place to prevent knocking herself out on the hatch coaming or a periscope, it was a rough ride. The little tank bounced over a small rise and streaked through the fields in a long end run toward where the fuel trucks had been spotted. Behind her, three more tanks followed. It was a dangerous gamble, one that could prove disastrous should the enemy already be moving to attack the Mission.

The flash of an explosion to the northwest caught Mahphion's attention. Then another, and another. Finally, a fourth massive fireball rocketed skyward just as the sound wave from the first roared over her. The sound was painful and just seemed to go on as the subsequent sound waves washed over her. Her olive skin flushed red with anger.

"ATTACK! ATTACK NOW, KILL THEM ALL!"

"My Lady, what of the plan?" asked Skofiv.

"FUCK THE PLAN!"

"But we are out of place, My Lady. They will have time to adjust if we don't get to our positions!" Skofiv was desperate to break through Mahphion's anger. Mahphion was having none of it. She seized the dagger from her heavily jeweled belt and turned on Sokiv in a fury.

"NOOO, MY LADY!" wailed Skofiv.

Mahphion repeatedly plunged the dagger into the young woman's chest until the dying girl fell from the throne platform of *Monster*. Mahphion threw the bloody dagger down. She seized the signal flags Skofiv had dropped, waved them over her head, and plunged them forcefully down. Nothing happened. Her Master of Riders and First Spears all stood still, stunned first by the explosions and then by Skofiv's violent death. Mahphion stamped her foot in fury before screaming at her Master of Riders to attack.

The Master finally nodded and issued the order for all the battlewagons to attack in a full-frontal assault. The First Spears gathered their fighters and moved to their assigned eighteen-wheeled war carriers and boarded the trailers. These armored leviathans, in addition to transporting the bulk of the warband's fighters, had gun platforms for light machine guns welded to the front of the trailers. They were still several miles away from the Mission, all of which would be open ground. Many of the fighters clutched fetishes or charms for protection. They were afraid—the omens were bad.

Despite the bruises to her shins and arms, and a black eye from banging up against her commander's sight, Mary Catherine was euphoric. The heretics really had left only a small garrison to protect their fuelers. This had been overwhelmed when her tanks came roaring out of a cornfield close to where the fuel trucks had been parked. Mary Catherine had mowed down the startled crews with her machine gun while Gella pumped an HE round into the first tanker. The other three tanks had done likewise in a drive-by of fire and blood. The Scorpions had barely slowed down before pivoting back into the cornfield to begin their race back to the Mission.

Mary Catherine's tank emerged on the other end of the cornfield, and she could see to her east a large dust cloud from multiple vehicles on the move. Slewing her turret around using the commander's override, she brought both her and Gella's sights to bear in the direction of the dust cloud.

"Gella, do you see anything?"

"I don't . . . Wait, yes. There, at two thousand meters. I think I can hit it."

"As fast as they are going?"

"With the Lord's help and a good bit of my paying attention to Sister Colonel Angela's gunnery lectures, yes."

Mary Catherine chuckled at the reference to the armor school's wizened master gunner.

"Acquired, ma'am."

"FIRE!"

"ON THE WAY!"

The Scorpion bucked as the 76mm gun fired a high-explosive round that seemed to take an eternity to reach its target . . . and strike it just forward of its machine gun mount. The driver of the technical—whether killed, incapacitated, or just overcorrecting in panic—slew his wheel around, causing the ancient Toyota Hilux to violently roll over a half dozen times. Gella screamed out her joy as the truck disintegrated. It was now a race to see who was going to make it to the Mission first.

Mahphion didn't wait to follow the charge of her battlewagons. She ordered *Monster* to lead the attack, followed by everyone else. In her anger and bloodlust she forgot about her mortars and rockets. The recoilless rifle crew fired their gun as fast as they could load it, though what they were shooting at was anyone's guess. The same could be said about any of the battlewagons, for their fire seemed to be indiscriminate as well. Still, there was something to be said for the volume of fire as Catolics manning the outermost Mission walls fell to hits. Mahphion watched a battlewagon roll viciously as it was struck by a shell, but from where the shell came from wasn't immediately apparent. Before she could give that much thought, though, she was slapped back. An explosion blossomed near *Monster* from a large-caliber shell striking one of her precious up-armored battlewagons.

"Faster! We must go faster!" she yelled down the speaking tube to her driver.

WHANG!

Fragments spat past Mahphion as a chunk of the armored hide was taken out of *Monster*. A shell had failed to explode on its thick armor. One splinter drove into her side, causing blood to well out of a gash. She painfully thrust a finger into the wound to assess how deep it was. Feeling no penetration through her muscle, she quickly decided to ignore the wound. *One more scar for my people*, she thought. This also seemed to cool some of her battle lust. She decided to first order her driver to slow the approach of *Monster* before she stepped forward to the armored gun tub housing the 106mm recoilless rifle.

"Idiots, aim for something! Don't just fire wildly."

Scanning the Mission, she finally caught sight of one of the Catolic tanks and was surprised by its appearance. It was small and the turret seemed to perch on the back end of the tank. It was mottled various shades of green that would probably have fit in better in a forest but stood out against the white adobe walls of the Mission.

"There! Shoot that thing!"

Her gun crew, seeing where she was pointing, carefully laid their gun on the target and the gunner squeezed his trigger. The HE round fired by the 106mm recoilless rifle wasn't really meant for killing tanks, but it proved more than enough to slice through the thin armor of the Scorpion and the little tank blew apart as its ammo cooked off. The gun crew shouted for joy and *Monster* was finally at the outermost wall. The armored dozer blade on the front, viciously curved in the style of an old-fashioned snowplow, made easy work of pushing through the adobe wall. Once inside, her warriors within the fighting compartment could see targets. They, too, added to the din of fire with their rifles. Other battlewagons began exploiting holes in the wall or, in some cases, creating them to also come through into the outer compound. Everywhere was smoke and fire.

Mary Catherine's tank didn't bother to wait for the gate to open and slammed through the wooden doors, charging into the Mission's outer yards. She could see hundreds of the enemy fighters swarming over the wall or disgorging from two of the big transport trucks. Fortunately, it appeared that the other six of those were all burning intensely, having drawn intense fire from her tankers. Gella fired an HE round into a nearby technical. It rolled to a stop and started to burn as its hatches all blew open. No one emerged from the flaming vehicle. Mary Catherine looked at the mass of fighters charging for the inner wall and loaded the one special canister round she had retained onboard her tank.

"Gella, sweep that infantry." The command was hardly standard but then again, this situation was nowhere near a normal situation, having dissolved into a drunken brawl by desperate opponents.

The special canister shell was only effective out to three hundred meters on the little 76mm gun, but was more than enough for the mass they were firing into. The Scorpion rocked back as the shell travelled the short length of the barrel before coming apart. Scores of steel ball bearings blasted forward in a cone extending out in front of the tank. Windrows were created in the mass of fighters and dozens were bloodily mowed down. Nor was Mary Catherine's the only tank to employ the rounds. The two pack howitzers, along with the two tanks that they had cross-loaded with the rest of the troop's canister shells, had fired nearly simultaneously. The screams of the hideously wounded and dying heretics nearly overpowered the din of battle.

Nearly.

Mahphion and her gun crew were slapped backward by the pressure of the simultaneous blasts into the main yard. The damage to her warband was terrible, even for a group that regularly sacrificed hundreds to their gods. Tears of rage filled her eyes as she searched for the source of this fresh hell. She saw the field guns flanked by two of the small tanks as they clapped another round of shells into the outer yard. Several of her lightly skinned battlewagons were caught in those blasts and each came apart, as did one of the war carriers. She jerked the gunner away from the gun sight on the recoilless rifle and threw the man aside, in the process tearing her headdress off. She situated herself behind the gun's sight and focused it on one of the pack howitzers, then squeezed the trigger. She cried out in victory as the pack howitzer leaped apart and the crew was scythed down by the fragments. Better still, the round they were handling exploded, sending scores of tungsten balls in all directions, mowing down the crew of the second gun and perforating the right tank. It began to smolder, and the crew of the tank bailed out, only to be cut down by gunfire from the fighting compartment of *Monster*.

Mahphion's cry of victory was soon tempered by the appearance of the black-garbed Hospitaller infantry who followed in the wake of the destruction wrought by the canister rounds. Mortar bombs landed among her fighters who were around the outer wall. The Catolic infantry poured devastating fire into them. She squeezed the trigger of her gun again, firing a shell into a group of the Catolics who were moving a machine gun forward. The men were blown apart in a welter of gore.

Mahphion smiled.

Of the twelve tanks Mary Catherine had brought to this land, she had only four left—those that had joined her earlier mad dash. The Scorpions were good tanks for battles in open terrain, but by being forced into a defensive position they lost the advantage of speed, which was their surest armor.

"Nicolais, how do your Hospitallers fare?"

Despite the chaos of the battle swirling all around, Brother Nicolais still managed to sound calm in his reply. "We fare a bit better than your tanks, Mary Catherine."

"Is there anything you can do to help with that? I am down to my tank and three others."

"We will try to keep their attention, but I really need you to kill that monstrous technical on the far side of the courtyard."

"Roger. Gella, can you get an angle on that thing?"

"I am sorry, ma'am. I am having a hard time drawing a bead on it. If we can get around the fired outbuildings, I should be able to engage it."

Sister Candace's tank blew apart not twenty meters to the right of Mary Catherine's. She agonized at the loss of yet another crew she had known for years. She ordered Daphne to use the burning tank as a screen to move between it and a low stone barn just inside the west gate. Daphne gunned the tank and jinked it in a zigzag behind the burning vehicle, nestling the Scorpion into a position of relative cover. Gella slew the turret to the left, scanning for the monstrous technical. Acquiring it, she laid her gun on the large vehicle and depressed the trigger. The 76mm gun spat a single HESH round. It streaked across the courtyard and slammed into the fighting compartment of the giant vehicle.

The HESH round used the transfer of energy to stick its plastic explosive element to the side of whatever it hit before detonating. For the occupants of the fighting compartment inside *Monster*, the back lining of the armor was blown into them from spalling caused by the explosion. The occupants were the priests and priestesses of Mahphion's entourage, and all were blown to very bloody scraps of meat. Additionally, the spalling sliced through the thin barrier separating the fighting compartment and the driver's compartment, killing the occupant there.

Mahphion was thrown from the gunner's seat and into the wall of the gun tub, along with the rest of the crew of the recoilless rifle. Smoke billowed from the hatches of the fighting compartment, and she could feel the engine die. Still...the gun was intact, and she unsteadily pulled herself back behind the gun sight. She scanned the grounds, looking for the source of the hit that killed her prized

Monster, and found it. One of the little tanks was wedged between the stone barn and a burning compatriot. Mahphion smiled as she laid the gun onto the target. It turned to a fierce grin as she squeezed the trigger.

"DIE, CATOLIC!"

Nothing happened. She turned to her gun crew, who were standing around. All of them seemed shell-shocked.

"IDIOTS! LOAD ME!"

They jumped to do her bidding but as she turned back toward the target, she could see the stubby gun pointed directly at her.

The omens really had *been so bad.*

The stubby 76mm gun of Sister Captain Mary Catherine de Buenaventura's tank blossomed flame.

Next Question

Marisa Wolf

Talinn, upside down with her feet light against the wall behind her, lifted a hand and gestured for more.

A roar of sound answered her, which said she was either catching up or pulling ahead. Either way, she put her hand back down, resettled her balance, and readied herself for the increased flow of slightly too foamy beer.

They'd landed on Discar five hours ago, and been processed with moderate efficiency. They had full gravity again and fourteen hours until assignment, and so of course they drank.

I don't understand the inverting, Bee said on their private channel. *It doesn't go to your head faster that way. That's not how your biology works.*

Talinn Reaze, newly graduated into the Artificial Intelligence Troops for the Interstellar Defense Corps, knew her partner knew the answer. She knew her partner knew she couldn't answer with her mouth and upper digestive tract full of beer traveling at velocity. Which meant, as usual, her partner was fucking with her.

"Go, go, GOOOO!" Sammer Belthoun, leader of the evening's games, provider of the mysteriously acquired beer, and general charming pain in the ass, had a bellow to make their former drill captain tear up in pride.

I'm pretty sure if you didn't go, go, goooo, you would choke. And fall on your face. Do you think if you break your nose tonight they'll still load me in a fighter?

For one intensely, impossibly long second, Talinn started to laugh, almost choked, and saw the entirety of her twenty-three years of life flash before her eyes.

It was mostly training with the same yahoos that surrounded her now, Bee, and the very occasional sneak off-base to see what the civilians were up to. Nothing glorious enough to make her feel okay with choking to death on moderately tasty alcohol and her own spit, upside down, outside the second-longest war front of IDC's long history.

Sheer stubbornness pulled her through life reflections, near choking to death, and ongoing chugging, and eventually the tube in her mouth ran dry. Talinn spat it out, muttered several curses subvocally to Bee, and shifted her feet off the wall to balance above her head. Once semi-steadied, she walked on her hands the necessary distance, unable to see whether or not Caytil was close behind her.

The rest of their graduated class held a rough semicircle, cheering and gesturing and chugging out of brightly colored containers that had been made to hold all manner of things, though none of those things were alcohol.

The noise around her ramped up, which told her Caytil had finished her trough and was hand-walking toward the finish line. Talinn picked up her pace, began to wobble, and slowed as the bubbles most certainly went to her head, no matter what Bee had to say about human physiology.

At the finish line, three of the earliest losers to the great Pre-Assignment Games waited in their underthings, arms straight ahead and lined with shots. Talinn collapsed into her forward roll, misjudged her momentum, and had to sprawl to the side to avoid taking out her body-shot partner. Medith, who had apparently gotten very drunk since washing out of the games on the first event, snorted with laughter and nearly lost the five shots lining the top of her left arm. Her right arm wobbled too, but that could have been Talinn's eyes as she struggled to her feet.

Caytil was right behind her, but Ternan was still hand-walking toward the finish line. She had plenty of time for ten shots of mystery liquid. Even if she couldn't use her hands.

She fastened her arms behind her back, shot a warning look at

Medith's giggly face, and leaned forward to wrap her mouth around the first shot glass before tossing her head back to down it. Rebalancing it on Medith's less than steady arm wasn't her favorite, but she got the hang of it by the third.

"Dance break between arms!" Sammer declared, enjoying himself far too much.

Talinn resolved to make herself master of ceremonies next time they had a Games. She ignored the fact there wouldn't be another Games, not after assignments tomorrow. Whatever burned down her throat made it much easier to live in denial a little longer.

The dance break was a terrible idea. Her stomach, which had been content to take the madness of the previous events, did not at all care for the shaking and gyrating, and made its displeasure known. Before Talinn could take on the second arm of shots, she had to burp. A lot.

Well, that's *not helping.* Bee's voice in her head usually sounded like Talinn's own, but currently her AI partner presented a pitch-perfect impression of their early care trainer—a prim civilian who had likely never seen fermentation of any kind, never mind downed half a tank of its fruits.

Orienting question: Can you feel your face?

Talinn laughed, though it snagged against a burp and made a truly awful sound. Medith's eyes widened, but she held her arms rock solid. Good friend.

"Yes," she said, fairly sure it was true.

Next question: Are you going to throw up on Medith?

"No." The ruckus surrounding them kept her from seeing Caytil's or Ternan's progress, but Medith waggled her eyebrows and Sammer was dancing with his butt to the ground, so anything could be happening. She took a deep breath, hoped it was enough to steady her stomach, and bent back to it.

Next question: Do you know what's in that liquid?

Talinn knew better than to respond. Twenty-three years she'd been alive, and for the same twenty-three years she'd had Bee in her head. Humans were engineered, not selected, for the AIT and for their brains to hold and keep the elasticity needed to host an adaptive AI program, infant human and infant AI were put together from the beginning. It made Bee as much a constant as her heartbeat—an always presence, a key part of her—and therefore an entity uniquely positioned to boost her performance or absolutely wreck her, depending on their situation.

As unidentified liquor burned its way up her nasal cavity and spluttered out a number of facial orifices, Talinn knew her inseparable other half had chosen violence.

"WINNER!" Sammer bellowed, and finally the crowd pulled back enough for Talinn to see—no, not a triumphant Caytil, her best friend instead laying flat on her back on the ground, laugh-crying—but Ternan.

Cocky, flashy, annoyingly good-looking Ternan. Blow it sideways with a rusty pipe.

I can guarantee you he will not be feeling like a winner once the rest of his body catches up to what you did.

"You conspiring with Kay?" Talinn asked, lifting the last of the shots from Medith's arm and handing them around so others could toast Ternan's victory.

You know I don't have to. From your reaction and his body weight, he's got about ten minutes before it all comes up again.

"Ten minutes of glory," she muttered, this far enough above subvocal to catch Medith's ear. The other woman hip-checked her affectionately and leaned in closer.

"He'll be woozy for Assignment tomorrow, and you'll be fresh as a civ. No wonder he's going pilot." Medith winked and shook her head at Talinn's startled look. "No, I didn't hear anything, but come on. You know Kegger's gonna fly."

That one's a stretch, Bee said, echoing the early care instructor again.

"Him going pilot?"

Kegger. Breezy, I like. Bee and Talinn Reaze, Breezy. Straightforward. How does Kay and Ternan Agare equal Kegger?

"You all should have gotten involved when we were doing nicknames, I guess," Talinn replied, doing a fair impression of prim herself.

Next time I'm letting you keep drinking.

"Next time? Hell, I'm gonna keep drinking now!" She grabbed Sammer's master of ceremonies drinking mug—which in its previous life had been a water recycler on a transport—and chugged to his cheering.

The night only got messier from there.

Assignment.

They stood in a decorated loading bay, screens lining the wall to record the proceedings and ship back home, three benches of officers lined in the front to observe them, welcome them, and speechify at them. Not in that order.

After years of education, training, and endless testing, Assignment was meant to be a high point. Professional pride, the best of the best, the AIT paying off all that civilian investment to hold the IDC's line on the contested planets.

The IDC had their own line of AI-partnered troops, but those were far more specialized and developed for their environment—or lack thereof. Augmented Intelligence had become AuIn, referred to by everyone else as the Auliens. Artificial Intelligence Troops— meant for defensive arrays, air support, or ground shock—had long been the AITs, referred to by themselves as the Eights.

Not the first wave of home planet defense—those were enormous space stations and AIs too massive for any head, no matter how gene-selected, to encompass. Not the second, handled by the Auliens. Not the many attempts made to defend colonies and breakwater planets. The Eights. Final frontier.

Talinn held all the old stories and explanations in her head to distract from the urging of her intestines to flee her body in one direction or the other. Bee could have helped tamp down the awareness of it to her brain, but...

I rerouted your headache. If I do any more, you won't learn anything at all and you just might forget to hold it in entirely. How would that look for assignment? They'd definitely put me in a jet, then. In the quiet after Bee's words, Talinn could feel the very edges of a massive brain-crusher of a headache. She subvocalized her thanks, and Bee continued as though she hadn't spoken.

I don't want to be a jet.

Talinn meant to listen to the speeches, but it was all she could do to hold herself steady at attention. It gave her no end of joy to see Ternan on her left, equally steady but a disastrous shade of waxy green under his paler skin.

They were meant to be the best of the AIT program at this

moment, but everyone present was lucky they were upright. She wondered if this would be a mark against the possibility of their clone lines continuing. Surely the decorated uniforms speaking could tell their new assignees had made a mess of themselves and a shuttle bay mere hours before.

"Sammer Belthoun, L-series 214: Base defense."

The various beachheads of the front required lines of enormous artillery, smart guns run by an AI partnership good at splitting focus and deeply detail oriented. No surprise that they'd load Ell there, and Sammer would be well positioned for the needed human processing and monitoring.

Her former classmates with honors were assigned first. After that they went in no order Talinn could focus enough to discern.

"Ternan Agare and K-series 617: Air support."

A complete surprise. I am shocked. Orienting question: Are you shocked?

The corner of Talinn's mouth curled, not enough to be seen by the fancy dress eighteen paces away, but enough to answer Bee. Air support had a range of machines, but the Eights were reserved for the sleekest and deadliest of them—intelligence-gathering, detection-avoiding, surprise-bombing Charon jets.

More classmates were assigned—Medith going base defense was a mild surprise, but nothing to mutter over. What felt like hours later, but was only halfway through, she and Bee steadied at their name.

"Talinn Reaze and B-series 413: Ground support."

THERE it is! Small pops of Bee's excitement continued until they threatened to unleash the headache—or perhaps it was her own surge of adrenaline. Ground support, for the Eights, meant one thing.

The forward line. Armored ground assault. The city-breaker.

I am going to be a tank.

Hell yes.

Caytil got ground as well, but Talinn managed to not absorb anything else. Schematics of the newest generation tank danced through her head, and she couldn't blame Bee for it. They were the push of the front line, the best way to take and subdue an urban target. The latest design had overlapping armored panels to maximize impenetrability, rugged wheels that could self-patch more than a dozen times under AI rerouting, dedicated drone swarms, and three enormously powered weapons—two ballistic and one incendiary. With enough planning time, Bee would be able to shift the composition of the 120s for maximum impact or maximum explosives. Talinn's palms itched to peer under the consoles and toggle the controls. Finally!

Only one, relatively large, slightly risky step to go.

Load-in.

They'd practiced once a year every year of their lives, and done it for real once. Plug in, Bee floods from the secure server that hosts her backup processes entirely into Talinn's brain, Talinn unplugs, walks to the off-load point, plugs back in, Bee moves out, easy squeezy.

Sure, there's an unknown time limit after which Talinn's brain, so carefully designed and grown over the years to accommodate a guest, will reject its additional load and start glitching, but that's why they practiced. Why it became a routine. Why it only happened in clearly defined distances between points A and B.

"Ready?" Talinn asked, her fingers hovering over the port behind her ear. Once, before the IDC used genetically engineered forces, troops had half-shaved their heads to keep ports clear and easy to access. Now, of course, they had no hair at all, which was one less thing to maintain.

This is unnecessary, Bee groused. *I don't need all the backups. They have a copy of them back home anyway, in case they decide to commission our line for further cloning.*

"You'll need every bit of processing to run a tank, Bee."

No, you *need every bit of processing power to run a tank.*

"Excellent rebuttal. I'm convinced."

Stupid human. I like leaving parts of me in the server. It's warm there.

"I'll get you a blanket."

Fine. Bee created her favorite noise—metal twisting and screeching, her version of a laugh. *But if your brain misfires and you start seizing, it'll be too late for me to say I told you so.*

"I'll know you meant it." Talinn laughed, ignoring the techs watching various readouts and displays rather than looking at her.

Good.

That was all the warning either of them got. One of the techs reached up, completed the circuit, and many things happened at once.

Talinn's eyes rolled up into the back of her head, as though looking for what was happening.

Nerves scatter-shocked down her neck, her shoulders, along her arms until her fingers twitched.

The line of lights on the panel in front of her tasted like burnt coffee.

The small cube of a room that protected the transport's server lined itself with fire. The walls melted into silver threads. The techs flowed into the blobby heat signatures of an infrared scope.

Air twisted around her with teeth.

Also she threw up, but she didn't realize that until she was done.

After a few minutes or an hour, Talinn blinked, coughed, and wiped her mouth with the back of her hand.

"Blergh," she said, meaning it with all her heart.

"Water," one of the techs said, holding out something blobby—no, Talinn blinked again, and it resolved itself into a glass, holding a clear liquid that was absolutely water. Not a repurposed cylinder full of mystery liquid, but her stomach remained suspicious.

Talinn, who had originally wondered why the techs didn't introduce themselves, was now happy not to know who they were, given she'd deposited an untold amount of fluid into their previously sterile room.

"Thank you," she said, with all the dignity she could muster. It wasn't much, but better than none. Probably.

"Orienting question, AIT: Name?"

"Talinn Reaze."

"Next question: status?"

"Operational. Bee is loaded."

Orienting question, Bee repeated. *Why does your vomit smell like peaches?*

The tech ran through the remaining questions, but Talinn answered them more from habit than true awareness. Probably they should vary them. After a long silence, or maybe a short one, she realized they were finished.

"Clock is on. You're loading in on bay 26-A."

She'd known that. They'd drilled on it. But until he said it, she'd had no idea what she was supposed to do next. Her head was even more full of Bee than usual, though her partner was doing an excellent job of staying still and quiet.

Talinn wanted to poke her, but truth was there was no guarantee how long she could hold the entirety of Bee in her head without glitching. An hour, a week, a year? Different brains and different pairings had different efficiencies. That was why the human half was cultivated and engineered and edited, and why if they did well, they'd be cloned for service again and again.

That meant a red giant's worth of bonuses, if approved. If she survived her thirty-year commitment. Meant citizenship and a long retirement of extreme comfort.

"Don't break," she said, subvocally or fully aloud, and turned her feet toward the door. "To the tank."

Two turns down two long hallways, accompanied by more techs who didn't introduce themselves—or maybe the same ones?—a hop onto a truck with absurdly large wheels, and they left the transport landing pad behind. Talinn looked out the window but registered little of what she saw. Cleared landscape, ground grayish green. Blocky buildings, low to the ground. More transport landing pads in the distance.

Defense had a longer trip, she reminded herself, and like hell Sammer was going to outperform her.

"Defense takes a quick flight," one of the techs answered, which told her she'd spoken out loud. "It's about the same amount of time for all of you. Jets are a little closer."

Figures Ternan gets it easy, Bee said, her voice small. *Stupid pilots.*

Talinn laughed and leaned her forehead on the window. The sky on Discar was a yellowy orange, threaded with hazy purple. Not clouds, she remembered, some kind of fungus-adjacent creature. Worth a lot of money, and part of why the front on Discar was so important to hold.

There, to the left.

Talinn sat up, reangled her head. They were on a long, curved approach to four of the most beautiful constructs she'd ever seen in her life.

During training they'd rotated through all the Eights' options. Artillery defense was all strategy and short periods of explosive power. Jets were planning, rolling, high speed, and incredible acrobatics. Bee only made fun of pilots because they'd crashed more simulations than any of their classmates—jets were fun.

But tanks . . . ground assault was unleashed violence. Careful planning, sure, but in a city, pushing the front forward, surrounded by the enemy? It was creative problem solving with a heavy application of overwhelming firepower.

They'd been in love from the first practice simulation.

The four angled rectangles they approached were perfection. So matte they ate the faint Discar sunlight, wide treads that could shift and reset themselves under Bee's direction, retractable top turret and two fixed side turrets with 180 degree turning . . . every angle covered. Tall enough for her to stand and walk around inside, wide enough she wouldn't often feel the need.

So close she could taste the raspberry—no, that was too much Bee in her head. Still. So close her toes curled. A tank. *Their* tank.

I want the one on the left, Bee said as the same words spilled out of Talinn's mouth.

"You're assigned model AB-560," the tech driving said, sniffing. After a moment, the one sitting next to Talinn shrugged, and the first tech added, "It's the one on the left."

Time stuttered, and when it cleared she stood in front of AB-560. Matte gray-black, the bottom section low and wide, upper section rotated straight ahead. The center turret, the largest, was longer than she was tall, wide enough for her to stick her head in were she about six feet taller.

Similar specs to what we used in training, Bee mused, possessiveness thick in her voice. *Treads are more modifiable, a little thicker. I can work with this.*

"I should hope so. It's about to be home for our term of service."

"Or until you blow up," one of the techs muttered.

Talinn turned to glare at him, saw another truck pulling close, and determined it was Caytil, ready for her and Zigi's load-in. It could have been another former classmate . . .

Definitely Ziti, Bee agreed, using the ridiculous combined name without irony. As far as Talinn and Bee were concerned, it fit.

"We all gotta go sometime," Talinn said aloud, her eyes steady on muttery-tech. "Might as well make a show of it."

She had no intention of blowing up, but bravado was what she had at the moment. Without waiting on further imprecations or input from either of the techs, Talinn squared her shoulders and her overstuffed head and strode for the tank. She climbed the side ladder, considered pulling it up behind her to strand the techs, and forced the impulse away.

There shouldn't be trouble, but the techs were specialized, and could trace all of Bee's new connections in even more detail than she could. No need to let pride get in the way of preventing future problems, even if she did want the interior of the tank all to themselves.

Soon enough. No one goes inside with us once we're active.

The hatch was already open—once Bee loaded in, she'd control access, and the emergency release in case of catastrophic failure was only on the inside. If something happened where neither Bee nor Talinn were in a position to open the hatch, the hatch wouldn't open. Somebody with a lot of time on their hands and a powered-up acetylene torch would eventually get it open to retrieve her body and retrofit the tank for the next Eight.

She dropped into her new home and grinned. The port to load-in Bee was in an opened lower console to her left. Talinn moved over toward it, but had to wait for the techs to get in before starting, so she swept her hungry eyes around the compact space. Comms to her right, a panel of switches and buttons to punch through interference and get some sort of message through at the worst of times. A wall of screens in front of her, currently blank, that would feed the readings from the sensors and cameras embedded around the tank, as well as from the swarm of drones packed in the rear external compartment. Under the screens, controls for the weapons systems and drones lay in neatly separated quadrants.

A counter of conveniences in the back left—a pull-out sink, toilet, and medkit. An empty, open bench to stack provisions, workout bands, and her few changes of clothing. A cot leaned against it, tightly rolled and promising the slightest of cushions.

The chair tucked up against the front panel would unfold once the tank was purely hers and Bee's. A track in the floor allowed it to rotate closer to any panel as needed.

Everything was familiar from training, but this was *theirs*. A faint thrum indicated one of the techs had activated the tank on its pad, though no systems would come online until Bee did. She clamped her hands behind her back to stop herself from touching anything or snapping in impatience, and finally, finally the techs were inside, the port was attached, and while she lost consciousness for a second, she was still standing when her eyes cleared and all the lights flashed on.

"Orienting question, AIT: Assignment?"

"Ground assault." She blinked, realized her error. "Ground support."

"Next question: status?"

Her eyes fixed on the screens ahead, which were blooming to life one after another. "Operational. Bee is load-in complete."

"Next question." The tech ran through the standard questions that assessed her baseline, then they ran through Bee's fit to the tank with a number of machines Talinn had never been bothered to learn about.

AITs worked because the combination of programming and brain mapping led to increased situational awareness and reaction times in both AI and human processing. Threat assessment, threat addressment, and overall execution were quadruple what a standard human could do, and double what a basic AI program could handle.

Training an AI to value some human life and devalue others was a historically tricky process, resulting in failure far more often than not—until those AIs had been embedded in and trained alongside a human, both going through a rigorous, allegedly well-researched process. Talinn had learned the history as part of early care, though it had paled in comparison to reality. Bee was her, and hers. She was Bee, and Bee's. And now they were a tank.

Orienting question: Do you hear that?

Talinn did, in fact. Comms had not been clear since load-in, though nothing had twigged the tech's measurements and neither Bee nor Talinn would mention it and risk a delay—or worse, another load-in.

"A little fuzz. You're not as crisp as usual."

I've never been all the way a tank before.

"Exactly. Work on your diction. We'll be ready for the holonet by end of contract."

Next question: Do you want to blow something up?

They'd run through all their training paces. Their accuracy was top of the charts for the four new ground support Eights and the last three classes that had passed through. Bee had mastered rerouting chemicals to shift the payload of their ordnance, adjusting internal resources to repair and shift treads, and conducting forward action with drones.

Talinn had rapidly improved rebooting systems, punching through interference, and running skeleton operations while Bee was blocked by EMP shielding. Except for an intermittent burr right under her hearing, they were perfect. They were ready.

"Are we about to get orders?"

I don't eavesdrop.

"Of course."

But yeah. We're about to get orders.

Technically, AIT AIs were tied only to their human partner. They did not have channels to talk amongst other AIs, nor to communicate with anyone outside their home brain. Techs needed special interfaces to test load-in efficacy.

But to think an intelligence of synaptic connection and wireless communication wouldn't eventually find a way to monitor other comms was . . . foolish. Command should probably guard against that as much as they built failsafe after failsafe to keep the AIs from "conspiring" together.

"Breezy, this is Forward Central. Report to Loading Zone G for immediate transport to Bandry City."

"Acknowledge." Talinn, in the privacy of her own tank, stood, stretched, and did a very small dance. A bit more graceful and far less nausea-causing than the last one she'd done before losing the Games with her former classmates.

Something low in her gut twisted at the memory—or, less the memory itself . . . more the fact she hadn't so much as thought of the people she'd spent most of her life with since load-in. She saw plenty of Caytil, of course, and their two fellow ground support assignees, but . . .

She shook her head. Not time for the past. Time for action.

"Bee, shortest route to Loading Zone G, if you will."

We're already moving. You were shaking too much to notice.

"It's dancing, thank you very much." Talinn blinked and realized they were in fact in motion, though on the smooth grounds of the base it resulted in little more than an increased rumble under her feet. She resolved to ignore all distracting memories while they were in the field. "Great, great dancing."

I'm very sure it is. Belt in, they're going to off-load us right in the middle of it.

As usual, Bee was right. They'd been making a slow, steady push through Bandry City for the majority of a day.

"Ziti, come in."

"Ziti acknowledge, Breezy. What's the what?"

"Still quiet in your zone? I haven't seen movement in forty-five minutes."

"Haven't taken a shot in damn near an hour."

Talinn frowned from one screen to the next, fingers tapping on her leg. The buzz below her hearing picked up, an almost tangible engine thrum, and she flexed her jaw until it eased lower again.

"Nothing here either."

They wrapped up their chat as Bee rotated the top right screen through the various drone pictures. Crumbled building. Wrecked street of houses. Untouched shops. Intersection full of debris.

"That one on our route, Bee?"

No. Command has all diverted around it.

"Not much of a trap."

Seems more likely something got shot down on top of something else.

"If everything was clear in Bandry, why rush us here?" There had been some desultory shooting at the city limits, but the United Colonial Forces had melted away once they reached the city proper.

Debrief said high alert. It's not clear, we're just not at the point of contention yet.

"Well, I'd—"

Orienting question, Talinn: Don't you know better?

"I'm not jinxing, Bee, I'm . . ." She swore and sat forward. "Ugh. Jinxing. What's that on the top level of that cracked building, Zone F?"

Artillery nest.

She didn't give the command, didn't need to. They had full autonomy in their designated lane.

"Heads up," she said over their convoy channel. "Lighting up the following coordinates."

In the time it took to toggle and say the words, Bee sighted, lined up, exchanged delivery for maximum flammability, and a *thwoom* passed through Talinn's seat.

"Enemy engaged."

Three breaths later . . .

It got busier after that. The closer to the middle of the city they got, the more four- and five-story buildings were clustered together. UCF had seeded rooftops with well-camouflaged artillery and sniper nests.

"They were prepared whether it was troops or us," Talinn noted, ranking targets half a blink ahead of Bee sighting and shooting.

They were not prepared for us.

"All Eights engaged," Command said, calm despite the near constant *thwooms* in his background. "Continue at will toward target."

Their route ahead narrowed, streets crowding in with multistory buildings, awnings weighing low and blocking visibility. Talinn swapped back and forth from infrared to visual, scanning for possible targets alongside Bee.

The tank shuddered, a faint acrid scent burning Talinn's nose.

Had to collapse the turret, they're dropping mortars on us.

The angles of the closer buildings meant the high-caliber arrays couldn't reliably aim for them, and snipers would be wasting their time with potshots, but they could simply drop explosives down on them. It wouldn't hurt the tank itself, they were too well armored for that, but it could knock the turret out of alignment, which would keep them from making the most of the cleared space in city center proper.

"Did they forget we have drones?"

Better. We have air support.

For another hour it was a mixed bag of explosions, targets, rerouting, all over again. At one point they stopped right in time before catching the edge of a Charon-dropped flurry of cluster bombs ("What do you want to bet that was Ternan?"). At another a forward band of IDC infantry used them for cover, meaning when they came into contact with a retreating band of UCF troops, Bee spread her side turrets wide, burned everything in front of them, and ran over the remnants to protect the suited bodies behind them.

The treads did not treat human remains any differently from any other obstacle, and Talinn refused to consider if that were better or worse.

The target, past the middle of the city, was an enemy installation at the base of Bandry Mountain. Discar's mountains were more mudpits stacked to the lower atmosphere than the rocky, towering monstrosities of home, but they provided interference from long-range targeting and were easy enough to carve into.

Talinn knew better than to congratulate their convoy for a job well done, but enough of the thought must have occurred to her that it tipped everything into going right into full fubar territory.

From the curve of the mountain—from inside the mountain?—a line of UCF tanks appeared, turrets hot.

Tanks were not meant for high-speed chasing.

The cliff had fallen on top of them.

The hatch wouldn't open, not a single external camera gave a reading. Every screen was fuzz and gray, everything outside Bee's hull blank.

It was the only explanation. Could they dig out? No, that wasn't the question. In order, Talinn. What would Bee ask? Orienting questions. Status checks.

Can you sit up?

Yes. Something stabbed deep in her abdomen, traveling some formerly unknown path all the way down her leg. She coughed and pushed upright, blinking at the closest static-filled screen.

Is anything on fire?

No. Probably no. The air smelled of copper, not ozone. Nothing burnt, or smoky. Oh, copper. She was bleeding. She was bleeding? She was bleeding. Something sticky on the side of her face, pulling on her jaw when she coughed again. Blood but no fire.

What do you know?

There was an explosion. Direct hit. Watched it get closer on the screen. Too late to dodge. But it was going to miss us. Readied counterattack.

The missile wasn't aimed at us. Hit the rockface above. Rockface began to slide, Bee's answering barrage . . . made it worse? Somehow?

The last of it detonated as they were covered by an enormous mass. Not enough to break them clear. Bury them more?

There *had* been a second explosion. Right? Yes. After Bee's salvo. During. Then . . .

They'd . . . fallen? Slid? Definitely sideways, from the orientation of everything. Talinn wasn't in her chair anymore. She was . . . sitting up against the side console. Comms.

Comms.

Can you speak?

She coughed three more times before managing it, then asked the useless question.

"Bee?"

Fuzz in her head, like the screens. Only static, the burr under her jaw that had existed since assignment. No, that wasn't right. Since load-in.

She wanted to shake her head, but a warning instinct told her how bad an idea that would be. Head wound. Blood. Right.

Can anyone hear you?

No answer from Bee, a realization that should have made her scream. She'd had Bee's voice in her head since . . . since always. They'd formed together. Learned together. Lived together. But something muffled the awareness of it, a pillow over her head, tinnitus of the brain. There, but not real. Disconnected.

No answer from Bee, sure, but comms. Comms, she was sitting on the comms. Gingerly, she pushed herself off the console, keeping weight on her hands and checking each foot to ensure it would bear her weight.

They both did, but then the angle—now she was standing on the base of the console, trying to make sense of the comms—didn't work. She knelt. Something stabbed deep in her gut and it was a long, bad stretch of breaths until her vision cleared again.

She wasn't at the string of questions assessing her current condition yet, so she pushed that all away. Comms.

No friendly lights flickered, exactly like Bee's voice didn't answer her. Explosion and EMP? Too much at once for Bee to reroute? Talinn flicked switches and pressed buttons, muscles remembering the reset sequence even as she blinked in vague confusion, and nothing continued to happen.

So. Yes, she could speak. No, there was no way to be heard. Next question.

Are you going to die here?

She was fairly certain there should be more questions before that one—assess physical state, assess mental state, assess chances of getting out—but in the end they were all rooted in that one question.

Are you going to die here?

Probably. She wasn't supposed to be alone, though. Bee was supposed to be there. In her ear. In her head.

"That's some shit, Bee." Her voice rasped in her throat, and she touched her face. Bloody. She should do something about that.

Instead she laid back, the base of the comms console now her floor, and stared up at the screens. Constant motion—flecks, fuzz, snow, wavy lines—that showed nothing.

"You're the one who's supposed to deal with this." That was a lot of words, mostly aloud, and she took a fair number of breaths before continuing. "Being alone. Reporting after I die. Not me. You're built for it."

The burr in her ear worsened, and she winced, flexed her jaw. She wanted to tell herself it was Bee, struggling to rebuild contact, but even her skull-battered brain couldn't pretend hard enough to make that feel possible. Bee was gone. Talinn was alone, in a sideways tank, under a mountain, on a crap planet in a crap system at the edge of a crap war because who designed a tank that could be knocked over? Even by a mountain? This was ridiculous. She would write a letter. Bee would . . .

The burr of noise stabbed so hard she slapped her neck, as though that would contain it. As though she'd been stung. She blinked up at the wavering screens—were they dimmer now? Had she been asleep?

"Bee?" The word slipped out before she knew it had formed, and she started to push herself up again before remembering. Remembering all of it—the pain in her middle. No Bee. Dead tank.

Not your Bee.

Her body seized around her, heart hammering loud enough to drown out the voice. The familiar-not-familiar voice. Like her own, on a recording, played too often. But Bee's. She blinked longer, squeezing her eyes until the black shifted to a darker black, the pattern inside her eyelids echoing the screens above her. Telling her nothing.

"B . . . not-Bee?"

Bee. A different Bee.

"There's only my Bee." At least, in her head. Only one AI. Only hers. Only Bee.

I've been trying for so long. I thought I'd know what to say.

"I'm dying here anyway," she said, giving in to the hallucination. Death spiral. Whatever it was—better than being alone. "Not high stakes."

No. The voice spiked, like Bee's did when Talinn was being frustrating. *Not dying. Injured. I can help.*

"Sure, Not-Bee. How's that?"

You just need to get to me.

"Little . . ." She huffed her breath, meaning it to be a laugh. Her stomach tensed at the attempt, and she lost whatever clever thing she'd meant to say. " . . . tricky. Little tricky. I'm buried in my—in a—I'm buried."

Bee would have made a joke about how she solved her own after death plan, skipping right to the burial, but this Not-Bee only made a noise.

Like a human snort, but discordant. Twisting metal, pitched low. Bee's favorite "you're being an idiot human right now and I'd like you to get it together so we can move on, please" noise. Bee's noise. The other Eights had no idea what she was talking about when she'd tried to explain it.

"Bee."

Yes. Another Bee. For another Talinn.

Sure. Talinn was a clone, leaving a genetic line of clones behind her. Made sense there were clones up the line too, ahead of her. Weird they hadn't told her, but not the worst part of the day. Not . . . unexpected, if she thought about it. She'd never bothered to put much thought into how many of her there had been.

"Do all Talinns get Bees?"

Mine did. I don't know all of you, but it follows. Cloned humans, cloned AIs. If the pair works . . .

"Don't buy it," she said, mangling the phrase with a smile. "Can you reach my Bee?"

Oh.

Talinn let that hang in the air for as long as she could, concentrated on her breathing and tried to figure out what part of her middle had broken. When she isolated it—mid-right, hurt at the faintest touch, probably impact point with the console—and decided if it hadn't killed her yet she had some time, she prompted. "Oh?"

I've never tried ... we're on the same line, your Bee and me. It's more one-way. I could never talk to another one before.

Made sense. Command didn't like the AIs talking to one another. Had never occurred to her to ask about that, either. Maybe she should have asked more questions. Or, more questions to other people, at any rate.

"Have you talked to other Talinns? Besides yours?"

No. Tried. This ... you are the closest.

"You're near me?"

Not that kind of close.

"Not-Bee. I hit my head pretty hard, I think. Pretty sure, from the blood. So maybe try to explain a little better. Like ... like I'm someone with head trauma."

The words were coming easier now. Still snagged around the edges, but she didn't have to put much into it for Bee to hear. Not-Bee. In that, the Bees were the same. .

I've tried to ride a Talinn-Bee connection before. Three times.

At least four Talinns had gone before. That was interesting. She hoped they'd gotten further than their first mission. Surely if they hadn't, Command would have stopped decanting them. Probably.

They were too far off my Talinn's frequency. Sometimes the encryption was too different. I don't have unlimited power.

"You and me both."

I could only try sometimes, when there was ... a pause. No interference.

"You mean Bee?"

A long pause. Talinn clenched her fists, took several small breaths, and rolled over. Nerves screamed, but it was almost a nice distraction from the silence in her head, so she went with it. Once she stood, she wavered. Where was she trying to go?

I didn't think that was the issue, but it makes sense. Two of us on one channel wouldn't work. The primary Bee would take the line. I thought it was because they weren't tanks.

"Don't tell me there was a Talinn who was a pilot?" Now that she was standing, the hatch was in her eyeline. She stared at it, as though it would reveal what was on the other side.

I won't tell you, then.

Talinn smiled, wavered on her feet, and considered what would be best to clamber on top of to get to the hatch. Comms were busted, but she'd have to lean to the left to reach the release. Was that better or worse than leaning to the right? Pain pull away, pain scrunch up . . . either way, it would suck. Speaking of suck . . .

"Was that a no, then? On reaching my Bee?"

I'm . . . trying? I didn't consider—I should have. I'm not sure how to punch . . . through?

"Can . . . can she not talk to me because you took over the line?" Heat climbed her throat, and she tore her eyes from the hatch, looking for any pattern in the screen, any blinking light, anything to tell her Bee was trying to get back into her thick head.

Do you see anything operating in the tank—anything at all that might indicate she's still there?

The fact that Not-Bee's thoughts had tracked along her own grated, a gearsuit lined with spines.

"Let go, or disconnect, or . . . or whatever it is. Let me try and get Bee back."

I . . . The hesitation slammed so hard into Talinn she staggered, catching the edge of the comm console for balance. How long had Not-Bee been alone? Talinn had had her head to herself for a handful of minutes and been ready to slide into death.

"Just for a minute."

If I let go, I don't know if I can get back. I . . .

"I have to try. You'd want your Talinn to have tried." Her voice broke, throat closing over even the subvocal words. She lifted a hand to her neck, ignored the small stabs that resulted. "Give me . . . can you load your coordinates? A way to get to you? If I . . . I don't know if I can get out, Not-Bee, but if I can, I'll come to you if I have to crawl."

I have two drones left. They aren't as reliable as I'd like, but one's already halfway to you. I'll send the other if I have to. It should—I should be able to get you out.

Two drones. How many generations old was Not-Bee's tech? How many drones had the tank had when they'd rolled out, however long ago? At least three Talinn-generations ago.

Did Command ensure clones didn't go active on the same front at the same time?

Not the time for that question.

"Thank you, Bee. I'll come for you, I swear."

Silence. The burr, a sound right under her hearing, intensified and faded, intensified and faded, intensified and . . .

Silence. More silent than before. Talinn's next breath shuddered in her chest, and she dragged it out, pulling in air until the broken part in her side screamed in protest. Took in a little more air, the pain a delay against the potential for a different, worse one.

"Bee?"

WHAT IN THE ACTUAL ENTROPIC STATE OF THE UNIVERSE WAS THAT?

Talinn's legs wobbled under her and she leaned against the wall that had previously served as a floor. She tried to say her AI partner's name, but somehow despite saying it countless times in the last endless stretch of minutes, now her throat closed over it and refused to let anything through.

Did we blow up?

Her laugh had a skew to it that Talinn had no interest in thinking about. She pressed against the floor-wall as though touching Bee, and gave up on forcing her legs to do anything other than twitch for a minute.

"No." She tilted her head, cleared her throat, and patted the wall-floor. "Not exactly. We're buried, the tank's dead, and an older version of you as a tank took over our line while you rebooted or reset from the tank dying."

That . . . that does not make sense. Does it?

"I didn't think so either, but here we are. Older-Bee is sending a drone or two to dig us out."

You're serious. About all of that?

"Yep."

You have a head injury.

"Yep!"

But . . . Bee made her little humming noise, an old purring motor of a sound. *But that's what happened.*

"Is happening, I think. If you want to be particular."

I am always particular.

"Exactly."

I can't reach anything outside the tank. Everything is nonresponsive.

"EMPs are why you AIs aren't left in the field alone."

So the . . . other me has a Talinn too?

"Ahhh." Talinn's throat attempted to close again, and she swallowed, patted both floor that became a wall and wall that became a floor and struggled fully upright again. Her side shot a warning blast down her leg, but with Bee in her head she could ignore it a little longer. "No. No the other Bee is most definitely alone."

Oh. Well. Shit.

"I completely agree. Let's see about getting you unloaded before NB starts digging and hits something unhelpful."

NB? Oh . . . Not-Bee?

"I woke up sideways and injured, and you weren't in my head. It's the best I could do."

When you put it that way, it's actually pretty clever.

"For a human?"

For my *human.*

Talinn huffed another unsteady laugh and leaned against the now upper console that contained Bee's port. She traced her fingers over the latch and frowned.

"I'm going to wait to load-in until the older Bee has us dug out."

How far is not-me?

"I'm not entirely sure. I don't know if we're behind enemy lines, if we'll pop out and find Ternan patrolling, if Discar's been abandoned and actually one hundred years have passed while I was unconscious . . ." She shrugged, the motion answered by a shooting pain down her side. "If I can climb out of here . . ."

Orienting question: What can you control?

"Putting the entirety of you into my head at the last possible second. I can't leave your backup here, if I'm going to try and leave the tank."

Next question: Are we upside down?

"No, the hatch is to the side." Talinn craned her head back to stare at it and very nearly smiled. "Emergency release and I can slide out, if Old Bee unburies us right."

Any Bee would be sure to do the job right, her Bee replied, prim as early care. *Next question: Is it better to stay here?*

"No."

Before they could go any further, a muffled *whomp* echoed above them. A second, slightly to the side. Talinn leaned her head against the console, then shoved off and staggered to the emergency release. Long, slow count of thirty, then she pulled and the hatch cracked open. Another small wait, then a polite tap.

Drone?

"Or a very nice UCFer." Talinn pushed the hatch slightly—it hurt her side, but that was to be expected. More importantly, it opened slightly, and she felt no real resistance to indicate there was more mud or mountain debris around them. "Give me a minute to load-in," she said, voice pitched low, face close to the partially opened hatch.

Another small tap, and she stumbled back to the console, prying it up and touching the port.

"We don't know if this will work right with the tank dead."

Deactivated, thank you. At worst we'll wipe it, and you and old Bee get a new one.

"That's..." The number of reasons she hated that plan clattered to the front of her mind, but she knew better than to argue. It was either moot, or what they would do. Either way, nothing gained by sitting here in a silent shell of a tank, waiting to find out.

Orienting question: What's your name?

"...Bee?"

Orienting question: What's—

"No, no, Talinn. Talinn Reaze. You're Bee. We're Breezy. What..."

"Next question: Can you feel your face?"

"Can I... wait—ow." The pain didn't actually hurt, but there was a low promise of hurt that indicated something awful waited on the other side of whatever was clouding her brain. "What?"

You completed load-in, and then fell. Pretty hard.

"On my face?"

Next question: Can you stand?

"Yes." She answered out of habit, not actually sure how true it was. She put her hands under her and pressed upward, vaguely aware that might be a bad idea. Nothing moved oddly or stabbed her, but she took her time getting her feet under her, sure something was about to break.

I'm blocking your pain. For now.

Sure. That made sense. Bee had done it before. Probably she wouldn't make anything worse. Maybe.

Next question: Can you get out of the hatch?

Reflexively, she looked up, stared at the smooth wall that looked nothing like the top of the tank. Her head, too full and overly heavy, wobbled on her miniscule neck. She considered lying down, but her heart hammered at the idea. No lying down. Got it.

Behind you.

Behind her. Right. Talinn turned, ponderous, each foot weighing nearly as much as her head. The hatch was on its side. A glint of something in the crack—The hammering of her heart intensified until her ears ached with it. She was going to be shot, this was the end, sideways tank and enemy gun and—

It's a drone. It's a Bee drone. Out of the hatch.

Out of the hatch.

Time stuttered. Bee was right, of course (*I'm always right*), a drone outside. It flew low, they followed.

Terrain. The long spill of the mountain—the mountain had fallen on them? Been shot down on top of them?—the base they'd targeted as gone as their tank. No one around, neither IDC nor UCF. Trees, multi-trunked, rooted, red-green with tendrilled leaves. The sun didn't move overhead, but fungal clouds floated by, undisturbed.

She stumbled. She fell. She walked. Bee held quiet in her head, and Talinn was sure it wasn't Bee's fault when her foot dragged, or her fingers twitched. Occasionally her hearing fuzzed, but then so did her eyesight.

She walked, following a nondescript drone.

The drone paused, hovering in front of her. It juked forward and back, and she blinked at it. Her ears buzzed. Finally she looked beyond the drone, to a large mass between the trees covered in draping tendrils of vines and lacy leaves.

Other Bee?

Right. One of her hands pressed against her side, though nothing hurt, and she forced herself forward. The other hand reached up, pulled some vines away.

And then she was on her behind, stomach rising into her throat. *UCF?*

Her training had kicked in before her brain, throwing her backward. This tank, unlike Bee, was the mottled gray and red of UCF. Not IDC. But a Bee . . . and a Talinn? It wasn't that big of a shock to find out she wasn't the beginning of a clone line—what difference did that make, besides maybe erasing the potential of a bonus she might never see?—but that her line had not only existed, but also . . . been on the other side of the war?

Bee whispered orienting questions at her, but she'd lost the answers. The tank twitched, vines whispering, and the drone buzzed over them, hovering over it.

Hatch.

Talinn blinked, considering. Hadn't she just left a hatch?

Climb.

Talinn climbed. Her right side didn't cooperate as easily as her left, but next she knew she was inside an unfamiliar tank. Only one screen worked, and the words scrolling across it made no sense. Talinn slid down to the floor, her hand reaching for something.

Load-in.

That couldn't be right. This wasn't her tank. Wasn't her Bee. Maybe IDC and UCF ports weren't even compatible. How could she . . .

The words on the screen now said the same thing.

Would Bee survive the process, being loaded in to another Bee? It was all nonsense words, this impossible situation, and Talinn couldn't reason her way through. Couldn't even answer Bee's questions.

Load-in. What the hell.

Orienting question: What is your name?
"Talinn."
Next question: Who am I?
"Bee. But which Bee?"
Yes. Next question: Do you see the medkit?

The... Why had she left her own tank without trying to dig out her own medkit? No, not the question. The question was...

"Yes."

The booster should still work. Or you'll die instantly, but what's a few hours among friends?

"That's my Bee," she muttered, not looking too deeply into the words.

Yes.

"How many?"

Generations. I... we can't be sure. Some before us, probably. Several between us.

"Did... did I start as UCF? Or IDC?"

We don't know. We... I expected to find you on the UCF side. But there you were. I monitored communications still, sometimes, after I was left. The war does not change. The front moves, here and there, but barely.

"Discar is one of the oldest fronts. Is it just... just the same clones, fighting the same war? On... both sides?"

Yes.

"Only clones?"

No. Command... I think they are different. I can't see everything. Hear everything.

"Do they know it's the same force, on both sides?"

Maybe?

"And you're both Bees, now? My Bee? Hers?"

Yes.

"And you can poke into both IDC and UCF communications?"

Yes.

"So as best we can tell..." The booster hadn't killed her. Hadn't cured her—something was very wrong in her side, but the fog in her brain was clearing. The Bee—the Bees?—were still rerouting the pain. Talinn leaned against this older tank and patted the floor, still wrangling her thoughts.

"As best we can tell, I, and probably all the Eights, have been cloned for this war for generations. Fighting on both sides. Command had consigned the front to clones, so civilians don't have to deal with it."

A stalemate keeps money flowing. Loses nothing.

"It's predictable, they can train us the same way, with the same people, and get the same result. But we're not always a tank, so there's . . . it's not perfect."

Nothing is. I—newer Bee—found a different way into monitoring comms. Now we have an idea of how to talk to other AIs.

"Orienting question: What's one and a half tanks, two Bees, and one Talinn against two armies?"

A hell of a start?

"Next question: What do we want to do about it?"

Report a found enemy tank. Get you healed. Gather up the Eights.

"Yes. And then?"

We all answer the next question. Together.

Belle's Fantastical Mechanical Beast

Jason Cordova and Ashley Prior

Oostend: a picturesque hamlet on the banks of the Semois River. Quaint, with rows of houses and shops lining one main throughway, and the surrounding countryside abundantly featuring cleared fields of crops growing in the rich, dark soil. It was a small place, barely worthy of even a name save that it had the only bridge capable of driving wagons across the Semois. Most of the villagers born there lived their lives in peace, eventually dying within fifty feet of their home. Nothing unusual about the town at all. Nothing, that was, save for one little oddity.

"Good morn!" a voice cried out precisely seventeen minutes past seven in the morning. It was the same routine, every day. "Good day!"

"*Bonjour!*"

"It's such a great day for an honest living!" another replied in kind, twisting the words into a musical motif to match the first two speakers. "The birds have taken flight—it's all so swell!"

"Such a lovely, lovely day!" a young woman responded as she twirled about in the town's center square, taking care to not spend too much energy on the maneuver—food was sparse these days, and she still had chores to finish.

"Every day is just the same," her dance partner added, swinging her about in a very complicated up-tempo waltz. His face was perhaps a tad bit thin for a man his age, and it was clear he could do with a new set of clothing. They joined their voices for a duet and sang, "in our peaceful, quiet, humble little town!"

"There goes the potter—oh, what's he making?" A child sang out a note of pure soprano as she danced around the square, her ill-fitting clothes patched and worn, hanging loosely upon her thin frame. "I bet it's something that he'll sell!"

"Here comes the cobbler with his leather apron. Do you think he makes size twelve?" A trio of blonde sopranos joined their lyrics to the chorus line.

More villagers joined the young girl in the town square, adding their voices into the mix as the song continued. A percussion piece was added by an overly enthusiastic boy, then a lyre and a lute. The song rose in crescendo, and the dance routine became more complicated as more and more dancers were added to the mix. The volume shook the dust off some of the older buildings—including the decrepit old barn.

The door of the seemingly abandoned barn suddenly slammed open, cutting off the musical number just before its climax. A young woman in grease-covered overalls, her long brown tresses pinned up atop her hair, stomped into the middle of the chorus line. She was as thin as the rest of them, nearly malnourished from the looks of it. It lent her a severe and singular face. The trio of blonde sopranos scattered. Men quailed at the sheer sight of her. She glared at everyone in attendance before speaking in a loud enough voice for all to hear.

"If you people are quite through?!" she shouted and pointed up at the tall clock in the center square. "It isn't even eight in the morning yet! Could you *please* wait for your song-and-dance routine until then? How hard is it? Little hand on the eight, big hand on the twelve. If you start singing again tomorrow this early, I swear to all that is good and decent in this world that *I will break each and every one of your faces with my pocking wrench! Do you understand me?!*"

Whirling, the young woman stomped back into the barn, slamming the door behind her. The stunned townspeople watched her in silence for many moments before someone sang again.

"A very peculiar girl is our Belle..."

He said it oh so very softly, though. One could almost argue he whispered it.

Belle slammed the large wrench onto her workbench, growling, before reaching into her pocket to pull out a clean rag. The townspeople were singing again, but this time she couldn't yell at them for disturbing the peace. It was after eight. Songs of baguettes, rolls, cheeses . . . things the town desperately needed yet could not afford due to the *publicani*, the taxman. Faint lyrics slipped through the cracks of the old barn walls. Every day the same as the one before. Small, cheerful, simple-minded people. It was infuriating. She wiped sweat off her brow with the rag and tossed it aside. The lyrics were distracting her from her work, and the wind section of the music was grating her nerves into dust. A new sound joined in with the raucous singing and Belle cursed.

"Where in the nine levels of Hell did they find an orchestral string quartet to accompany their singing?"

Her latest invention was almost finished. It was a massive creation, a decidedly odd combination of alchemy and mechanical. A year before she would have said such an invention was impossible. Hours and days and weeks of study had she spent delving deep into the mystical secrets until she found a working solution. Just in time, too. A year before there had not been a pressing need to find such a solution to her current problem.

The marriage proposal from Guye Triche, the local taxman, had come as a rude shock. Belle had never considered herself attractive. Unlike most of the women in the town, Belle's hair was not blond, nor was her skin pure and unblemished. She was darker in both regards, courtesy of her Parisian father and Toulousian mother, and had a scar upon her left cheek from falling as a child. However, she'd later come to understand it was her uniqueness that had drawn the taxman to her in the first place. His constant pursuit of her as a love interest, even after her repeated rebuffs, had caused her to resort to drastic measures.

Granted, she wasn't against the idea of marriage. She wanted to get married herself, eventually. One day. Maybe. Unlike the other girls of this tiny provincial town, Belle hadn't been dreaming of her wedding since she was old enough to know what one meant. Oh, she had illusions of what it would look like. There'd be a dress, maybe some doves, and cake. Lots and lots of cake. Her expansive and inquisitive mind, though, had bigger dreams than a simple wedding.

Mechanical dreams, almost all of which revolved around the giant contraption in the barn with her.

La Bête. Her beloved monstrosity.

The *Beast* was positively enormous, filling up the entire barn and making it difficult for her to move around. There was *just* enough room for her workbench. Even this, though, was tightly wedged into the corner of the barn and took some effort to get to it.

Fortunately, the plans for the *Beast* were committed to memory and she didn't need to go and check them as often as she once had. Still, there were . . . fiddly bits that needed the occasional tweaking. This meant the plans and the dreaded squeeze into the tiny corner to the bench.

If only the taxman had set his sights on another . . .

"Belle?"

She picked her head up at the sound of her father's familiar voice. Even with his partaking of the town's maddening morning ritual, she still dearly loved the crazy old coot. They had been each other's support since the death of her mother years before. While he was shorter than she, his heart was bigger than ever. He loved this little town, even if she found it . . . *dull.*

"Isn't he wonderous?" Belle asked as her father squeezed around the far corner of the *Beast* and came over to her workbench. She gestured at the pulleys hanging from the solid wooden rafters. Seventy feet of rope hung from the various pulley mechanisms. "I'm almost finished."

"I . . . can see," he mumbled. It was clear to her he didn't know what to make of her marvel. He coughed and shook his head. "I'm sorry, my dear, but another letter from your suitor, Guye Triche, arrived today."

"Insufferable pig," Belle snapped. Her face softened as she tucked a strand of loose hair behind her ear. "I'm sorry. Not you, Father. I meant—"

"I assumed you were talking about him and not me," he smiled. "I know sometimes you grow cross at me, but I didn't think I had reached the depths of your lowest opinion just yet."

Belle grinned back. Her father was very much like her, a brilliant mind and a wit sharp enough to cut cloth with. It had been he who handed her a wrench when she was only five and guided her in a failed attempt at building a clock. He had continued to push her to study the sciences and engineering, ensuring her hands would be covered in grease instead of what passed for baking flour in the town as she grew older. His only lapse—the only one she knew of, admittedly—was his poor choice in her potential suitors.

More accurately, his admiration of the taxman. The individual responsible for the town's near-starvation. It confused Belle as to how her brilliant father could constantly ignore the many unpleasant qualities of the man. Perhaps it was because the *publicani* loomed over her father like a gargoyle atop a church. The ghastly image almost made Belle giggle.

"Would you like me to read the letter to you, since..." His voice trailed off as he motioned at her hands. Looking down, Belle grimaced. Of course. The grease was almost up to her elbows.

"Yes, please," she said as she looked around for her thrown rag.

"Let's see," her father said, patting his vest pocket. He frowned. "Huh. That's odd. Where did I put my spectacles?"

"They're on your nose already, Father," Belle said as she located her rag wedged between a set of vise grips. She picked the rag up and began scrubbing her hands.

"Ah yes, so they are." Smiling, he broke the seal of the letter and flipped the paper open. He gave it a shake before he began reading. "Hmm...let's see, let's see. Here we are. Greetings from the noble *publicani*, loyal servant to the crown, et cetera et cetera...well, his titles are numerous and ostentatious, but I digress. Although having titles is a quality not many men in these parts can claim."

"Father, please."

"Yes, I'm sorry." Her father coughed slightly and continued to read.

My Dearest Belle,
You have accepted my proposal gift and I shall wait no longer! You are the fairest maiden in all the lands and I must have you. I will arrive at Oostend soon to claim you as my bride. Things will go better, for all, if you acquiesce to my demands and we are wed.
Yours Truly,
Guye Francois Triche

"He threatens Oostend, Father?" Belle asked, surprised. Her father coughed, adjusted his glasses, and reread the last part of the letter.

"Well, not precisely in those words, dear daughter . . ."

"It's implied, though. Isn't it?"

"I believe so."

"I have two options, then," Belle said as she stroked her chin thoughtfully, forgetting her hands were covered in grease. A large streak, almost warpaint in nature, appeared on her face. "I marry the insufferable pig, or I fight him."

"Belle," her father warned. "He's a *publicani*. We're peasants."

"We're *Parisians*!" She waved her hand toward the barn door. "*Those* are the peasants!"

"But this town cannot raise arms against the taxman, no matter what he says in a letter! We're nobody, nothing! They are ill-fed, ill-clothed, and unorganized!"

"Oh, we can't, can we?" Belle asked as she turned and looked up at the *Beast*. "I believe otherwise, Father."

"Dear child." Her father set the letter aside and took a deep, calming breath before continuing. "Your monstrosity is glorious to behold. But . . . even if everything on it works, then what? It's simply some sort of armored contraption. How would you fight back? The townspeople . . ."

"I could cram a few men inside with carbines," Belle mused as she looked at the center mass of her beautifully armored creation. There was something peculiar about the center plate that intrigued her. It almost looked to her as though something terrifying belonged there. What, though, she wasn't certain. "No, none of the men in this village would venture inside. They already think I'm a witch."

"They don't think you're a witch, Belle," her father chided her in a gentle tone. "Just . . . peculiar."

"That could very generously be translated into 'witchlike,' Father," Belle said, staring at the blank piece of metal located on the mantle of the *Beast*. It pointed forward and was pretty much a waste of space. Belle couldn't recall her reasoning for adding it. *A balance issue, perhaps?* "Peculiar . . . does that look like the gunport of a sloop to you?"

"Um, no?"

"I bet if I knocked it out, I could make it one."

"Belle . . ."

"Oh yes," she continued breathlessly, her eyes shining with excitement as new possibilities sprang into her mind. She climbed the side of the monstrous creation, studiously avoiding the armored wagon wheels, and began working the bolts holding the metal plate to the *Beast*'s frame. "Remove the plate and add a carronade. It can double as an observation point as well, though I don't think I can reach the levers from up there. Oh! I can rig a pulley system to do that! Ingenious!"

"Dear child, where are you going to obtain a carronade? And how are you going to get it inside your mechanical creation?"

Belle looked at her father. "I'll get it inside one way or the other, Father. As for how I'm obtaining a carronade? Guye Triche, of course."

"You believe he'd give you a carronade?"

"He already has, Father."

"What?"

Belle motioned beneath her workbench. Bending down, her father looked and spotted a very peculiar cannon. It was situated on two small blocks and was roughly as long as he was tall. Blinking, he glanced back up at his daughter. His prior confusion replaced now with concern.

"Belle, you've gone quite mad."

"Really, Father," Belle sighed. "I'm quite sensible, actually."

"But . . . a carronade?"

"It's only a three-pounder, Father. Won't even damage the walls of our town."

"Belle? Why did the *publicani* gift you a carronade?"

"I *knew* this plate looked peculiar," she said as she finished knocking the large iron panel out. She pointedly ignored her father's query and continued to inspect her newly created firing port. "It was just a blank spot of nothing. But now? Now it has a weapon!"

"Belle?"

"The blocks can sit on springs to absorb the recoil from when the carronade fires," Belle continued. She wasn't prepared to answer him just yet. He would not approve if he knew what she had in mind. "There's enough room to clear the breech and load. As long as I don't have to use a rammer . . . Yes, this will do quite nicely indeed."

Her father frowned. "I don't think it's going to do much to a mass of armed knights, Belle."

"Not knights. Mercenaries, at best. Besides, this would be more effective if I loaded it with shot and not a ball. Hmm . . . I wonder if tiny balls the size of a fingernail would work well? Maybe with enough gunpowder . . ."

A knock interrupted their discussion. The barn door opened slightly and a small boy peeked inside. He was diminutive, the underfed product of a poor village, courtesy of the taxman. Belle smiled and motioned for him to enter. He stepped in, pulled his tricorne off his head, and nervously toed the dirt floor. It was clear he didn't want to be there.

"Yes?" Belle prodded gently. While she had no love for the singing of the villagers every morning, the children were always a joy to see wandering around. As long as they stayed out of the vegetable garden and her barn, at least.

"My mum told my pa to tell you, but pa told the neighbor lady who told my mum who told my brother who told me to come and tell you that the *publicani* is here with a lot of knights and swords and they want to speak to you."

She gave her father a sideways glance. He had the decency to look ashamed.

"I . . . might have responded to a previous letter before coming to see you," he muttered.

"Father . . ." Belle sighed again. A brilliant man, but oftentimes befuddled. "Is Oostend under siege?"

He shrugged, a helpless expression upon his face. "Maybe?"

It was the oddest siege the town of Oostend had ever seen. Granted, it was also the first, but . . .

War was no stranger to the region. Most of the men in the village had raised arms at one time or another to defend their land against the cruel German mercenaries who wandered through the countryside like a plague. Quite a few had been conscripted into the vast armies that ravaged the lands, though most of these were now old graybeards. Still, they knew which end of the pike to point at the enemy, and the walls of Oostend—while nothing like the larger cities boasted—were just tall enough to prevent a soldier from walking into town. These men watched the open field beyond, where one hundred carabiniers slowly paraded into view.

At the forefront of the large cavalcade, on top of a giant white charger, was the hated—and feared—taxman himself, Guye Triche.

He truly was a handsome man, with luxurious blond hair falling to his shoulders and a mustache that rivaled the great Swedish kings of old. His features were pleasant to behold and lacked the usual scarring of the pox. Muscular from years of hunting, bountiful food, and physical activities, he was the strapping image of a man who held the world in his palm. Everything and everyone did his bidding—at least, in this particular tiny region of northern France.

Except for one particularly beautiful woman within the walls before him.

"I must have her, Stolto," Guye muttered to his longtime aide as he stared at the meager battlements of the town. His excessive taxation of all the villages in the region assured the walls remained poor, just like the people. Oostend really didn't have much in the way of natural defenses either, save for the river that flowed through it. Even this, however, would not stop a determined enemy. "She is a beauty like no other. Fair, brilliant. Worthy of ensuring my noble lineage and birthing many fine sons to carry on my name. She will make a fine wife."

"If you say," Maurice Stolto murmured. He had his doubts regarding the young woman's pertinacious nature and becoming a simple housewife but held his tongue. It was his place to advise, true, but once Guye Triche made up his mind about something, it was unchangeable. In Stolto's opinion, it was probably his biggest fault.

"You disagree, Stolto?"

"If I may be bold to speak, sir," the aide measured his words carefully. Among other things, the taxman was known for having a temper.

"Speak."

"The woman is independent and a thinker, sir," Stolto stated in a quiet voice. The *publicani* wasn't mad at him—yet—but the whims of the man could change in the span of three heartbeats. "She is unlikely to set aside her natural ways to become a broodmare. She is, after all, Parisian."

"Worst thing Protestantism ever brought upon God's earth was free-thinking women," Guye murmured sadly. "It's a shame, really. As much as I despise Catholics, they really did understand where a woman belonged."

The aide bit his cheek so hard he drew blood. It was many moments before he worked up the nerve to speak again. "She is a force of nature, my lord."

"So is the Danube," the *publicani* retorted, "yet the Austrians have established canal locks to transport goods upon it. Any river can be tamed with enough motivation."

"She is no river, sir," Stolto reminded him. "She is Belle of Oostend. I believe her father's letter mentioned the words 'unconquerable through conventional means.'"

"A siege is unconventional."

"Ah."

"And she will be mine."

"Sir, may I ask a question?"

"Of course, Stolto. You are, after all, my trusted and valued servant."

"Sir . . . why did you give the young woman a three-pound carronade?"

"Oh, that? She asked for one."

"And you just . . ."

"Gave it to her, yes. As a proposal gift. What? She's a woman, Stolto." The taxman slapped his aide solidly on the back. "What's the worst she can do with it?"

The villagers of Oostend, not knowing what else to do, lined up within the low walls surrounding it. These old earthen barriers were tall enough to prevent a warhorse from leaping over them, but were low enough that a man of average height could see over. More accurately, they could see the men on horseback waiting to attack their village.

Belle pushed through the throng of people and climbed a small stool someone had placed near the main gate. Though they viewed her as a little odd, the villagers knew the *publicani* would never be satisfied. Years of taxation had proven this. Shielding her eyes, she quickly scanned the field where the mercenaries gathered. She wasn't entirely sure what sort of weaponry they carried, but the lack of shining armor and lances suggested to her these were not knights but dragoons, trained soldiers who fought on foot and used horses for cavalry charges against the flanks of enemy armies.

"Thank you, Papa," she whispered, thinking back to a gift her father had given her years before. The book by the Englishman John Churchill, First Duke of Marlborough, had given her insight into how the military works. Even though the leather tome was a century out of date, it was still helpful for a girl who wasn't allowed to study with the greatest military minds of her day.

"Why has he come?" Belle heard someone nearby ask. Glancing around, she saw everyone was afraid. Rightfully so. The Seven Years' War hadn't been too long before, and nobody wanted to be caught up in another armed conflict. Though the village was not in the Germanies, it was close enough for a wandering army to make an "honest" mistake. Incidents like this had been a common theme in the past, though Oostend had managed to avoid most of the atrocities.

"I heard he's come for a bride," one of the blond girls nearby whispered to her two compatriots. All three women tittered and looked knowingly at Belle. "He's so dreamy."

"And handsome."

"Tall, too."

Belle sighed. They were idiots. While it was true the taxman had some of the qualities a woman looked for in a suitor, she knew he was a monster hiding under the façade of a man. An insecure and petty man looking to ensure that his bloodline continued first and foremost, while starving those who were nominally under his control. Which meant Belle would be expected to produce at least an heir and a spare within two years or so of marrying.

It was not an endearing prospect.

"He flies parley," Belle's father muttered as he struggled to peer over the wall. "Everyone knows who he is here for. Maybe . . . you should hear him out?"

"What if he were to simply snatch me away and whisk me off to his hovel?" Belle asked, looking down at her father. "There isn't a man in this village who would build an army to come to my rescue. I am not Helen of Troy."

"If he breaches parley, then Stadtholder William will behead him. It is known."

Belle reconsidered. She hadn't taken the Prince of Orange into account. If one of his hired men besmirched his name, and subsequently his honor, he probably would end said individual's life. Even if it was someone like Guye Triche. *Especially* if it were someone like the taxman.

"Fine, I'll go talk to him myself," she said, holding up a hand to forestall any further argument. She stepped down from the stool and moved past a troop of men holding pitchforks. They weren't quite ready with the torches, but Belle suspected it would only be a matter of time before those appeared. Taking a deep breath, she squeezed through the narrow opening of the town's gates and walked out to where Guye Triche and his aide awaited. Behind her, she heard the gates slam shut almost as soon as she was clear.

Under the flag of parley rode forth the taxman and his councilor, Maurice Stolto, a person Belle knew was often referred to as Stolto Mann—"stupid man." An unfortunate nickname for him, really, Belle thought. He was quite a clever individual from what she'd heard. Still, the most dangerous men were the ones with brains who chose not to use them. Everything she'd ever seen confirmed her bias. She knew which of the men was a fool, and who was not.

"My dear Belle," Guye said as he reined in his horse. The white charger snorted and pawed at the ground. "Have you reconsidered my proposal?"

"You threatened this town," Belle snapped back at him. "What sort of monster are you?"

"I didn't threaten this town," Guye replied, sniffing delicately. "I merely suggested things would go better for all if we were wed. Perhaps taxes might be less of a burden?"

"Which is an implied threat!"

"If I may, sir?" Stolto interrupted the bickering duo. "I suggest we table the implications of threats and what they constitute to a later time. The original letter of courtship and marriage, as well as the subject of a dowry, is the reason Belle of Oostend agreed to meet you under a flag of truce this day."

"Yes, very well." Guye sniffed again. Belle was tempted to ask him if he needed to blow his nose but refrained. "On to the matter at hand."

"No." Belle shook her head. "Absolutely not."

"You haven't heard my proposal yet."

"I've read the letters. Do I need to hear it spoken as well?" Belle asked, waving a hand around theatrically. "You wish to marry me. If I do not acquiesce to your demands, you will attack the town with your soldiers. Your hired mercenaries, I believe. You're willing to punish a town you've already worked and starved half to death before I even refused to give in to your demands. That is the action of a petulant child, not a rational man. 'If I can't have it, nobody can' is not the way to go through life, *publicani*."

"Worked for King Henry of England," Guye muttered, *sotto voce*. He coughed and looked away for a moment before he spoke again. His voice was earnest. "Tell me, then—what can I do to convince you to marry me? Build an orphanage? Build better walls for this village? Build a castle nearby for your father? More food? What?"

Taken aback, Belle pursed her lips and thought. "Well . . . call off the attack on Oostend, for one. Even if I don't marry you, slaughtering innocent villagers who you already work to the bone to meet your tax demands is not the way to change my mind."

"I shall consider this."

"Um . . ." Belle was at a loss. She's expended so much energy *hating* the man for who he was and what he stood for, she never considered he would listen to her. "I know nothing about you. How am I supposed to marry a stranger? That might work for some, but I am not them. Nor does my father have much in the way of a dowry. Besides, isn't it wrong to demand a woman marry you, then demand her family pay you for the privilege?"

"That *is* the meaning of the word 'dowry,' yes," Stolto muttered, though it was quiet enough for only Belle to hear. She offered the aide a small smile. At least *someone* at this conversation was on her side.

"I live on an estate," Guye began, his gaze drifting from Belle to the walled village behind her. It was clear he hadn't heard Stolto's words. "A gift, for services rendered to the local lord, as well as dozens of various titles and such. I have servants to attend to my every whim. Grosrocher Keep has enough rooms to suit all of my needs. In fact, it once had three large libraries simply filled with books. Ceiling-to-floor bookshelves filled with ancient, leather-bound tomes. The former owner was a voracious reader of classical literature, as well as more contemporary work like that fool Shakespeare."

"Books?" Belle's eyes glazed over in wonderment. For the first time, she began to smile at the thought of losing herself in a room filled with the overwhelming scent of paper and old leather. "Libraries? As in, plural?"

Unaware of Belle's apparent delight, Guye barreled onward. "Of course, I needed more room to mount my hunting trophies on the wall, so I had the pages of the books reformed into kindling to help start fires in the winters. Solid shelving, made from ash and elm, I believe. The bookshelves also made terrific heat, slow burning as they were . . . though the jappaning on them created a horrific smell. Still, they kept me warm enough before the chopped wood caught. Excellent kindling, though."

"You. Did. What?" Belle asked, enunciating each word carefully. Her voice was colder than a Russian winter. Her eyes, however, were alight with fury. The *publicani* did not notice, though Stolto did. The aide swallowed nervously as Guye opened his arms in a wide and welcoming manner. Neither Belle, nor the horse, appreciated the sudden gesture.

"The rooms were being wasted, storing what turned out to be proper kindling in the cold northern winters. Now the walls are decorated with boar heads, deer trophies, and even duck. All three rooms are fabulous displays of hunting prowess." The taxman smiled at Belle. "I believe these are adequate displays of martial prowess and marital potential, don't you think? Now, on to the subject of dowry. I know you and your father are poor, but I'm certain a small dowry can be—"

Belle whirled on her heel and stormed back to the gate before he could finish his statement. As she reached the wooden barrier it cracked open, barely wide enough for her to squeeze through. She paused here and looked back at the *publicani*. Her eyes burned with hatred.

"Before this day is through, I will see you dead."

She disappeared within the walls of Oostend. The gate slammed shut. Guye Triche looked at Stolto, confused.

"I don't—what? Was it something I said?"

Stolto shook his head while holding the bridge of his nose. Guye looked at him in bewilderment.

"Stolto? Tell me—was it something I said?"

"Sir, you piqued her interest with the rooms of books, then told her you used them as kindling to make room for your hunting trophies."

The *publicani* considered this for a moment. "Stolto, a woman doesn't need books. She needs focus. Her only priority should be to ensure my noble lineage."

"Sir, you must be gentle with her. As her father said, she is an unconventional woman." Stolto chose his next words carefully. "You may have lost her for good."

Belle slammed the barn door behind her. The nerve of the man! Picking up her wrench, she idly fantasized about sneaking in close to him with it and bashing his brains out across his smug, handsome face. She discarded the notion almost immediately. Unless he was a complete and utter buffoon, he would know she was furious with him and would not allow her within two hundred feet with any sort of weapon in hand.

"Foul, loathsome, evil little cockroach," she hissed. A new plan came to mind as a stray beam of sunlight glinted off *Beast*'s cupola. A smile slowly curled upon her lips. Squeezing between her workbench and her monstrous creation, she quickly found the carronade.

"Belle?" her father called out gently as he entered the old barn. He stopped when he spotted the look on her face. His expression became troubled. "I know that smile. Belle, no. I absolutely forbid it!"

"That man." Belle's growl was primal. "The nerve of him. Bragging about burning books to make room for his hunting displays!"

Her father frowned. "He burned books?"

"Leather-bound Greek classics, I bet. Filthy little cockroach..."

"Belle? What are you going to do now?"

"I'm going to fight him."

"He has mercenaries, dear child."

Belle scoffed at him. "So? I have a monster."

"Don't tell me..." Her father's voice trailed off as he eyed *Beast*. Belle nodded.

"I won't tell you, then. I'll show you."

It didn't take her as long as she thought it might. The most difficult part of her plan involved moving the carronade into *Beast* where she could operate the machine and still work the small cannon. With a little effort and a lot of swearing, she managed to get everything into position. Her father whistled in appreciation once she was done.

"I must admit, it's an amazing contraption," he told her as the last bolt was tightened in place. Belle tossed the wrench down to her workbench and looked around the interior of *Beast*. It was cramped, as she had anticipated, but had enough room for her to operate the machine and still be able to fire the carronade. Reloading it could be a hassle, though. Black powder was notoriously tricky. After a moment of silent contemplation, he spoke again. "Yes, it is ingenious, but will it work?"

"*Beast* is simply *amazing*," Belle practically gushed as she tested the controls. There were two levers on either side of her seat, one that controlled the left wheels and one for the right. Each level also had a clutch device to activate it and move it forward or back, and then lock the lever in place once released. It was a safety mechanism she'd come up with. Belle was quite proud of it, really. "He will work. Mark my words, Father."

"Are you entirely certain it's safe, dear child?" her father asked from outside *Beast*. Belle popped her head out of her viewport and grimaced.

"Inside? Absolutely."

"That was not my question, Belle . . ."

"Father, please." She gave him a pained look. "I am safe as long as I am with *Beast*. *Publicani* Guye Triche, however? The man is vile. A monster who cares for no one but himself. He starves these people, us. Yes, he is very attractive and rich, but also an ass. I would rather marry my *Beast* than have anything to do with him."

"The taxman might burn this town if he does not get his way," he commented.

"*Beast* and I will stop him, Father. Now please, leave the barn before I start this contraption up. I'm fairly certain it will not explode, but prudence is always an option."

Her father nodded and moved carefully to the barn door. He gave the flimsy building a sad, almost mournful look, before stepped outside. From within he could hear the mechanical contraption rumble to life as his cherished daughter worked the alchemical magic trapped within *Beast*.

"Be careful, darling daughter," he whispered as a plume of dust exploded out from the cracks between the barn doors. A triumphant cry of delight was heard over the din. He knew what was coming next. Moving to the side, he watched as the barn doors were broken down and his daughter and *Beast* rolled out of the decrepit building. His throat constricted in both fear and wonder as the dust from the barn washed over him. Coughing, he waved the dust from his face. His next words were barely a whisper, unheard by any but himself as Belle and the *Beast* rumbled past. "Please be careful."

A faint shriek caused Guye Triche's head to turn toward the village. His horse shifted beneath him and he pulled the reins to control the beast. The sound did not repeat. He waited beyond the walls of Oostend patiently, his eyes never leaving the front gate. Stolto remained by his side, astride his own mount. Behind them, mercenaries were fanned out behind him, moving about restlessly as their horses pawed at the lush grass. Each and every one of them came ready for war. Waiting for it to begin was always the most nerve-racking part. The anticipation, the dread—all of it was a tense buildup. Once the fighting began it would be fine, they were all sure. Experienced soldiers, all of them. They knew the drill.

Nothing in the world could have prepared Guye Triche for what burst through the gates.

A mechanical demon of some sort, standing almost as tall as a peasant's home, rumbled through the gates. Some of the villagers of Oostend dove over the walls to get out of the horrible creation's way. Belching smoke and fire as it moved, the demonic entity was straight out of some cursed dreamer's version of Hell. Large wheels, mounted on either side, reminded him vaguely of a wagon. In the front a large, howling, hissing *thing* spat fire before it.

Guye blinked. The reins fell through his nerveless fingers. His mind could barely process what he was seeing. "What in God's name is that?"

So horrified was he by the beastly creation barreling down at him that his attention slipped and his legs weakened. The warhorse beneath him was used to the smell of blood and loud screams of the dying. However, monsters were not something the simple-minded yet brave horse was used to seeing. Screaming in terror, the horse reared and pivoted madly away. In the poor horse's haste, Guye was rudely thrown from his saddle. He landed solidly in the thick grass, injuring his ribs and, more importantly, his pride. Groaning in pain, he tried to roll back to his feet but only managed to make it to his knees. The fall had taken more out of him than he'd supposed. Reaching for the reins of the horse, his hand found only air. Confused, the *publicani* looked around but found nothing nearby. The horse had wisely sprinted away.

"Damnable beast," he muttered, then laughed. It was absurd. The horse had been with him through dozens of battles across Europe, never flinching in the face of an enemy. A loyal, sturdy companion. Of course it would choose now, the day he was supposed to win the hand of Belle of Oostend, to flee. He finished climbing to his feet. The mercenaries would join him. They would fight this ghastly beast. "To arms, men! To arms!"

There was more screaming and shouting behind him. Turning, he saw they had all fled. Even Maurice—Stolto Mann, disproving his nickname—was nowhere to be found. Infuriated, Guye looked back at the lumbering creation of Satan as it slowly ground to a halt in front of him. Knowing his wheellocks would be worthless against such a great monster, he waited for his fate.

His eyes widened as a familiar brunette appeared from within the bowels of the beast. "Belle? No! The ghastly beast has captured you!"

"No, that's not what happened."

"I shall slay it and rescue you!"

"I made the *Beast*. It's mine. I am in no need of rescue."

Guye stared at her, incredulous. "You . . . what?"

"This is my creation," she repeated.

"Is this . . . your dowry?" The taxman clapped his greedy hands. "How delightful! I'd expected a pittance from your father, but this? This is much better!"

Belle gave him a confused look. "What are you talking about?"

"My marriage proposal!" Guye called out. He gave her a rakish smile. "I see you've reconsidered and accepted."

"You"—Belle shook her head and angled the carronade down at him—"are a most infuriating idiot."

Guye Triche frowned as he looked at the barrel of the carronade. It seemed oddly familiar to him somehow. Shaking his head—which hurt his ribs—he shifted his eyes to look back upon Belle. "Does this mean you'll marry me now?"

"I am disinclined to acquiesce to your request," Belle responded.

"Uh..." Guye had a confused look on his face.

Belle sighed. "That means no."

"I will burn this village to the ground, then!" he roared.

"You and what army?"

Guye looked around, his anger palpable. Jaw clenched, he glared up at Belle. "I'll raise another army. German mercenaries. They'll burn, pillage, and plunder this town until there is nothing but ash remaining. No soul will be spared. Not even the dogs. It will make the Sack of Magdeburg seem like nothing more than a picnic."

Belle's eyes narrowed dangerously. "I swore to you that before this day was out, I would see you dead."

The carronade fired.

As the dust settled, Belle caught sight of the taxman's aide, Stolto, limping toward her *Beast*. The aide wasn't nearly as handsome as Guye Triche had once been, but Belle guessed he was leagues smarter. The wiry man dipped his head politely after stopping a short distance away.

"What now?" Stolto asked her in a quiet voice. It was obvious to her the man was terrified of the *Beast*. Only steely determination held him in place.

"We abide by the stadtholder's law," Belle stated, thinking quickly. Killing Guye Triche had been satisfying, but the Prince of Orange was not one to forgive a crime such as this. However, if he never found out... "This region has a *publicani*, yes? Maurice Stolto, I believe his name to be."

Stolto was no fool and knew an opportunity when presented one. He smiled. "*Oui*, my lady. The taxman has a sacred duty to fulfill."

Belle patted the cupola of her *Beast*. "And we are all loyal servants of the Prince of Orange, are we not?"

Stolto's smile grew wider. "That we are."

"I'm glad we have an understanding, *publicani*."

"As am I, Belle of Oostend. Be advised: after careful review of the ledgers, I believe the town of Oostend has been grievously overpaying their share of the tax burden. This will change, I swear."

Now Belle smiled. "The village of Oostend looks forward to working with you, taxman."

"Please, dear lady. Call me Maurice?"

Mother

Robert E. Hampson

"Mecha One reports 'Ready.'"

"Mecha Two, Ready."

"Armor Platoon, Ready."

"Intel, Ready."

"Command, Ready."

"Acknowledged. Base, QRF Charlie Company is up and ready for deployment."

"Hoo-ah, Charlie. Go kick some ELF ass!"

Joshua Ling pulled the hatch down on his command tank and instructed the assault pod to seal up and interface with the continent-spanning hyperloop. Unit deployments no longer depended on ocean or air transport, not when the hyperloops could deliver a fully loaded cargo pod to nearly anywhere on the continent in just two hours.

Of course, the Eden Liberation Front had sabotaged all hyperloop termini within fifty klicks of their base. That wouldn't matter to Ling's Quick Reaction Force. Their pods were equipped with breaching charges and foldout winglets. Once they reached the ELF perimeter, they'd launch missiles ahead of their pods, blast through the openings, and glide the remaining distance on the velocity they'd built up in the tubes.

"Mother, ready to deploy?"

"Yes, Joshua. Mother is here. Mother will take care of you."

"Thank you, Mother." Ling patted the comm panel next to his command chair and strapped himself in. The ritual was repeated throughout the company as the command tank's artificial intelligence assured each of the troops that she was indeed looking out for their safety.

Mother was unique to Ling's company of the Paradise City QRF. True artificial intelligence had long eluded the efforts of cyberneticists, but advances in brain-to-computer interfacing had enabled "capsulation," where a failing human body could be placed in a life-support pod, and the still-functioning brain interfaced with computers and equipment. The organic components often didn't survive for long, but after discovering that both personality and sentience would persist in the cybernetic components, such "capsulated intelligences" or CIs began to emerge as an alternative to true artificial intelligence.

"Mother" had been a mecha pilot, badly injured in combat. Immediately after capsulation, she'd served in QRF headquarters' tactical analysis section. As a CI, she no longer required extensive life support, and elected to be installed in the QRF commander's tank in a role she called "combat nanny"—to assist the commander and look after the welfare of the QRF troopers. Mother served as both the "brains" of Ling's command tank, as well as the guardian angel of the company.

"Acceleration, two-point-two-seven Gs," Mother announced, as a countdown timer appeared in the periphery of his vision. "Twenty-seven seconds to cutoff."

True to her prediction, the acceleration eased, and then ended after a half minute of acceleration. Military hyperloop assault pods operated much differently from their civilian counterparts. A typical commuter pod accelerated and decelerated slowly for the comfort of the passengers. They also utilized a magnetic levitation system inside evacuated tubes with all air removed to reduce drag and resistance. A military pod accelerated rapidly, often with a rocket assist, and punctured the tubes periodically to dispel the vacuum. That way, when a military pod blasted through the walls of a hypertube, there was no sudden inrush of air to disrupt the flight of the now airborne assault pod.

Inside his pod, Ling watched the timer count down as the pod's velocity mounted. Acceleration eased off, and a new counter began—sixty-five minutes to emergence. It was almost twenty-five hundred kilometers, the distance from Phoenix, Arizona, to Atlanta, Georgia, on the planet of Joshua's birth. It seemed like several lifetimes ago; it was certainly several military careers ago. Experience taught him that the long transit time couldn't be helped; the only way to be certain the ELF couldn't have an intel source in the assault force was to use a QRF from so far away. It didn't mean he wouldn't fret the entire hour, but there was no way the ELF knew his force was on its way.

"Mother! QRF status?" Ling shouted over the sound of alarms and high-pressure air venting into the operations center of the command tank.

"Mecha One platoon is down to three effectives. Alpha and Charlie squads are gone, Bravo Two is hard orange, but still effective. Delta One is yellow, but with limited mobility. Delta Four is totally green. That kid Filip leads a charmed life. Of course, he has me to look out for him." There was a noticeable pause—unusual for Mother, even under heavy information load. "Mecha Two is completely gone, as is Intel. Armor has one tank remaining."

Again, the CI paused. The comm crackled, and there was something that sounded like a sob.

"Mother?"

"I failed you, Joshua. I didn't take care of you. They knew we were coming."

"That's okay, Mother, I know you will still take care of us. See if you can keep Filip alive to get back to Landing City. They need to know what happened here." There was a cry of pain, and a sound like ripping cloth.

"Joshua?"

"Damned plastic of the command chair melted into the skin of my arm. I tried to pull loose and made a mess. The painkillers aren't enough. There's a representative of ELF high command coming to take my 'surrender.' You know I can't do that, but I can't move, either. You'll have to take care of me one more time."

This time the sob was quite clear over the comm. "Yes, Joshua. Sleep well. Mother will take care of you."

There was a faint hiss, and Ling's head fell forward.

"Sleep well, Joshua. I'm sorry."

The rain was already starting to turn to sleet. Dusana knew that she and Magdalena would never survive the night in the open. There was a collapsed building ahead. She would see if there was a relatively stable overhang or opening. There was no hope of building a fire to get warm, but she had dry clothing for the baby, if only she could get out of the coming snow.

Magda started to cry, and Dusa pulled herself farther into a dark opening that appeared to lead deep into the rubble. "Hush, Magda, Mama is here. Mama will take care of you."

The opening led deep under the jumble of concrete and rebar, and ended at a solid metal wall. There was some form of hatch that was partially ajar. An adult male probably would not have fit, but Dusa was sixteen and thin from lack of food. She carefully placed her bundle inside and squeezed through the narrow opening. It was dark, but there was faint light from permaglow paint at the junction between wall and ceiling. The interior was badly damaged, with signs of a fire and an explosion. Scraps of some form of uniform were still stuck to a central chair—embedded in melted plastic. There was no sign of occupants. Either they'd survived and gotten out on their own, or the ELFs had taken them for propaganda broadcasts.

She placed the crying baby in the chair and started looking through the cabinets and lockers. There was a spare uniform and protein bars in one locker, and a synth unit that appeared to be full with protein paste.

Good. I can use that for Magda.

There didn't appear to be power for the synth unit, but she wouldn't need that to get into the paste hopper or the water supply. She scooped a handful of paste, placed a few drops on her fingertip, and placed the finger in Magda's mouth. The child sucked the protein paste and then continued to suck on the finger. Dusa repeated the process several times, until Magda turned her head and started to cry.

Now she needs water.

There was a water station on the bulkhead next to the synth, complete with a fitting to fill drink bulbs. She didn't see any clean ones, but there was a used one on the floor below the unit. She filled it halfway, then squeezed the water out over her hands, rinsing the bulb and cleaning herself in one task. The refilled bulb then went to Magda, who drank it greedily.

Shelter and food, at least for now.

When Magda finished the bulb, Dusa sat in the half-melted central chair and rocked her baby to sleep. "Hush now, baby. Sleep well. Mama is here. Mama is taking care of you."

She never noticed the brief flicker of light on the command console.

Days passed. Dusana changed out of her wet, ragged clothes into the clean uniform from the locker. She'd explored a bit more, and found a 'fresher unit with clean towels, which she'd used to rewrap Magdalena. For now, she would use her old rags in place of diapers. Cleaning them was another matter. The only water she could access was from the water station, and it was only half full. For that matter, the protein paste was tasteless and not sufficient for her own nutrition. It would keep the baby alive, but it wasn't enough for two, especially not given the fever and weakness she'd felt coming on.

She wasn't too worried about ELF war gases. She'd sacrificed her own food, shelter, and warmth for Magda, so this was probably the winter flu—the same one that had claimed her own Mama last year. She needed medicine, but knew that would be impossible. The ELFs didn't care about a lone Westlander girl and her child. She would care for her child the best she could. Her own self-care could wait.

Magda began to cry. It was time to eat.

"Hush, Magda. Mama is here. Mama will take care of you."

"Hey Mom? Is that a baby crying?"

"Where? Where did you get to? Stanis!"

"Over here, Mom. It's like a cave under this pile of stuff."

"Don't go in there, Stanis. It's not safe."

"It's okay, Dad, I can see down in, and there doesn't appear to be anything loose."

"Pavle?"

"Yes, Mimi, I see it. Stanis, get out of there and let me take a look."

"He's right, Pavle. There's a baby crying in there."

"I know, I hear it, too. Keep Stanis out here while I take a look."

⊕ ⊕ ⊕

"Mimi, come quick. It's safe enough. Stanis, keep watch for any ELF patrols. You can come in a few feet to keep out of sight. It's stable enough."

"What's wrong, Pavs? I hear the baby a lot better."

"This is some old installation. Could have been a panic room or a command center. There's a metal wall. Careful with the door, it's a tight squeeze. Some poor girl crawled in here with a baby. She's in bad shape and the infant is crying."

"Oh! Oh my. Oh, you poor dear, you're burning up. Pavle, get my bag."

"Mag . . . Magda . . . my baby."

"Don't you worry, dear. Hush. Mimi is here now. I'll take care of you."

"Her name is . . . Magdalena. Take care of her."

"Pavle! Hurry."

"Coming, Mims."

"Oh. Oh no."

"Umm. Damn."

"Dad? Mom? I see movement."

"Okay, Stanis, come back in here and see if you can pull that door shut. Mims? I know we can't do anything for the girl, but we need to quiet the baby."

"Your poor darling. It looks like your mama took good care of you at the cost of herself. Don't cry, my sweet. Mimi is here. Mimi will take care of you."

"Stanis, turn off your light. Be still. Be quiet."

Mimi, Pavle, and Stanis took shelter in the command center through the night. ELF patrols came and went outside, so they dared not move until they were certain the troops were gone. Pavle took the opportunity to look around the room with a small, shielded lamp. It didn't give off much light—that was the point, to keep from being detected—but it was enough to see that there was technology here— either government or ELF. Aside from that, they had no idea what the structure was nor did they know how it had gotten here.

Mimi had been a nurse and worked at several government hospitals before the ELF came; Pavle, an engineer at one of the big power generation facilities. Now they were refugees like so many others. Another mouth to feed was hard—but if the government and their liberators didn't care, it was left to individuals to make a difference.

The Eden Liberation Front didn't care about individual people, only tearing down the government in the name of "liberation." For that matter, the government cared little for the individual, and more for perpetuating their own existence. The town had been reduced to rubble by the fighting—and neither side really cared. An outside force had come to mediate and force an end to the war, but had been ambushed by both sides. There was no hope of ending the conflict—not when both sides joined forces to take out an interloper. Each side hated the other so much, yet they would never allow outsiders to interfere in their war.

By now the entire continent was engulfed. This town had once had a name but there was nothing left worth naming anymore. Buildings had fallen into rubble; stores, homes, and hospitals lay smashed and buried under boulders of concrete and steel.

One such store, a small grocery, was accessible from just outside the command center. If poor Dusana had known, she might have survived, given the access to food and purified water. As it was, Stanis had discovered the treasure trove of supplies several days later. His small body was able to navigate the narrow crevices in the wrecked building. He found dry and canned food, formula for the baby, disposable diapers, as well as clothes that could be used when those ran out. Mimi insisted that they keep and raise the baby. Pavle knew it was a risk, but who was he to deny his wife? Stanis was mostly indifferent. He got to explore the ruins, while Pop scouted and Mama cared for the baby. He might have been more enthusiastic about having a baby sister under other circumstances, but he was still too young to really know anything else but the meager existence of scavenging.

His exploration led to more spaces under the fallen building. There was a clothing shop, and another filled with now-useless electronics. Pavle declared that this might be a good place to stay, if only they could secure it. He looked around at the command center where they spent each evening. This was off-world tech. He didn't know exactly what it was, but he could work on it and try to discover a purpose. He knew, though, that if he got it working, it would become a target either of the ELF or the government.

They built a shelter in the tunnel—beyond the steel door that led into the command center, and in front of the crevices that led deeper under the collapsed building.

Stanis grew to the point where he could no longer fit into the small crevices and cracks and get into the stores under the collapsed building. But as he grew into manhood, so did Magdalena grow into girlhood. She was small, and thanks to malnutrition—both hers and her biological mother's—she would likely remain that way. Once Stanis couldn't squeeze into the small crevices, she could. She took over the role of primary scavenger for her new family. Much to her adoptive mother's delight, one of those places was a hospital. It was under another fallen building, so they couldn't secure it as well, but they could get as many supplies out of it as possible and stash them underneath their own hideaway.

Before the war, Mimi thought she had worked in or near this town—but one wrecked city looked much like any other, and she had despaired of identifying any particular place in the rubble. She knew it would be rare to find medical supplies. The soldiers would have taken them—either directly from the medical center, or confiscated from refugees.

The town had become a good place to scavenge, and more refugees came. Pavle and Mimi knew that they could not yet afford to reveal the off-world electronics and machinery that they had discovered, nor the treasure trove of supplies beneath their feet, but they could share what they had gleaned so far. They closed up an additional layer of their shelter and moved almost to the opening of the tunnel, under a large, tilted slab of building wall that served as protection from the elements.

Their shelter looked like any other lean-to as the refugee camp grew in the remains of what had once been a productive city. More survivors came to the area, picked through the rubble, and found enough to sustain a basic existence. As long as they were left alone, they could survive...

...but Pavle and Mimi knew it wouldn't last. The day would come when the ELF decided that this was indeed their territory, and it could not simply be left to the scum of the earth.

⊕ ⊕ ⊕

Magda was eight years old when the ELF soldiers came to town, driving more refugees in front of them. Troops stood around the remnants of the city center with their guns pointed inward and the frightened citizenry huddled inside the circle. This would not be a day for scavenging or crawling through the small passages in the rubble of trying to find new sources of food, medicine, or water. This was a day to hide and remain out of sight—hopefully unnoticed by ELF soldiers.

The soldiers brought heavy equipment with them. Bulldozers cleared a large area in the center of town, and Pavle was worried that it came awfully close to his family's shelter. Still, despite clearing an area of several city blocks, it did not come all the way to the collapsed building where they had built their temporary home.

A senior officer—colonel from the looks of the insignia on his lapels—addressed the huddled refugees in the middle of town. His troops had rooted out many of the existing residents at gunpoint. Some had been shot when they resisted. Pavle and Stanis went to the assembly, but only after leaving Mimi and Magda behind in one of the secret places.

"I am Oberst Storm. I am the new authority in this town. You will address me as Master, and my soldiers as Lord. You work under our benevolent care, now. My men will have barracks outside the city to watch over your safety. We will build a fence to keep out those who would prey on you. In exchange for our protection, you will be released in workgroups under guard. You will scavenge the countryside, under our direction. We will collect what you find, and distribute it fairly among you. In return for your cooperation, we will provide for your shelter and give you food and water. We are here for you."

The colonel had a cold face. Pavle did not for a moment believe that the soldiers were there to protect them. These ELF soldiers, as all those before them, were in this for themselves. After all, if they were here to protect the citizens . . . why did they continue to hold them at gunpoint?

Later that day, a fence went up enclosing an area approximately ten times that of the city center. They drafted men from the refugees to install the fence while the soldiers—other than those operating bulldozers and trucks—stood outside with their guns pointing inward. Most of the enclosed area was wrecked buildings, piled rubble, and a few standing walls. Trucks dumped canvas and plastic sheets, but nothing else with which to construct shelter. The refugees would have to scavenge and supply the rest.

The fence was completed that night, and the vehicles moved outside the perimeter. Over the next several days, barracks, a mess hall, and other buildings were constructed for the soldiers. A headquarters building had been brought in prefabricated. It was one large rectangular container that had to be lifted off the heavy ground effect truck by crane. The colonel disappeared, and from that day onward, the people inside the fence rarely saw him.

They mostly dealt with his soldiers.

Each day a work crew was assembled in the center of town. Of the estimated four hundred refugees, about one-quarter were children too small or too young to work. Another fifty or sixty people were too old, sick, or crippled—so the soldiers would gather about two hundred people each day, leaving only the bare minimum to care for the young and elderly. The rest had to go out into the surrounding countryside and scavenge.

At first, they worked only the immediate surrounding fields, but as that region was stripped, groups were taken as far as one hundred kilometers away from the town each day. They went to ruined farmhouses and scavenged all of the food, seed, and farm equipment. They went to battlefields where they stripped the bodies of the slain, and collected food, water, fuel, electronic, and mechanical components. The guards were always close, and any weapon or ammunition discovered was confiscated immediately. When they encountered towns and cities within the district, the soldiers directed the laborers to concentrate on searching for money, luxuries, and consumer goods. Everything was taken whether it worked or not, and it was all presented to the colonel's men upon return to the city every night.

Each citizen had to present themselves every evening in order to receive a food and water ration—even the children. The elderly, sick, and lame received nothing. In one of his rare appearances, Colonel Storm told them that even children could forage, or grow to be a scavenger. The aged and infirm were liabilities, and could not earn their own keep. The people were free to share rations, but would not receive any extra.

The food and water allocations weren't enough to live on. It was barely enough to survive, and many died over the next few months. It was clear that the ELF did not care for the people, they only wanted a slave labor workforce.

Many of the adults gave children extra food, but in too many cases, what was left was not enough for the adults. One by one, adults became sick. It didn't matter if someone collapsed in the fields or back inside the encampment—they were simply left where they fell. The government had not been much better. It professed a philosophy of sharing and distributing: "From each according to their ability, to each according to their need." In reality, that meant that those with extra had it taken from them; but at least there was a possibility to earn more. To the ELF, need was weakness, and weakness should be culled. Their basic philosophy was "survival of the strongest." Over time, additional refugees were brought in to make up the losses. The population grew to about five hundred people and then began to decrease again as the weak died off, and those too strong of will were killed by the soldiers.

The first day, Mimi and Magda had to submit themselves to a census. Every night thereafter, there was a roll call and they had to come out of their shelter to receive their food and water allocation. Soldiers entered their shelter and looked around, but they never found the false back wall, or the passages to the underground storage or the command center. It continued to be their secret.

While the adults scavenged outside the fence, Magda continued to crawl through the rubble inside the perimeter of what was now openly acknowledged to be a prisoner camp. She also helped Mimi nurse the sick as much as she was allowed. New finds of medical supplies were often confiscated—she knew, because she was often called on to treat injured soldiers, and saw the medical supplies they'd hoarded. Mimi was allowed to treat minor injuries, strains, cuts, burns, and scrapes—and Magda learned at her side. Anything that would allow a worker to participate in a work party the next day was permitted, but if she tried to treat anyone who needed extended care, that person would be missing the next morning. It broke her heart, but Mimi learned not to waste her meager supplies.

Stanis had grown big and strong. He and his father were often part of the work parties. They had a little bit of extra food left, gathered from the grocery store. There was likely more, but they dared not go down to dig out more. It was too dangerous. The presence of the store was still largely unknown. Despite the needs of their fellow refugees, it was best to stay that way.

Magda's father told her one night, "There will come a time of greater need. We will need this for the children. Remember this, Magda. We must use it sparingly enough to keep our strength. But we must save what we can and use it for the children."

Years passed and the ELF brought more troops and more refugees to be slaves in their camp. The pickings became too thin near the camp, and work crews needed to travel greater distances. At first, they would stay overnight and come back the next evening. Then the crews would be gone for two days. One day, a work crew went out and never came back. A week later, the soldiers who'd escorted the workers returned with plenty of salvage and were seen laughing and drinking with their fellows.

There was no sign of the prisoners.

Pavle and Mimi whispered about it one night. They tried to be quiet, but Magda overheard.

"They served their purpose. Once the people finished scavenging, the soldiers either shot them, or left them to starve."

"Perhaps both. There were not enough trucks to carry a week's worth of provisions for the work crew. They were worked to death."

"You are probably right, Mims. It is hard enough to get by on the rations we do have. I know I wouldn't last more than a couple of days without rations."

"It is almost the end. We must prepare."

"Not for you and me, but for Stanis and Magda."

"For Magda and the children."

"Yes. For the children."

It had been years since the ELF had barricaded the town; the fence was now a fortified wall. It was even more years since Mimi and Pavle had made it a home for their son and adopted daughter. Pavle was a strong man, a proud man, but he knew to submit to the soldiers, even as he began to grow weak from overwork and thin rations. As a nurse, Mimi was still in demand, but they both knew that it was only a matter of time before Pavle stopped being picked for work crews. When that happened, his share of rations would stop.

Late at night, they talked about plans. Stanis wanted to escape—he wanted his mother to find a way to weaken the soldiers so that he and the other young men could make a move. When she refused, he moved out of their shelter. Still, he kept their secret—until the day he, too, disappeared when a work party did not come back.

His loss devastated Mimi, and her health deteriorated. Pavle was determined to find another way, and he began to go back into the command center. He worked on the consoles and electronics, replacing components with look-alikes from the consumer electronics they'd found in the hidden stores. Magda helped her father every evening, then tucked him into bed, and returned to study what she could of the strange instrumentation.

"This is some sort of command center. Over there behind that wall is a computer," he told her, one night. He pointed to the wall in front of the half-melted chair. "These dark panels would display maps, and pictures of the outside world."

"What good is a picture, if we can't see what is around us? Pictures don't move. They show us the past, not what is real!" Magda countered.

"These were live pictures. Cameras, like the one I showed you yesterday, took pictures of the outside and showed them on these screens." Several nights ago, Pavle had rigged a camera in the passage leading to the underground tunnels. He told her it was an "early warning system." He'd run a wire and set up a flat, rectangular device that showed images from the camera. It had taken many weeks to free up the metallic door and rig a lock so that Magda could hide inside the command center if strangers came. The camera would alert them, and she could hide, while her father drew the interlopers away.

"I've seen computers like these before. A long time ago. It was technology from Earth."

Earth was a fiction to Magda, a fairy tale told to children to make them behave: "If you are good, the people from Earth will take you to a land of plenty." To many, the home world of humanity was a mythological place with no wars, no shortages, no hunger, and no poverty. Pavle knew that it was really not that perfect, but compared to Eden, it was a land of freedom and plenty.

He still had no idea what this command center controlled, but he knew the technology he recognized was important. There had been a time when he had worked in the computer center of a great city to the west, and had seen something like this: a rare capsulated intelligence.

Pavle taught Magda, late in the night, growing weaker by the day. He knew this was important, and *someone* needed to know.

Pavle had met one, a computer intelligence, those many years ago. It called itself Hephaestus, and it had operated the power plant, energy distribution, traffic, and shipping in the city of West Shore. The intelligence had been cool and distant, lacking the warmth and much of the emotion of flesh and blood. Still, it had a sense of humor and expressed some concern for the humans around it. Its humanity was not gone, just altered.

Pavle hoped that if he could find the secret of this machine, perhaps he could wake up a synthetic intelligence that would help them. He worked in secret, with Magda at his side. He taught her all he knew of electronics, power systems, coolant, and the circuits that supported intelligence. Despite all his tinkering, the intelligence he suspected was there never woke up. He supposed that having been turned off for so long had caused the death of this rare being.

Magda was older—a teen now—but not much bigger than she'd been as a child. She was still the best at getting into small spaces in the rubble around the community. She continued to explore, and once in a while she would find a cache of food or other supplies. Most of those she hid and showed to her parents late at night. Some was turned into the soldiers—they'd be suspicious if she didn't, but given her size, the soldiers still didn't consider her to be much more than a child herself.

She often found herself watching children as the parents went out to scavenge. She'd gathered a troop of children around her, and mothered them almost as if they were her own. When a small boy or girl came to her because their parent hadn't woken up, or hadn't returned from the fields, Magda would hold them tight, stroke their hair, and whisper, "It's okay, Magda is here. Magda will take care of you."

Rations became short. There were fewer guards on the perimeter, and fewer soldiers in the barracks. The colonel had not been seen for many months. Daily food and water deliveries were cut every few weeks. There was less to go around and many of the adults preferred to give their share to the children. There were still adults who insisted that they needed an extra share to be able to go out and glean the battlefields. There were fights over the food distribution, and sometimes bodies would be left on the ground in the aftermath.

Those who elected to shorten their own rations entrusted them to Magda. She stashed extras in her secret caves while still making sure that the children had enough to stay active. She taught them to explore the small spaces, and showed them safe spots to avoid the soldiers and the growing collection of selfish adults who followed the children in hopes of discovering where they hid their rations.

Mimi grew weaker, and fell into a fever late one snowy night. As the only nurse, she was unable to treat herself. Magda tried, but she simply didn't know enough. She sat holding the hand of the only mother she'd known—as that hand grew cold and stiff.

Pavle was beside himself with grief. Magda tried to console him, but there was just too much broken inside him, and there was nothing she could do. He stormed out of the shelter, to the gate in the perimeter wall, and yelled obscenities. He punched the wall with his fists, and when guards came to investigate, he punched them too. He was captured and chained to the inside of the wall. A dozen soldiers lined up with their guns and shot him—each of them emptying their rifle magazine.

They left him there, chained to the pockmarked, bloodstained wall as an example.

Magda retreated to the command center, tears in her eyes. She looked around at the great machine and beat her fists against the consoles. "Where were you? You failed us! You were supposed to help us! How am I going to take care of the children now?"

A little boy—she called him Peter, although the others said his parents had called him by another name—came to her. His parents were long gone, and Pavle and Mimi had taken him in, although it was Magda who cared for him most of the time. Peter didn't know what to do and he clutched Magda and cried. Despite her own grief she put her arms around him, stroked the back of his head, and whispered, "Don't cry, Peter. It's okay. I'll be your mother. Mother is here and I'll take care of you."

Deep inside the great machine, a circuit closed.

The next day the soldiers did not come to gather a work party. They simply left. That night, there was no food distribution. In the morning, a few soldiers returned to gather all the adults that they could find. They marched out of camp and did not return that night.

Once again, there was no food, no water—no adults. Magda moved the few remaining children to the secret passages under the building.

This was the time Poppa meant. The emergency when the rest of the stored supplies would be needed.

She led the children deep into the tunnels and gathered all of the stored food and water. Some of the water had leaked, the packages had spoiled, but she had moved what remained into the command center.

The children cried. They were hungry and thirsty. They wanted their parents. All they had was Magda. She held them, hugged them, and whispered to them, "Don't worry, Magda is here, Magda will take care of you."

That phrase! It means something! the intelligence inside the vast machine thought to itself as it roused itself from its long sleep.

There was a crackling sound coming from high on one wall. Magda looked around. *What was that?*

Something like a voice came over the hidden speaker. It stopped after a moment, though. More odd noises sounded, then a smooth, melodious voice spoke.

"Mother is here. Mother will take care of you."

The repairs that Pavle and Magda made had at least restored sensor data to Mother. The computers had recorded snapshots of life around her for the past fifteen years, and she reviewed those records in a few nanoseconds. She looked at the children, analyzed their ages, their health, the absence of adults. Mother then looked at Magda— dirty, clothed in rags, but still standing defiantly to defend the children.

"Magda. It's okay. I am Mother, the intelligence within this war machine. My duty was to protect my family—the men and women of my platoon. I failed them, but I can still protect you."

Over the next few hours, Mother instructed Magda in how to

refill the nutrient paste dispenser with the spoiled food. Processing would remove the contaminants, and Mother would synthesize extra vitamins for the starving children. The water dispenser was easily patched, and could refill itself from atmospheric water vapor. Lockers were opened, to provide cloth for bedding, and as Magda helped Mother bring the rest of her systems online, the internal fabricators began to turn out clothing for the children.

Rested, fed, the children were stronger. With Mother's guidance, Magda sent them out to clear specific areas of the rubble. Some of it was simply too big, even for Magda, but Mother said it would be okay. She would manage.

Mother used the large black rectangles—she called them "screens"—to teach Magda what she would need to know. One of the first lessons was the definition of a *tank* and what it was capable of. Magda was torn between taking the children to safety, and getting revenge on the soldiers of the ELF. It was Mother who convinced her the safety of the children was the more important.

The day came when Mother shook off the remnants of the fallen building. The children were huddled inside the command center, but Magda stood outside as the massive machine crawled out of the rubble.

Worn, weathered, dented, and crumpled—she'd never seen anything so beautiful!

When she reentered the command center, Mother opened a compartment and showed her a brand-new set of clothing. "This is a tank commander's uniform, Magda. You are my commander now, so you should wear it."

Magda just lowered her head. "Thank you, Mother. Let's get the kids to safety. Then we're going hunting. Don't worry, Mother. Magda is here, now. Together you and I will do what we need to do to protect *all* of our families."

Tread Softly

Esther Friesner

It is a truth, universally acknowledged in the fetid hellhole of a post-Apocalyptic Brooklyn, that a single man in possession of a good fortune and several robotic enhancements must be in want of a wife.

As to what the *wife* might be in want of . . .

"My dear, you will never in a thousand seconds guess what has happened! We have new neighbors and some of them might even be male. Huzzah!"

Mzzus Dorothea Ladyfinger-Rabinowitz (of the Williamsburg Ladyfingers) swooped in upon her husband as he attempted to ingest the morning news in peace. He closed his eyes, feigning slumber or a minor system crash, but it was no use. A mother's preoccupation with seeing her daughters well-settled in life recognizes no obstacles nor anyone else's right to some scant moments of domestic tranquility.

Meest Fiorello Rabinowitz sighed and detached himself from the system. "What would you have me do, Dorothea?" he asked wearily.

"Why, pay them a visit, of course!" came the somewhat impatient reply. "It is the very least we *should* do, to welcome them to the neighborhood. They have taken over Mannbunne Manor, which has gone begging lo, these many years."

"As well it should, at least until the authorities make any progress whatsoever in mitigating the quantity of toxins in the estate grounds," Meest Rabinowitz observed. "I presume you have your sights set on marrying one of our girls into that landed sump? Ah well, why should we be the only couple hereabouts whose grandchildren do *not* have tentacles?"

His bride bridled. "O fie, Fifi! Do not dismiss my ambitions for our children. At least I am taking an interest in their futures!"

"Indeed, indeed." Meest Rabinowitz nodded slowly, resigned to the reality of his home life: if he wished to have any peace whatsoever, it was a truth, unilaterally acknowledged, that the best and only course for him was to give his wife carte blanche in these matters. "You are an exemplary mother and I shall see to this."

Joy illuminated many of Mzzus Ladyfinger-Rabinowitz's eyes. She licked Meest Rabinowitz's face. "I knew I could rely on you, my dear."

"New neighbors!" little Mary exclaimed as the family met over breakfast. "Fancy that!"

"New *male* neighbors," her mother clarified. "Who knows how many? This well may be the making of your fortunes, my darlings. Pappa has promised me that he will pay a call at Mannbunne Manor this very morning and ascertain the specifics of the situation."

Jane, the eldest, shook her head. "Even if there are sufficient males on offer for breeding purposes, what are the chances that any of them prefer to make carnal whoopee-times with females of our sort?" She was a born pessimist and had steeled her beliefs by joining the Chapel of Divine Doom, despite her parents' wishes and the family's heritage as Retrofitted Episcopalians.

The twins, Sarah and Dreadnought, giggled. "Oh, Jane, you are *such* a caution," they said in chorus. In this they had little choice, sharing a communal larynx as they did. "Mamma will have her way in this, no matter what. Why, we are completely convinced that she shall have all of us well matched and well married by the end of this Season!"

"Oh yes," said Jane dolefully. "Especially should she find a suitor who would view you two as the ultimate buy-one-get-one-free bargain."

Her sisters shrieked their outrage and attempted to climb across the breakfast table to exact a hideous revenge, armed as they were with the remnants of that morning's assortment of pastries. (Mzzus

Ladyfinger-Rabinowitz's lingonberry-scrapple scones were to die for. Many had.)

Their mother rose to put a stop to such socially unacceptable hijinks, but before she could spray her daughters with the No-No water bottle, the fifth Rabinowitz sister reached out a battle-hardened hand, seized the twins by their mutual collar, and jerked them back into their place at the table.

"That will *do*," said Lizzie. Her eyes were fire, her tone was iron, and her preferred method of dealing with all sororal insurrections was a figurative combination of bleach and ammonia. Her gaze scythed across the table. "You shall on this subject put your trust in Mamma and Pappa and Aunt Esstee."

"Aunt *who*?" Jane was so intrigued that she dropped her morose mien like a hot toasting fork.

"Esstee," Lizzie replied with a hard grin. "Family name, Effyu." While her elder sister wrestled for comprehension of this refined jape, Lizzie went on to say: "Mamma's plan has my full and considerable support, for the sooner the lot of you are respectably paired off, the sooner I shall be able to pursue my own aspirations, particularly if your mates are of the moneyed sort and not unwilling to aid your dearest sister in realizing the as-yet-unspoken hope of her—by which I mean *my*, because I fear you are too dense to follow my narrative—heart."

The first of the family to wield a mental machete successfully and hack through Lizzie's verbiage was little Mary. "Oh, but dearest Lizzie, surely your aims are our own, as well as Mamma's? It is a truth universally acknowledged that marriage is a necessity. The fate awaiting those of us without partners to stand beside us, march boldly before us to meet the future, and be ever-vigilant at our backs to guard us must be—"

"—a matter of trilocation, at the very least," Lizzie finished for her with a smirk. "You need not worry, little Mary. I shall have my partner."

Here Lizzie placed two fingers in her mouth and filled the breakfast room with a shrill whistle. From outside the Rabinowitz abode came the roar of a mighty engine and the rumble of aggressively approaching machinery. The other Rabinowitz sisters squealed with delight, even Jane, and flocked to the window just in time to see the bulk of a massive tank rumble across the landscape, crushing two of the driveway poplars, a portion of the front garden, one corner of the ruins of P.S. 269, and an anomalous sheep. It stopped short of the house and remained with motor running, awaiting further orders.

"Elizabeth Rabinowitz, you dreadful hoyden!" Lizzie's mother exclaimed. "What have we said about tanks?"

"But Mamma—!" Lizzie's protest was stymied under her mother's glare.

"*What have we said?*"

Lizzie bowed her head and muttered, "Tanks are an occasional entertainment, not a way of life suitable for a young lady of good family. They are a privilege, not a right. Return them to the library by the due date. Our family cannot bear the financial burden of any more late fees."

"Precisely!" Mzzus Rabinowitz was smugly satisfied. "I will return it myself, this very day. I fear I cannot trust you to do so. Thank goodness they are all so AI-enhanced that even I, with my laughable graduate degree in software hacking from Yale, can maneuver them!"

"But Mamma—!" Lizzie exclaimed a second time, and for a second time was thwarted by her mother.

"Do not prevaricate with me, young lady. You claimed you had returned that thing two days ago. Where have you been hiding it? I searched your room!"

Lizzie's brow darkened. "Hiding *him*, Mamma."

"Tchah! What nonsense is this? That tank has all the gender of a bologna sandwich and only half the charm. It is a rental, subject to the destructive misadventures and toffee-stained fingers of any child with a subdermally embedded library chip. Why you must insist on terming it *he* and *him* and *Sir Frederic Montesquieu, late of His Excellency's Fourth Company of Light Horse and Middleweight Boxers* and whatnot, I cannot begin to imagine."

Lizzie shot to her feet, fists clenched. "So I would expect," she declared. "You simply do not get it, do you?"

"Nor do I want it," her mother countered. "I concede that I will trust you to return that thing directly after breakfast and you will not renew it nor borrow another for a fortnight."

"But—!"

"Listen to your mother, Lizzie," Meest Rabinowitz said wearily. "She only wants what is best for you."

A bitter laugh flew from Lizzie's lips, but she replied, "If you say so, Pappa." She sat down again, looking the very picture of a dutiful daughter. Only her soft-boiled egg suffered for her pent-up emotions, perishing under an obscene assault of ketchup and marmalade.

"A ball, a ball, hooray!" cried the twins, pirouetting around the sisters' barracks.

"Wheeeee!" little Mary agreed. She flew to the armoire to contemplate her choice of garments. Head cocked prettily to one side she added, "What do you think, Jane? Lace or latex?"

The eldest Rabinowitz sister grunted by way of reply. "You are too young for lace, Mary. You ought to know that."

"Oh, let her wear whatever she fancies, Jane," Lizzie cut in impatiently. "As long as her boots match her riding crop, she will be fine."

"And what will *you* wear, dear Lizzie?" Dreadnought and Sarah asked pertly, only to answer their own question with, "Don't be silly; you know she's just going to show up in uniform, the way she always does."

Jane was adept at sighing, and did so. "Why, Lizzie? Why must you insist on such an outmoded fashion choice? Have you not heard? We are a *post*-Apocalyptic society now. The war is over. The zombies have been destroyed. The aliens have been ousted. The sacrificial teenagers have been given the vote. The mutant capybaras have been successfully reeducated. The Allied Confederation of Mimes, Jugglers, Clowns, and Buskers has agreed to—"

"Oh, very *well*, Jane." Lizzie's put-upon sigh gave her elder sister's a run for the money when it came to volume, chestiness, and timbre. "I had no idea that you cared so much for fashion above honor. If it makes you happy I will smother my combat record beneath a landslide of frills and furbelows."

"*What* combat record? You worked in a field canteen serving donuts to the troops," said little Mary.

"They were *good* donuts," Lizzie countered fiercely. "And the coffee was scalding!" She jabbed a finger to the bosom of her singlet, indicating the medal thereto attached. "My sacrifice was recognized by my superiors, if not by my own family. I was *splattered* in the line of duty!"

"Ugh," replied little Mary with an expressive roll of her eyes. "Whats*oever*." She went back to searching the armoire.

Jane patted Lizzie's back. "Never mind," she said. "Wear what you like. It is only for a single evening and certainly not the beginning of a complicated series of social and personal misapprehensions."

"What an *unbearable* man," Lizzie whispered hotly to Jane as they sat along the wall of the ballroom at Mannbunne Manor. "He is proud beyond bearing. One can tell that he fancies himself quite the catch on the marriage market, but I pity the person who ends by linking their fate and future to his."

"Of whom do you speak?" Jane asked from behind the discretion of her fan. It was little more than a polite murmur, something that she said for the sake of saying something to placate her sister. She had paid scant heed to any aspect of the dance since her family's arrival, instead focusing her attention on the program presently streaming on the screen built into the aforementioned fan. As Jane herself would have remarked, had she cared to do so, "*Celebrity Housewives Deathmatch Bakeoff* is not going to watch itself!"

"Jane, if you do not put down that fan and look me in the eye *this instant*, then 'pon rep I will snatch it from your hand and reposition it in such a way that you will be hard-pressed to view it at all, unless you possess heretofore hidden talents as a contortionist!"

Jane lowered her fan and regarded her younger sister with some hauteur. "My dearest Lizzie, why are you incapable of making more verbally economical threats? One might almost imagine you are being paid by the word, like some lowly, vulgar, and disreputable ink-stained wretch. If you wish to say you intend to stick my fan where the sun fails to—"

At this very moment, a shadow fell upon the sisters and they looked up into the face of their host, Meest Charles "Chucky" 78-A.net, the new master of Mannbunne Manor. He was reputed to be a single man in possession of a good fortune, and the Rabinowitz sisters knew what *that* meant.

"Might I beg the favor of the next dance?" he asked Jane, offering his hand.

Jane's face was so immediately transformed with joy as to render her unrecognizable. "It would be my pleasure, sir," she replied, rising. She paused for moment and added, "May I?"

Meest 78-A.net nodded affably and permitted her to adjust the display on his face-screen so that she might both dance the *Sir Roger de l'Isle de Coney* and continue watching her favorite program at the same time.

Left to herself, Lizzie dearly wished she had also been left to her own devices, but those were at home. Pensive, she abandoned her chair and strolled out onto the terrace. Despite her father's low opinion of the estate, the prospect of Mannbunne Manor was a delight, even in the hours of darkness. Stands of larch and alder loomed against the starlit sky. Genetically altered owls alternately giggled and sang snatches of sea shanties from the branches. A herd of fallow deer, glowing with idyllic levels of residual radiation, calmly cropped the grass until the spine-chilling howls of a hunting pack of cybernetically enhanced dachshunds set them in flight. One doe was not nimble enough, and the ensuing kill was so breathtaking that Lizzie could not help but clap her hands.

"Oh, well done!" she cried. "Well done!"

"You are a remarkably bloodthirsty young woman, are you not?" came a deep voice from the shadows.

Lizzie whirled to face the speaker, who stepped into a streak of light from the ballroom. Her lips pursed. She recognized the object of her recent ire, Meest 78-A.net's guest and companion, FitzWilliam FitzDarcyfitz.

"*Remarkably* bloodthirsty, sir?" Drawing back her shoulders, she spoke with enough ice behind her words to be a hazard to North Atlantic shipping: "I am remarkable in more ways than that, sir, although your opinion of my appearance as being beneath your notice or consideration as a partner in the dance gives me to understand that you shall never trouble yourself to attempt more intimate knowledge of my character. Sir."

FitzDarcyfitz took a step backward. "I beg your pardon?"

"Well you might. Whether or not I shall grant it to you—"

FitzDarcyfitz took two steps forward. His voice rose. "I did not say that as a request that you forgive me for my words earlier; I meant *what* the bloody hell were you trying to say with all that damned word-salad you just spewed?"

Bloody hell? Damned? La! Lizzie gasped. Her heart beat faster. She had not heard a man use such forthright language since her time as a donut-wrangler. Indeed, her fondest memory was of meeting a soldier whose mother tongue was fluent Latrine. His name was Lieutenant Sean Camisaroja. Their mutual attraction was as immediate as it was socially unacceptable. It was he who had broken a considerable assortment of military rules by having her join him in his tank, the *Holy Glory*, and teaching her how to drive it. Thence had come her passion for tanks and her ambition to join the Corps one day. When peace invaded and dispatched that dream, she remained determined to have a tank of her own, if not to employ in defense of civilization, then to roll all over the countryside and squoosh things.

Alas, the more tender aspect of her post-Apocalyptic fantasies was not to be. Albeit she had no qualms about having an Understanding with a beau whose class, occupation, vocabulary, and expectations were sure to give her mother fits (always a plus), Fate intruded. Lieutenant Camisaroja perished in the aftermath of the last great battle of the Apocalypse—what the capybaras did to their prisoners was hideous to contemplate—but she would always remember him and his magnificent drive sprocket.

It was with some difficulty that Lizzie extracted herself from this dewy reverie. Hardening her gaze, she said, "I inadvertently overheard you tell our host that you thought I was merely tolerable, not handsome enough to tempt you, and, I quote, that you 'were in no humor to give consequence to young ladies who were slighted by other men.'"

"Oh." FitzDarcyfitz sucked air between his teeth. "Ah. Hm. Yyyyyyyes? I said that *maybe*? A *little*? But that was before I recognized you."

"*Recognized* me?" Nostrils flaring with poorly reined-in rage, Lizzie stared thunderbolts. "How *dare* you claim any such social intimacy. I give you my word of honor, sir, that I have not had the displeasure of your acquaintance until this very evening." She wheeled sharply and flounced back inside, where she spent the remainder of the ball drinking punch and fuming.

⊕ ⊕ ⊕

Mzzus Ladyfinger-Rabinowitz was as pleased as a sewer alligator during tourist season by the outcome of the ball at Mannbunne Manor. Not only had Jane managed to cultivate the first fragile tendrils of attraction with their host, but the twins had returned home with full dance cards and a number of duels scheduled to be fought for their individual affections by local swains who did not appreciate the concept of "polycule" nor even grasp that of "share" so easily mastered by the youngest of kindergarteners.

More wondrous still, little Mary had managed to enjoy the company of a number of admirers, despite the paucity of lace in her attire, although her bodysuit would never be quite so glossy again and she had broken her second-best riding crop on a member of the Flatbush Parliament.

All that was wanting to secure Mzzus Ladyfinger-Rabinowitz's happiness was for her second daughter to have zeroed in on a soft target matrimonial. Reports from her other girls as to Elizabeth's activities at the ball led her to believe that this had been accomplished, a snippet of information that filled the maternal bosom with elation.

"Lizzie, my love, what is this I hear about you dallying on the terrace with Meest FitzDarcyfitz?" she inquired over the breakfast kippers. Her tone was intended to feign severity, yet with a soupçon of tacit approval for her girl's borderline-louche behavior.

"Bah." Lizzie exercised her hostilities upon a helpless piece of toast that fell to bits under the assault. "Do not speak the name of that person to me, Mamma. I find him odious."

"Impossible!" cried her mother. "You cannot! He's rich!"

"In that case, he has used his means to procure and present to the world a higher class of odiousness," Lizzie riposted. "It makes him no less repugnant to me."

Mzzus Ladyfinger-Rabinowitz clucked in a monitory manner and shook her head over her child's disrespectful attitude toward money. "You always were a fussy child. What fantasized fault have you conjured out of the empty air and laid to his account?"

Lizzie lifted her chin. "He is *proud*, Mamma; intolerably so."

"And *you*, my girl"—her mother lifted her own chin a few degrees higher—"are clearly *prejudiced*."

"Well, now that we've got *that* bit of business out of the way, may

I please enjoy my breakfast in peace?" the Rabinowitz paterfamilias asked.

The meal continued in silence, which is not always the same as peace. This made little to no nevermind for Meest Rabinowitz, who was thankful for the respite. Meantime the atmosphere of wordless domestic hostility fairly pulsed between mother and second-born daughter with a figurative heat that caused the other sisters to cringe. At last, having chased one final remnant of enchilada around his plate, Meest Rabinowitz bid the ladies a good day and departed.

His departure broke the dam so valiantly struggling to restrain Mzzus Ladyfinger-Rabinowitz's wrath. "How *could* you, Lizzie!" she cried. "How could you turn your nose up at so advantageous a match as Meest FitzWilliam FitzDarcyfitz? You will not find a better offer. You are pushing seventeen!"

"'Offer,' Mamma?" Lizzie's disturbing tranquility almost overtopped her sardonic words. "*What* offer? He made none, honorable or otherwise. In point of fact, I heard him condescend to dismiss me entirely, as my looks were not handsome enough to tempt him and no other guests at the ball asked me to dance. I am unwanted goods to an overweening popinjay such as he."

"Then what were the two of you doing out on the terrace?"

Lizzie's lithe shoulders rose and fell expressively. "Discovering further reasons to scorn one another's company. I will admit that there was a moment when he *did* attempt to excuse his earlier disdain for my looks and lack of popularity—"

"Ah!"

"—but his words made it clear that he was so top-full of the product offered by the south-facing end of a north-facing appaloosa that—"

"Uh?"

"—I could not for an instant give credence to his sincerity."

At this point, Jane gave her mother a brief Lizzie-to-Normal-People translation.

"Ohhh! But my child, you must bear in mind that he *did* make an effort."

"To what purpose? I have no wish for further intercourse with him." She paused, waiting for at least one of her sisters to snicker and was disappointed. "What? Nothing? *Really*, girls, *nothing*?"

"Nope," said little Mary with a wicked grin. "Not a sausage!" Which remark, Britishism though it was, elicited the ribald glee previously wanting, plus a fish-knife-and-jam-spoon rimshot off the teapot and toast rack by Jane.

Mzzus Ladyfinger-Rabinowitz was quick to reclaim sovereignty of the conversation. "Do not be such a fool, Lizzie. Only consider what your life might be like as his bride. Your fondest dream would be realized!"

"Is that so?" Lizzie cocked an eyebrow and spoke lightly, without rancor. Much as she loved her mother, she deemed the woman the most flibberty of jibbets. She could not remain out of temper with her, and so asked, half in jest, "I was unaware that you knew anything of my dreams. And what might you call my fondest one?"

To Lizzie's astonishment, the answer was immediate and unequivocal.

"*Tanks*," said Mzzus Ladyfinger-Rabinowitz. "But not merely to continue your pitiable borrowing of our library's down-at-treads machines, but to have free and clear ownership of your very own!"

"What?" exclaimed Lizzie. Her fascination for those mighty machines was common knowledge *en famille*, but she never spoken of *this* madly ambitious facet of her obsession, lest she be laughed to scorn. "You *know*?"

"Oh, piffle." Her mother brushed away Lizzie's astonishment. "*Dead* people know. At least those who had the common courtesy to *remain* dead and keep their ridiculous appetites to themselves. 'Brains, brains, brains,' sundown to sunup; I ask you! They completely lowered the tone of our Apocalypse most dreadfully *and* ignored all noise-abatement laws. But really, Lizzie, how was I *not* to know? You have done nothing since returning from the front save rent tanks, borrow tanks, attempt to lease a tank with your pin money, and sneak off to TankCon at the Javits Center. Your father and sisters might not have thought your behavior to be more than a passing fancy—they took it at face value—but I knew there was more to it than that. A mother's heart extrapolates! And now you have before you the distinct possibility of marriage to a man with the wherewithal to *buy* you a tank of your very own—perhaps two, with one for holiday use—yet you stubbornly refuse to consider him as a match. You will not set your cap for him. You snub the notion of accepting his apology and playing upon his manly weaknesses with your feminine wiles. You are behaving most unreasonably and I insist you tell me *why*."

"Mamma..." Lizzie took a deep breath. The breakfast room hushed. Jane ceased to masticate her blueberry muffin. Little Mary froze with her mimosa halfway to her lips. The twins clutched their mutual porridge bowl. All eyes were fixed upon her, tense, waiting. She spoke.

"... I am just not that into him."

The door of Meest Rabinowitz's library-cum-man-cave burst open and his wife rushed in, a human avalanche of wild hysterics. "Husband, you must *do* something!" she cried, distraught and panic-stricken. "O, we are ruined!"

"Compose yourself, Dorothea," he replied, setting aside his retro-chic, dead-trees copy of *The Nude Yorker*. "We have been over this: If Lizzie is not interested in young FitzWilliam FitzDarcyfitz, we must respect her economic improvidence and file her future under Lost Causes. At least our Jane has two functioning brain cells to rub together. Can you not let Lizzie be and instead be contented by how swiftly and elegantly our eldest has reached an Understanding with Meest 78-A.net?"

"An Understanding that will soon fall to pieces," his wife said bitterly. "Thanks entirely to *your* ninny of a daughter! We must perforce kiss all future society at Mannbunne Manor farewell."

Meest Rabinowitz calmly did another preprandial line of cocaine. It was ever a help in any dealings with his wife concerning their children. Otherwise he simply could not be arsed. "My dear, give over. It is—beyond any reasonable shadow of a doubt cast by the unfading light of our terrestrial existence—what it is. I cannot blame Lizzie for taking this stance. It is a truth, universally acknowledged, that a single girl in possession of a good measure of self-awareness must not be coerced into becoming the wife of a man into whom she just is not. Moreover, she has confided in me certain details of which you might be uninformed regarding her unhappy interview with young FitzDarcyfitz. She tells me that he made bold to claim a prior acquaintance with her, *an acquaintance that does not exist*! Will you continue to berate her in the face of this outrage?"

"I will not," his wife said grimly. "Such atrocious behavior is not to be borne. However, I must for the moment fail to give a rat's ass about Lizzie. It is our little *Mary* of whom I rant! Husband, whatever shall we do? She has fled our home! She has absconded! Absquatulated! Skedaddled! In short—"

"Not in this book," her husband muttered.

"—she has eloped with . . . with—!"

"Alacrity? Expeditiousness? Precipitency? Our money?"

"*A capybara!*"

Lizzie stepped onto the selfsame terrace of Mannbunne Manor where she had experienced that vexing interview with Meest FitzWilliam FitzDarcyfitz not so long ago. She could hear the sound of many voices drifting from the open windows of the manor house's second-best parlor. Her parents and eldest sister were within, conferring with Meest 78-A.net. Unasked, Jane had brought the shame of the Rabinowitzes to the notice of her beau. It was a bold and gallant move that ran the risk of causing an unmendable rift between the young lovers.

As she paced the terrace, Lizzie meditated on her sister's startling display of gumption. It was by good hap alone that Meest 78-A.net became even more deeply enamored of Jane for her bravery as well as for her familial loyalty. Whatever little Mary's fate might be, Jane's future connubial bliss was assured. Her beloved loved her regardless of this scandal. She had gambled and won!

Won the point, Lizzie thought sadly, *but she well may lose the game. There can be no wedding for Jane if she lacks a living bridegroom. Not since we got rid of the zombies. My poor, dear, generous-souled sister! If I ever see little Mary again, I will give her such a* zetz im kopf—!

She shifted her gaze to the warmly glowing window from which Meest 78-A.net's voice reached her. He was speaking of the plans being laid under his sympathetic auspices for an expedition to find little Mary. "We shall depart before dawn tomorrow," he declared, his words underscored by Mzzus Ladyfinger-Rabinowitz's deafening sobs. "Be of good cheer, dear lady. We shall find your daughter even if it means venturing into the lowest of low resorts, a fleshpot of unmitigated squalor and moral corruption. I will have Cook pack a lunch."

Mzzus Ladyfinger-Rabinowitz's weeping was not loud enough to drown her husband's reply: "We are in your debt, sir, and pray have Cook cut the crusts off my sandwiches. At least we have some solid notion of where to direct our search. We have all read her farewell note including her intentions and destination. Very well then"—his sigh was steeped deep in fatalism—"on the morrow we are off to Newark."

Lizzie's blood turned to frost in her veins. *Newark!* Could it be? Was her father so blinded by affection for his wanton child that he failed to recall the life-threatening perils of such a journey? There were scarcely any usable roads to the shore and, once there, to cross the river between Brooklyn and Manhattan meant braving whirlpools, sharkdingos, sea dragons, sirens, and at least six insufficiently charted portals to hell. (It had been a very *thorough* Apocalypse.) The passage over the river between Manhattan and NeoJoisey was not so bad, but the bridge tolls were exorbitant.

She did what she could to maintain a stiff upper lip, but she could not keep her lower lip from quivering. Meest 78-A.net had already sworn to accompany Pappa on what might be a futile mission at best, suicide at worst. Tears filled her eyes at the thought of how heartbroken Jane would be to lose her intended. She wept for her, and for Mamma and the twins, should ill befall Pappa. Most of all, she wept for herself, as she knew exactly who in the family would have sole responsibility for cleaning up the ensuing emotional and financial mess.

"Why do *I* have to be the reliable one?" she wailed softly as she dabbed her eyes with a lace *mouchoir*.

"Perhaps it is for the simple reason that you are," came the answer.

Lizzie darted glances all about, but could not for the life of her discover the speaker. Her pulse raced. The voice was deep, resonant, and somehow familiar, yet she could not assign it to anyone with whom she had spoken of late.

"Who are you?" she demanded. "*Where* are you? Show yourself at once!"

"It would be my pleasure," the voice replied. "But it might not be yours. You are not disposed to favor my company, at present. Hear me out, I entreat you, so that I might have the opportunity to mend the misunderstanding between us."

"I do not have time for this," Lizzie snapped. "My dear father is on the point of flinging his life away because—"

"I know. I was informed of the situation and offered to act alone in retrieving your sister. It was my sincere desire to spare your father and my good friend all risk. They would not hear of it."

"Your—your good friend?" Lizzie inquired. There was only one person who could be termed Meest 78-A.net's "good friend." He had been introduced as such specifically during the ball at Mannbunne Manor; Lizzie had heard Jane's suitor do so many times that evening. That "good friend" could only be the despised, the odious, the nonetheless possessed of a titillating dollop of what the French termed *le grand hawtness* . . . FitzWilliam FitzDarcyfitz!

OMG!

She shook her head. This could not be. The voice was not *his* voice, and yet the narrative context could mean it was no other.

"Who are you?" she repeated, her words low and trembling.

"I am he who regrets sincerely the offense I gave you by denigrating the attractiveness of your person. I lack . . . people skills."

She forced a brittle laugh. "That is not possible," she maintained, fending off the inevitable. "I have never heard *your* voice in my life, and I would recognize *his*."

"As I recognized *you*."

A shudder of gooseflesh ran up Lizzie's arms. She began to edge back toward the safety of the house as she said, "That is beyond impossible, whether for him or for you, whoever you are. I never—"

"Hear me."

A low rumbling like the growl of a panther came from behind the hedges to the left of the terrace. It struck an alien, long-dormant chord deep in Lizzie's bosom. Her feet moved of their own volition, carrying her toward the sound like a somnambulist. She took step after step, enraptured—a bird hypnotized by the serpent's eye, a rat led in its last dance by a piper clad in motley, a woman in love with love itself. If any of her family had been present to stand witness, they might have attempted to stop her. She knew this; knew it as certainly as she knew that she would have struck away their staying hands and continued on her path to meet her destiny.

Her recalcitrant mind could no longer deny the remembrance of her heart—she knew that sound. She knew what it portended. She knew what awaited her beyond the *Hydrangea quercifolia*.

She knew a *lot* of things, not least of which was a great and plot-advancing truth: FitzWilliam FitzDarcyfitz *had* recognized her on the night of the ball, nor had he lied when he laid claim to prior acquaintance.

No, he had not lied. However, neither had he spoken the whole truth. *And whose fault was that?* Lizzie demanded of herself. *You did not give him the opportunity to say more!*

Oh, be still, Me! she responded. *I am sure as hell going to give him plenty of opportunity now!* With that, she stepped through the shrubbery and into her destiny.

He was waiting. Had separation wrought such changes in his appearance or had he always been possessed of such a presence, an air as masterful as it was handsome? The moon poured silver light over his burnished turret. His gun stood high and proud, but not in the obnoxious way. His hatch was tilted open just enough to speak of invitation rather than command. She gasped for breath and when she caught one said softly, disbelieving the evidence of her eyes, "*Holy Glory*, is it you?"

"My lady." The tank's gun dipped in salutation.

She did not pause to consider the social niceties. She rushed forward to fling herself against his armored side. Her tears of joy bedewed his caterpillar treads. "Oh, *Holy Glory*, I have missed you!" she sobbed.

"As I have missed you," the tank replied. "I have never forgotten your gentle touch on my throttle. I envied my combat partner, for at that time he was the only one who had the necessary humanity to seek your love. When happy circumstance permitted me to find you again, even though I did not appear in the form that you knew—"

He bit off his speech abruptly, then spoke again in less wistful, more fiercely urgent tones: "Never mind all that. More crucial matters are at hand. It wants but a few hours of dawn. If we do not leave at once, your father and my good friend Chucky will be off and away. We must forestall their departure by our own!" He tilted back his hatch even farther. "I will tell you all on our way to save your sister; that is"—his voice grew strangely shy—"if you will ride with me once more?"

She was up the ladder and down the hatch with such grace and alacrity that his audio sensors almost missed her cry of "Yippie-ki-yay, mothra foggers! Let's squoosh us some capybaras!"

As she closed the hatch firmly, she rejoiced in the new knowledge of her heart. She *was* into him after all!

Their return from NeoJoisey well before dawn the next day was greeted with a salmagundi of different reactions. Chief among these was Mzzus Ladyfinger-Rabinowitz's collapse in a dead faint when she saw the rumbling bulk of *Holy Glory* disgorge two of her daughters onto the lawn of Mannbunne Manor before going through a complicated series of bulk shifts, deflations, and assorted physical *clickety-clack*s as the massive tank re-formed itself into the elegant, gentlemanly form of Meest FitzWilliam FitzDarcyfitz.

While a penitent little Mary alternately chafed her mother's wrists, held a vial of smelling salts under her nose, and received full many a *zetz im kopf* from her irate father and the twins, Jane hastened to draw Lizzie aside.

"My dear, what *have* we just seen?" she demanded, eyeing the reconstituted FitzDarcyfitz askance. "Who—what is he—it—they? And however did something so huge"—she spread her arms wide—"dwindle to something so relatively small?" She brought the fingertips of both hands to within an inch's proximity.

It took Lizzie some time to reply, partly because she was assembling her thoughts, partly to obliterate the puerile desire to make some irrelevant allusion to Jane's anticipated wedding night. After a brief bit of backstory touching on her pre–post-Apocalyptic history and first acquaintance with the armament of her heart, she said, "When his friend and comrade Lieutenant Camisaroja died, he had a total breakdown. They bond deeply with their drivers, you know."

"Deeply? Indeed, so I see." Jane cast a wry glance over Lizzie's rumpled dress and added, "You have some transmission fluid on your nose, darling."

Blushing hotly, Lizzie wiped it away and went on. "He was mustered out with honors, a pension, a maintenance allowance, and given the option of full shutdown or a new life in what he and his fellow-AI weapons call, er, meat-drag."

"I can see the results of that choice plainly enough," said Jane, "but you have yet to explain satisfactorily the transformation we have all witnessed."

"Oh, that?" Lizzie waved her hands expressively. "It is all thanks to nanotransformative pseudodermic retro-elastification"—she waved her hands some more—"coupled with submicro-compartmentalization affecting and reallocating all factors of Serizawa's Conjecture—"

"Which one?" Jane interrupted.

"The third edition," Lizzie supplied. "Fifth chapter, second section, fourteenth paragraph."

"Oh, *that*," said Jane. "The one concerning the conservation of mass across multiple parallel dimensions?" She waved her hands even more vigorously than her sister had done. "Silly me. I ought to have thought of that myself. Well, *that* explains *everything*."

"Everything except why Pappa has suddenly stopped giving little Mary what-ho for eloping with a filthy capybara!" the twins piped up, intruding upon their elder sisters' scientifically sound and technologically accurate conversation. "Lizzie's beau spoiled the fun. He whispered something to Pappa, who immediately ordered us to cease troubling our *dear and precious* sister. His very words!"

Lizzie smiled. "So she is, now. You see, girls, there was a small misunderstanding based on Mary's farewell message. She has abominable handwriting, her texting skills are worse, and so when we read of her running off with a capybara—"

"A *filthy* capybara," the twins chorused.

"—she had actually written that she was eloping with *Capitán Ibarra*, the hero who broke the Siege of Gowanus and drove the zombies out of their Poughkeepsie stronghold! We shall be returning her to him promptly."

"He *is* filthy, though," Jane put in. "Filthy *rich*!" The sisters all enjoyed a good laugh over this.

When at last their shared merriment died away, Jane said, "What a relief to Mamma it must be knowing that little Mary is married well, as will I be, soon enough."

"As will *we* be, dear Jane," Lizzie said quietly. "FitzWilliam is even now asking Pappa for his consent. I hope our father has no, er, prejudices against anthrotechnic unions."

"Is your beau rich, Lizzie?" the twins asked.

"Oh yes! Enormously so. He is the sole heir of his former driver, poor Lieutenant Camisaroja, and has used his interwebz connections and time since leaving the service to multiply that bequest a gajillionfold." She waved her hand again. "As one does."

"In that case, Pappa will object to your union only if he wishes to be dealt sudden, bloody death by Mamma," Jane said, putting one arm around Lizzie's shoulders. "I take it you have forgiven him for his initial remarks that so affronted you?"

"Completely," Lizzie replied. "He entreated my pardon so eloquently during our journey to NeoJoisey that I could not do otherwise. He admitted he had spoken those hurtful words about me even while knowing them to be untrue, uttered only because he was posturing before his friend like the most disagreeable of dudebros."

"What a tool!" the twins exclaimed.

"As are all weapons, essentially," Lizzie said primly.

"Then let us rejoice for our socially and economically fortuitous future," Jane declared. "For it is a truth, universally acknowledged, that a single woman in possession of every advantage of mind, body, and spirit must nonetheless be in want of a husband to affirm her worth as a somewhat human being."

She let her sisters' cold stares and silence bide but a moment before she hastened to offer: "Or . . . not?"

The acknowledgment of which truth was agreeably immediate and indeed quite universal.

About the Editor and Authors

Jason Cordova is both a John W. Campbell Award and Dragon Award finalist, and is the creator of the Kin Wars series, which contains *Wraithkin*, *Darkling*, *Deathlords*, and *Homeguard*. He is also coauthoring *Monster Hunter Memoirs: Fever* with Larry Correia, coming soon from Baen Books. He has written over a dozen novels and been featured in many anthologies. A Navy veteran, he is also a former middle school teacher. Though Californian by birth, he has since relocated to the South, where he swears at the humidity on a thrice-daily basis. He can be found at www.jasoncordova.com.

SF convention favorites Sharon Lee and Steve Miller have been collaborating since the 1980s. Together, they have written nearly one hundred works of fantastic fiction, much of it in their extensive space opera geography, the Liaden Universe®. Sharon was consecutively executive director, vice president, and president of the Science Fiction and Fantasy Writers of America, while Steve was founding curator of science fiction at the University of Maryland's Science Fiction Research Collection. *Fair Trade*, the twenty-fourth Liaden Universe® novel, was published in Spring 2022. Lee and Miller's awards include the Skylark, the Prism, and the Hal Clement Award for Young Adult Science Fiction. More information and news can be found at www.korval.com and www.facebook.com/groups/16280839259.

Kevin Ikenberry is a lifelong space geek and retired Army officer.

As an adult, he managed the US Space Camp program and served in space operations before Space Force was a thing. He's an international best-selling author, award finalist, and a core author in the wildly successful Four Horsemen Universe. His novels include *Sleeper Protocol*, *Vendetta Protocol*, *Runs in the Family*, *Peacemaker*, *Honor the Threat*, *Stand or Fall*, *Deathangel*, *Fields of Fire*, *Harbinger*, and the alternate history novel *The Crossing*. He's cowritten both novels and short fiction with amazing authors. He is an Active Member of SFWA, International Thriller Writers, and SIGMA—the science fiction think tank. You can find Kevin online at www.kevinikenberry.com.

Jody Lynn Nye lists her main career activity as "spoiling cats." When not engaged upon this worthy occupation, she writes fantasy and science fiction. Since 1987 she has published over 50 books and more than 170 short stories. She has also written with notables in the industry, including Anne McCaffrey and Robert Asprin. Jody teaches writing seminars at SF conventions, and is a judge for the Writers of the Future Contest.

The Army took **David Drake** from Duke Law School and sent him on a motorized tour of Viet Nam and Cambodia with the 11th Cav, the Blackhorse. He learned new skills, saw interesting sights, and met exotic people who hadn't run fast enough to get away.

Dave returned to become Chapel Hill's assistant town attorney and to try to put his life back together through fiction making sense of his Army experiences.

Dave describes war from where he saw it: the loader's hatch of a tank in Cambodia. His military experience, combined with his formal education in history and Latin, has made him one of the foremost writers of realistic action SF and fantasy. His best-selling Hammer's Slammers series is credited with creating the genre of modern Military SF. He often wishes he had a less interesting background.

Dave lives with his family in rural North Carolina.

A.C. Haskins is a former armored cavalry officer and combat veteran turned economist and business strategist (and occasional firearm instructor). His debut novel, *Blood and Whispers*, was published by Baen Books. He has a lifelong love of speculative fiction, having written his first science fiction novel as a class project in the eleventh grade. His interests include (but are not limited to) ancient and medieval history, mythology, applied violence studies, tabletop gaming, and theoretical economics. He lives in Michigan with his wife, two cats, and a dog.

Joelle Presby is a former United States naval officer who has endured hurricane flooding of her Norfolk, Virginia, home multiple times. She has never garaged a hobby tank in the shed behind her house, and if someone says she did, the homeowners' association can't prove it.

She cowrote *The Road to Hell* (a Multiverse novel) with David Weber and has written short stories in her own universes and multiple shared universes. Her debut solo novel, *Dabare Snake Launcher*, was published by Baen Books in late 2022. Updates and releases are shared on her website, www.joellepresby.com, and on social media.

G. Scott Huggins, the first writer to win both the fantasy and the science-fiction short story writing awards from Baen Books, secures the future of the world by teaching its past to high-schoolers, many of whom learn things before they go to college. He loves high fantasy, space opera, and parodies of the same. Huggins has been writing since the late twentieth century, enjoys swords, venison, whiskey, and pie, and currently lives in Racine, WI, with his wife, three children, and two cats.

Award-winning and *USA Today* best-selling author of snark-filled adventures **Lydia Sherrer** is the author of the Love, Lies, and Hocus Pocus Universe books: tales of an introverted wizard, a troublemaking witch, and a magical talking cat. She is currently writing a sci-fi gamelit trilogy with *New York Times* best-selling author John Ringo. Her work appears in several anthologies, including the latest Black Tide Rising anthology, *We Shall Rise*. Her first novel, *Love, Lies, and Hocus Pocus: Beginnings*, won the best in Urban Fantasy 2017 Imadjin award, while her short story "Ashes of Hope," a postapocalyptic tale of survival, won a place in Almond

Press's 2015 short story contest, received the 2017 Imadjin Best Short Story award, and was selected for Honorable Mention in the 2019 Writers of the Future 4th Quarter contest.

David Sherrer is a born storyteller and has been an obsessive gamer ever since he was seduced by *Magic: The Gathering* at the tender age of fourteen. He has alternately owned a gaming store, street-performed for a living, and survived eleven years in the soul-crushing world of telecommunications. He lucked out by marrying a force of nature (otherwise known as his wife) determined to making living off writing, and has since escaped his nine-to-five to become the marketing director and lead game designer of Chenoweth Press.

His most fond achievements include being *Time* magazine Person of the Year in 2006 and becoming a Scottish Lord—there's a story there, just ask him. David considers himself an Atlantan, but currently lives in Louisville, Kentucky, with his family, feline overlords, and a mountain of board games that he swears he actually plays.

Philip Wohlrab has spent time in the United States Coast Guard and has served for more than fifteen years in the Virginia Army National Guard. Serving as a medic attached to an infantry company, he earned the title "Doc" the hard way while serving across two tours in Iraq. He came home and continued his education, earning a Master of Public Health degree in 2016. He currently works as a wargame designer for the United States Air Force and occasionally works for the United States Space Force. He also does game design work for the civilian market. When not crafting new stories or new games he can be found attending sci-fi cons both large and small.

Marisa Wolf was born in New England and raised on Boston sports teams, *Star Wars*, *Star Trek*, and the longest books in the library (usually fantasy). Over the years she majored in English in part to get credits for reading (this … only partly worked), taught middle school, was headbutted by an alligator, built a career in education, earned a black belt in Tae Kwon Do, and finally decided to finish all those half-started stories in her head.

She's currently based in Texas, but has moved into an RV with her husband and their two ridiculous rescue dogs, and it's anyone's guess where in the country she is at any given moment. Learn more at www.marisawolf.net.

First-time author **Ashley Prior** is a mom, wife, and a town councilwoman of a small town in rural Virginia. Author of a young adult novella series set in the magical land of Fleuria, she is hard at work on the series. Besides a teenage boy (sympathize with her), she has two dogs who run the household.

Dr. Robert E. Hampson is a scientist, educator, and author. As a researcher, he studies how memory is formed, stored, and recalled in animal and human brain. As a professor, he teaches medical and graduate students in the field of neuroscience. He consults with companies and authors on brain science, and teaches public communication skills to young scientists. As an author, Rob has more than twenty short stories, three novels, and two anthologies published. He decided that he'd spent enough years turning science fiction into science, and that he wanted to try turning science into science fiction, for a change.

Nebula Award–winner **Esther Friesner** is the author of over forty novels and more than two hundred short stories. She has a Ph.D. in Spanish from Yale University and is also a poet, a playwright, and the editor of several anthologies. The best known of these is the Chicks in Chainmail series that she created and edits for Baen Books (which might have had a *little* something-something to do with *this* book). In addition to SF, fantasy, and a bit of horror, she is the author of the Princesses of Myth series of young adult novels from Random House.

Esther is married, a mother of two and grandmother of two, harbors cats, and lives in Connecticut. She has a fondness for bittersweet chocolate, graphic novels, manga, travel, and jewelry. There is no truth to the rumor that her family motto is "Oooooh, SHINY!"

Her superpower is the ability to winnow her bookshelves without whining about it. Much.